PEOPLE
OF THE
BIBLE

PEOPLE
OF THE
BIBLE

Three Volumes in One

John Phillips

TESTAMENT BOOKS
New York

This 1999 edition is published by Testament Books™,
an imprint of Random House Value Publishing, Inc.,
201 East 50th Street, New York, New York 10022,
by arrangement with Loizeaux.

Testament Books™ and colophon are trademarks of
Random House Value Publishing, Inc.

Random House
New York • Toronto • London • Sydney • Auckland
http://www.randomhouse.com/

Printed and bound in the United States of America

Library of Congress Cataloging–in–Publication Data
Phillips, John, 1927–
[Introducing people of the Bible. V. 1–3]
People of the Bible / John Phillips.
p.   cm.
Originally published: Introducing people of the Bible,
v. 1–3. Neptune, N.J. : Loizeaux Brothers, c1991–1995.
ISBN 0-517-20421-5
1. Bible—Biography.   I. Title.
[BS571.P52   1999]
220.9'2—dc21
[B]   98-37055
CIP

Originally published as *Introducing People of the Bible, Volumes 1, 2, and 3*

8 7 6 5 4 3 2 1

VOLUME 1

CONTENTS

1
Adam,
the First Man

Genesis 1:26-31; 2:7-8,16-25; 3:6-24;
Romans 5:12-15

I. ADAM AND HIS WORLD
   A. How God Created Him
   B. How God Cautioned Him

II. ADAM AND HIS WIFE

III. ADAM AND HIS WOES
   A. One Man's Disobedience
   B. One Man's Descendants

Think of the most handsome man you have ever met—handsome as a son of the gods. Think of the manliest man—the man with the most splendid physique, an athletic kind of man, keen of eye, muscular, coordinated and skilled. Think of the most brilliant person of whom you have ever heard—a Shakespeare, an Einstein, a Beethoven. Think of the man with the most spellbinding charm, the man with the greatest personality and charisma. That was Adam. Adam was fresh from the hands of God. Adam, in his unfallen state, was the crown of God's creation—destined by God to be the father of the human race. Adam was inhabited by God; he was man as God intended man to be.

I. ADAM AND HIS WORLD

It was a world of bliss and beauty, a world of harmony and peace. It was a world of perfect balance, where all the forces of nature were matchlessly poised. It was a world of glens and gardens, of mountains and meadows, of rushing rivers and deep, mysterious woods. It was a world like ours, but with nothing gone wrong.

A. How God Created Him

The Bible makes no apology for introducing God into the nature of things. The theory of evolution, which leaves God out of everything, is not so much a science as a propaganda offensive—a convenient tool in the hands of the atheist, the communist, and the humanist for postulating a universe without God. That is why the theory of evolution is so popular. It gives the unbeliever a working hypothesis for atheism. He can (at least to his own satisfaction) explain the universe without including God. Either the humanistic scientist is right or the Holy Spirit is right. The believer would rather trust the Holy Spirit than men's ever-changing opinions.

The Bible teaches that God made each creature that inhabits this planet as a separate order, species, or "kind." Each kind was separate from every other kind. Divine fiat created them. God simply spoke them into existence. When it came to the creation of man, however, God acted in a personal and distinctive way, making him by divine formation. God stooped down and fashioned Adam's clay. A great gulf exists between man and the animal creation.

God utilized the same general principle and pattern of creation, so far as man's body was concerned, that He had used for the animals. But God made modifications for Adam who was to be in His image and crowned as creation's lord.

The complexity of a functioning human body is a compelling argument against the theory of evolution. Suppose we were to try to make a human body. We would go to the store and bring home the raw materials: fifty-eight pounds of oxygen, two ounces of salt, three pounds of calcium, twenty-four pounds of carbon, some chlorine, phosphorous, iron, sulfur, and glycerin. We would now have our "do-it-yourself" kit; all we would need to do is put it together.

We would begin with something relatively simple—skin. In most places it would have to be paper thin and made to be stretched evenly over some eighteen square feet of the body. We would have to build into the skin some two million sweat glands to make sure that the temperature of the finished body would be kept within a degree or two of its normal 98.6 degree mark. Each sweat gland would have to be a tightly-coiled little tube buried in the skin's inner layer, with a one-fifth-inch-long duct rising to the surface. A piece of skin the size of a postage stamp would serve as a sample of the whole; it would require three million cells, a yard of blood vessels, four yards of nerves, one hundred sweat glands, fifteen oil glands and twenty-five nerve ends.

Something as relatively simple as skin is not simple at all. So how would we manufacture and assemble the ears, eyes, hands, and feet? And what about the blood, veins, arteries, kidneys, liver, heart, and stomach? What about an immune system? The complex disease of AIDS illustrates what happens when a person does not have one. This disease has baffled our best medical scientists for years.

Before we could begin making any of these organs, however, we would have to make some cells—a mere quadrillion of them (10^{15}). But to make just one cell would be an exercise of mind-boggling complexity. We would have to be able to work on a very small scale, for the nucleus of each cell would need to be less than .0004 inch in diameter. The components of the cell would have to be enclosed in a membrane only .0000005 inch thick. The core would have to contain the genes and chromosomes, and we would need to imprint these with the "master plan"—the blueprint or "code of life" containing all the information necessary to determine whether the cell would be that of a cockroach, a camel, a horse, or a human being. This would involve arranging some twenty amino acids in an almost endless order to make the awesomely complicated assortment of proteins needed to build the body.

Another thing we would have to keep in mind: every minute some three billion of these cells would die, so we would have to arrange for them to be replaced at that rate.

And so the calculations go on. To believe that all this astounding complexity evolved by chance is to believe the impossible. Evolution is the atheist's inadequate "explanation" for the universe. It explains nothing. For example, add up all the component parts in a body. Remember that each one has to be in its right place at the right time, flawlessly performing the function for which it was designed. The odds against all this happening as a result of the blind working of the forces of chance are about the same odds against *Webster's Unabridged Dictionary* resulting from an explosion in a printing plant.

So we return to the Biblical account of creation. God created Adam. God set him apart from the rest of creation and gave him a *spirit*—something He had not given to bird or beast, fish or fowl. God made it possible for man to be inhabited by Himself; man in his nature, person, and personality could live, move, and have his being in fellowship with God.

An animal does what it does because it is what it is. It acts and behaves the way it does because of what we call *instinct*. Nobody has to teach a salmon to seek out the river of its origin in order to spawn and die there. The salmon does what it does because it is what it is—a salmon. Nobody has to teach a spider to weave a web. The spider weaves a web the way its mother

wove a web—by instinct. Nobody has to teach a bee to build
a hive with hexagonal chambers tilted at the correct angle to
the sun to keep the hive at a constant temperature. Nobody
has to teach a bee to maintain a colony with exactly the right
relationships between the queen, drones, and workers. Nobody has to teach a bee how to locate nectar or how to pass
the word to the colony. All this work is done by instinct. A bee
does what it does because it is what it is.

In other words, the governing principle in a creature—
whether it be an insect, a four-footed mammal, a fish, or a
bird—is instinct. The creature is locked into a special pattern
of behavior by the wisdom and power of the Creator. Some
of the higher creatures show signs of personality and manifest
an ability, within limits, to learn. They exhibit such emotions
as joy and sorrow. In other words, they may have what we call
a _soul_. Even so, instinct controls their behavior.

God could have created man the same way. We could
have been created to do what is right by instinct, but then God
would have only had another breed of animal—a superior
breed, but still an animal. Instead, God built into man a
different governing principle. He gave man a _body_ to make
him world-conscious, a _soul_ to make him self-conscious, and
a _spirit_ to make him God-conscious. In man, the body was to
be governed by the soul—by the intellect, emotions, and will.
The soul, in turn, was to be governed by the spirit, the new
ruling principle that sets man apart from the beasts. The human
spirit was to be indwelt by the Holy Spirit, so that man—in
fellowship with God, indwelt by God—would do, say, and
think in harmony with God.

B. How God Cautioned Him

In order for man to be a self-governing, rational, morally
accountable, volitional being—a _person_, not a _puppet_—he
must have the power of choice. He must also be placed in an
environment in which that power of choice can be exercised.

So when God planted the garden of Eden, He placed within it the tree of the knowledge of good and evil.

In effect He said, "Do you see that tree, Adam? That one is Mine. You can go where you like in the garden. All things are yours to enjoy richly, except for that one restriction. That tree is Mine, and you are not to eat of it. If you do, you will die. Now, then, enjoy your world."

II. ADAM AND HIS WIFE

The Holy Spirit intends the story of Adam's love, courtship, and marriage to be the divine prototype of all love, courtship, and marriage. The boundless freedoms, the experimentation, and the trial-and-error system of our modern world find little or no approval in the Bible. When Jesus spoke the last word on the question of divorce, He added this significant statement: "All men cannot receive this" (Matthew 19:11). The same is doubtlessly true concerning the divine pattern of love, courtship, and marriage found in Genesis 2. There we see illustrated the divine ideal, although not everyone has the grace to be governed by it.

In the beginning, Adam was celibate and was happy and content to be single. He went about his work in Eden, enjoyed daily fellowship with God, and lived a full-orbed life as a single person. He was engrossed in the hundred and one things that made up his daily life. He had evening times of communion with God and went to bed conscious of a need for nothing. Then God awakened in him a sense of lack.

God brought the animals to Adam to receive names. The purpose behind this stimulating, highly complex, mental exercise was to make Adam fully conscious of something: every animal had its mate. He alone, of all God's creatures, had no one his equal with whom to share life's joys. So Adam became acutely aware of a missing dimension in his life. For the first time, he was lonely.

Then God put Adam to sleep, and he went to sleep in the will of God. Doubtless Adam had committed this whole area of his life—his missing love life—to God. He did not run frantically all over Eden, beating the bushes to find someone to fill this newly discovered longing. He went to sleep in that "good, and acceptable, and perfect" will of God. Such reliance on God is wholly foreign to most people in our western world. Our ideas of love, courtship, and marriage are molded more by movies and fiction than by any thought that God might have a better way. This is largely true even when the single person is a believer and anxious to marry a believer. Dating is our pattern; dependence on God is the Biblical pattern.

When Adam awoke from his trustful rest, it was to look into the face of the woman God had created especially for him. If Eden had been a paradise before, it was ten thousand times a paradise now.

Then Adam spoke his vows: "This is now bone of my bones, and flesh of my flesh" (Genesis 2:23). During the days that followed, the couple lived in the wonder of an Edenic honeymoon. Every day they discovered something astonishing. Every day Adam took joy in introducing Eve to a new marvel in that pristine paradise. In the cool of the day, hand in hand, they sought their daily quiet time with God.

So Adam was now happily married in the will of God. He was married to Eve whom God had designed to bring love and companionship, life and color, into his already glorious life. Such is God's ideal marriage. The Lord Jesus referred to this idyllic scene when He made His authoritative pronouncement on divorce. He endorsed the ideal.

III. ADAM AND HIS WOES

The idyllic conditions of Eden that could have lasted forever suddenly ended.

A. One Man's Disobedience

The Bible clearly speaks of Adam's sin. Actually, Adam was not the first to sin; Eve was the first. But God held him accountable. God always holds the man accountable for what happens to his wife. Adam, the ordained head of his home, was responsible before God for his wife's spiritual welfare. This principle still holds true today.

As Scripture records, the serpent entered Eden. It was not the serpent Adam had known from the day of his creation. It was not a beautiful, graceful creature named and known by Adam for its cleverness. It was "that old serpent" (Revelation 12:9; 20:2), an invader who came in the guise of a serpent with the express purpose of infecting the human race with the virus of sin. He found Eve alone, deceived her, and left her in nakedness and shame. Already shadows were gathering in the garden of Eden.

Adam found her, lost and alone, standing before the tree of the knowledge of good and evil, holding the forbidden fruit. She did not have to tell him what she had done; he knew. She was disturbingly different. Her beauty had a different, sensual quality. When she held out the fruit to him, there was allurement in the act—a mixture of provocation and pathos that struck a false but tantalizing chord.

We can picture Adam's consternation. He loved her, and now she was lost. Nobody had to tell him that. He knew it intuitively from the indwelling Holy Spirit. He knew the word of God: "The day that thou eatest thereof thou shalt surely die" (Genesis 2:17). He was about to lose this woman whom he loved—lose her forever. He loved her more now that he was about to lose her than he had ever loved her before in her sweet innocence. He was not deceived. The Bible clearly states that Eve *was* deceived and that Adam was *not* deceived. His keen intellect took in the situation at a glance, weighed all the factors in the equation, and arrived at the correct answer. His wife now knew good and evil. Moreover, in learning about evil she had become evil. Between Eve and Adam a gulf now existed as deep and as wide as that which separated the rich man from Lazarus in our Lord's teaching (Luke 16:19-31).

A door had slammed irrevocably on the past. Adam and

Eve could not go back to the idyllic Eden they had known. Eve was no longer innocent; she was guilty. She was no longer pure in mind, heart, and will. She was tainted and depraved. At once she had become both a sinner and a seducer. She was tempting Adam at that moment. She knew it; he knew it.

We do not know how long Adam debated the issues within himself, weighing all the factors in his brilliant mind. We only know the decision that he reached. His great love for Eve led him into sin. His heart went out to the woman he loved. His *logic* said, "No! No! A thousand times no!" His *love* said, "Yes! Yes! Ten thousand times yes!"[1]

As Eve had followed her *head* into sin, so Adam followed his *heart* into sin. He looked again at Eve—at his beloved wife, at the companion of so many blessed, blissful days. She was lonely and afraid. He could see the haunted look in her eyes. She was now under God's curse. Soon He would be abroad in the garden. Then would come His sentence—death!

Well, Adam decided to share her sin and sorrow. With one almost magnificent gesture, eyes wide open to the consequences, he took the proffered fruit from her hand, deliberately bit into it, tasted its bittersweet flavor, and became a *sinner*. He deliberately stepped down to where she was.

Thus, as Paul put it, "By one man sin entered into the world, and death by sin" (Romans 5:12). One man's disobedience ruined the human race.

B. One Man's Descendants

When Adam fell, all creation fell. We were all "in Adam" when he fell. He dragged the entire, unborn, human race with him into sin.

No sooner had Adam sinned than the light went out in his soul. His next act was one of folly. He made an ineffective,

---

[1] Adam was not deceived; he was disobedient. He knew what he was doing and his love for Eve was the only possible motive. His love for her, which should have been subordinated to his love for and trust in God, had become idolatrous. From a purely human view it seemed noble.

foolish effort to cover the nakedness of which he had just become aware. He sewed fig leaves together to cover his shame and the shame of Eve.

Thus false religion was born, for such an act is the essence of all false religion—man's attempt, by his own effort, to cover the guilt and shame of his sin in order to appear acceptable to God.

Adam's fig leaves served well enough for him and Eve, but the leaves were woefully inadequate in the presence of God. Adam and Eve had to learn that "without shedding of blood is no remission" (Hebrews 9:22).

Soon God's judgment fell; the gates of the garden clanged ominously behind the fallen pair. Now they faced a future in which no thought, word, deed, incident, accident, motion, or motive could be divorced from the terrible fact of sin. Nor could they forget that the only road back to God was by way of the shed blood of Calvary's Lamb.

Adam was not long in discovering what kind of seed the serpent had sown into the world by his fall. Adam himself was no longer inhabited by God; he was inhabited by sin; the controlling principle of the indwelling Holy Spirit was gone. And Adam's sons were born in sin and "shapen in iniquity" (Psalm 51:5). Sin leaped full grown on this stage of time.

Adam's first son, Cain, grew up to be a murderer. Cain, Scripture reveals, was very religious, but his religion was too refined to slay a lamb. However, his religion was not too refined to slay his brother Abel, of whom he was jealous. Abel disagreed with Cain's religious creed, but his simple trust in God and acceptance of God's way of salvation won Abel God's approval. Infuriated, Cain murdered Abel. Then, far from being repentant before God, he was insolent.

Adam lived for 930 years (Genesis 5:5). We do not know how many of those years he lived in Eden. Perhaps he lived there for thirty years, since Jesus (the Second Man) was thirty years old when He met the same old serpent with far different results.

In any case, Adam lived on and on in that world before the great flood. He saw evil men and seducers wax worse and worse. He saw harvest after harvest of wickedness reaped on the earth. He saw his oldest son establish an utterly godless civilization. He saw the knowledge of God linger for a generation or two in Cain's family and then die out altogether.

Adam also saw his sons' astonishing inventiveness. He saw them found great cities and discover the art of smelting. He saw them bring the world through an industrial revolution that changed the course of history. He saw man's cleverness with cattle. He saw arts and entertainment come into being, flourish, and reach full fruition on the earth. What din and noise it all was after the peace and quietness of Eden.

But side by side with all this splendor and achievement was unparalleled wickedness. "Every imagination of the thoughts of [man's] heart was only evil continually" (Genesis 6:5). Adam saw the rise of a pornographic society in which lust, lewdness, and license reigned supreme. It must have broken his heart. Indeed, by the time Adam was several hundred years old, he must have been the unhappiest man who has ever lived.

One redeeming factor remained—the godly remnant of Seth and his sons. Adam did not live to see the full fruit of their goodness, but when he was 622 Enoch was born. Sixty-five years later, when Adam was 687 Enoch began to walk with God. That must have tremendously encouraged Adam. Just 57 years after Adam died, Enoch was translated to Heaven. There he and Adam have been walking with God ever since. There Adam, Abel, and Seth wait for the coming of you, me, and the last of Seth's godly line.

2
Eve,
Mother of Us All

Genesis 2:18–3:24; 4:1-8; 5:1-3

I. EVE'S FUTURE

    A. Her Maker

    B. Her Marriage

II. EVE'S FALL

    A. The Challenge

        1. The Authorship of the Word

        2. The Accuracy of the Word

        3. The Acceptability of the Word

    B. The Change

        1. She Saw: The Look Became a Lust

        2. She Took: The Desire Became a Decision

        3. She Did Eat: The Choice Became a Chain

        4. She Gave: The Sinner Became a Seducer

III. EVE'S FAMILY

    A. A Messiah

    B. A Murderer

She was as fair as the morning, bright as the day, warm as the sunshine, and as sweet as honey in the comb. She was the essence of womanhood. She was brimful of life. Her husband lost his heart to her the moment that he saw her. Her name was Eve.

If we each think of the most beautiful woman we have ever met—a woman with grace and charm, wit and personality, charisma and appeal—Eve personified that woman.

I. EVE'S FUTURE

Normally when we meet someone attractive, we like to know something of his or her past. Eve had no past; all she had was a future.

A. Her Maker

God was her Maker. On this point even the so-called theistic evolutionist faces an insurmountable controversy with the Bible. The theistic evolutionist tries to accommodate the evolutionist by conceding that Adam could have evolved under God's directing hand. But what about Eve? There is no way she could have evolved. The Bible says that God created Eve from Adam's side as a special, final act in the creative process. This is either true or false. If the Bible is true, then evolution is false. If evolution is true, then the Bible begins with a gross, inexcusable mistake. Both views cannot be true. Here in Genesis 2 we have fact or fable—one or the other.

Moses hinted that Eve was almost an afterthought with God. Again and again in Genesis 1, the creation chapter, we read, "And God saw that it was *good*" (italics added). At the end of the chapter we read, "And God saw . . . it was *very good*" (italics added). Then, after placing Adam in the garden, God said: "It is *not good*" (Genesis 2:18, italics added). "It is not good that the man should be alone; I will make him an help meet for him." God went on to produce His masterpiece. He created a woman whom Adam called Eve.

Matthew Henry said of Eve that God took her from Adam's side—not from his head to rule over him, and not from his feet to be trampled on. God took her from Adam's side to be his equal, to be protected under his arm, and loved close to his heart.

One moment there was no woman. The next moment she stood before him: fresh from the hand of her Maker, with no past, with only a future.

B. Her Marriage

The first thing that happened to Eve after her creation was her wedding. There was a lightning-swift courtship when God introduced Adam to her. They met. They married. Just like that. And instantly Adam's paradise became a double paradise.

Jesus goes back to this Edenic scene when He states His sublime views about marriage (Matthew 19:1-8). Let us note that. Jesus believed in a literal Adam and Eve. If the evolutionist is right, then Jesus was wrong. It's unthinkable for anyone to claim to be a Christian and accept the view that Jesus, the incarnate Son of the living God, could be wrong about anything. During His earthly stay, Jesus was never wrong about anything. He is the eternal, uncreated, self-existing, second person of the godhead. He stepped out of eternity into time to be born as a man among men. While always never more than man, at the same time Jesus was never anything less than God. He was God manifested in flesh. As such, He was omniscient in His wisdom. He made no mistakes. Anyone who says that He did is a deceiver and an antichrist.

When the disciples asked the Lord to expound His views on divorce, He took them back to the beginning of creation. He went back beyond the prophets, beyond Sinai, right back to the garden of Eden, back to this first wedding. He, Himself, had officiated at this wedding as the father of the bride and friend of the bridegroom. Divorce, Jesus taught, had its roots in human hardness; marriage had its roots in divine love. "What therefore God hath joined together," Jesus stated, "let not man put asunder" (Mark 10:9). That was His verdict.

So Eve was created and Eve was married. Before her

stretched an eternity of bliss in an earthly paradise. She and
Adam lived in ideal surroundings. They had the delightful task
of tending and keeping that Edenic garden. It was filled to
overflowing with exotic fruits and flowers; it was graced by all
kinds of birds and beasts, each one perfectly tame and wholly
submissive to their will. There were wide rivers to explore,
forests to roam, and surprises and delights at every twist and
turn. Their days were full of wonder; their nights were filled
with starry skies. The cool of each day became a special time
when God came down to the garden to walk with them, to talk
with them, and to open up before them new and marvelous
mysteries of His handiwork in Heaven and on earth.

Then one day the serpent came.

II. EVE'S FALL

The serpent was none other than fallen Lucifer, who was
using the graceful serpent's form. Evidently he waited until Eve
was alone.

The Bible tells us much about this old serpent. Three
chapters in from the beginning of the Bible, we meet him for
the first time. Three chapters in from the end of the Bible, we
meet him for the last time. In between we discern his evil trail.
Before his fall Lucifer was "the anointed cherub"—the greatest,
most glorious, most gifted, and most gorgeous of all the
creatures God had made. Lucifer was the choirmaster of
Heaven, brilliant in appearance, and the highest of all created
intelligences.

After his fall, he retained great gifts of genius, only now
they were bent, twisted, and warped. His soul was soured by
sin. He was driven by an implacable hatred of God and by an
all-consuming envy of the human race. He came into the
garden of Eden to spoil. His one great passion was revenge.
He wanted to bend, twist, and ruin the human race because
man had been made in the image and likeness of God. That
image Lucifer desired above all else to deface.

On the surface of things, Eve was no match for this evil one. The Holy Spirit tells us that he was full of subtlety. Eve, in contrast, knew nothing of sin. She had never been tempted. All she had was the armor of innocence and the Word of God. But in herself she would be no match for the fallen Lucifer. If it came to discussion and debate, he could beguile her in no time.

Besides, God had intended her to be the heart of things, not the head of things. He had created, ordained, and commissioned Adam to be the head, not Eve. Her first mistake was in not calling for Adam, her federal and spiritual head, as soon as temptation began.

Even so, there was no reason why Eve should have fallen so easily into Satan's crafty snare. She had one weapon he feared—the Word of God. Of course her Bible was quite small indeed, consisting of just two verses (Genesis 2:16-17). But that would have been enough. One word from God, believed and obeyed, is a mighty sword.

To all the serpent's wiles, Eve simply would have had to say, "Thus saith the Lord." All she would have needed to do was fall back on God's inspired, inerrant, invincible Word and she would have been safe. It was all the protection she would have needed. Had she drawn and used that Sword, fallen Lucifer—stabbed and pierced through and through, his soul screaming with the cut and thrust of that Sword, his wounds burning and flaming from its fires—would have fled in mortal terror from the garden, from the planet, from the solar system, and from the galaxy. He would have put a million light years between himself and that Sword.

But look at what happened. In the first place, Eve was clumsy in her use of the Sword of the Spirit. She used it, it is true, but she misused it. She constantly misquoted it, she subtracted from it twice, and she added to it once. She thought that she could paraphrase it and improve it. She thought that as long as she had the general drift of God's thoughts in mind, the actual words did not matter. She set up her puny mind as the ultimate authority as to what God had said and what God had meant. Therefore she was putty in the devil's hands. Likewise, there is no hope today for the man or woman who thinks that the Bible can be handled like that. They are the devil's dupes from the beginning.

We are not going to labor here over the cut and thrust of that battle—for a battle it was, with the stakes being the rule of the world and the ruin of the human race. We will simply note that Satan challenged the Word of God along three lines.

A. The Challenge

He first challenged:

1. The Authorship of the Word

"Yea, hath God said . . . ?" (Genesis 3:1) Lucifer was, in effect, asking, "How do you know that God said it? Maybe Adam said it. What proof do you have that it is *God's* Word?" Of course, if there is doubt as to the authorship of the Bible, there is a question as to its authority. "Yea, hath God said . . . ?" Nobody has answered that Satanic challenge better than Dryden the poet. With his open Bible before him, he wrote:

> Whence but from heaven
> Could men, unskilled in arts,
> In different ages born,
> From different parts
> Weave such agreeing truths?
> Or how, or why
> Should all conspire to cheat us with a lie?
> When—starving their gains
> Unwanted their advice,
> Unasked their pains
> And martyrdom their price?

Next Lucifer challenged:

2. The Accuracy of the Word

"Yea, hath God said, Ye shall not eat of every tree of the garden?" The evil one was asking, "How do you know that the words you quote are exactly what God said? How do you know that there is no error in the transmission of this 'word' of God? After all, you weren't there when it was given. All you have is what has been handed down to you. It may not be inerrant after all."

Then Lucifer challenged:

3. The Acceptability of the Word

After listening to Lucifer, Eve saw that the forbidden tree "was good for food, and that it was pleasant to the eyes, and a tree to be desired to make one wise" (Genesis 3:6). "Why should anyone," he was suggesting, "place such a restriction on you? After all, you are a mature adult. You should do your own thing. As an intelligent, thinking, independent person, you should simply not accept such a narrow restriction being placed on your behavior."

Because Eve did not have a firm grip on the authoritative, inerrant, divinely inspired, Holy-Spirit-preserved and God-revealed word of Scripture, she was an easy prey for the tempter.

One moment she was free, magnificent, God-obeying, Bible-believing, and Spirit-exalting. The next moment she was a temptress and a seducer, determined to drag her nearest and dearest down to her level.

The sun still shone brightly in the sky. The flowers still shed their perfume. The four rivers still flowed out of Eden. But there was a difference. The alluring serpent had vanished, and the light of the Holy Spirit had gone out of Eve's soul. The Holy Spirit no longer indwelt her spirit. She was suddenly much more aware of her body and very much alive to all kinds of wickedness. Her imagination was quickened to things suggestive and seductive, and her soul was tinged by the first shadow of coming night. Instead of delighting her, thoughts of God disquieted her.

Eve had not anticipated that the knowledge of good and evil would be like this. It was both frightening and fascinating. Moreover, she had suddenly become a schemer. Deep within her, the light that had previously illumined her soul and bathed her body in a rainbow robe had gone out. She was naked. She knew that she had become evil. She did not like it and wanted to do something about it, but she did not know what to do. Her sense of exposure filled her with a desire to run away and hide. She experienced shame. A terrifying thought haunted her: *What will I do when God comes?*

God had said, "In the day that thou eatest thereof thou shalt surely die" (Genesis 2:17). *What did that mean?* she wondered, her fears rising. Eve already knew that something had died within her and she did not like it at all. She was suddenly greatly afraid of God; she was a sinner, and would become the mother of a whole race of sinners.

Maybe Adam would help her. But how could she explain to Adam what had happened? How could she tell him how she now felt? How could she describe this tumult of emotions that now surged in her soul? The scheming part of Eve decided at once that Adam must become like her. Then he would know what she knew. Then he could bring his magnificent intellect to bear on the problem of nakedness, exposure, guilt, and fear.

B. The Change

Notice the four downward steps in her fall:

1. She Saw: The Look Became a Lust

There are certain things we cannot help but see, things on which we ought not to look. They are the very stuff of which temptation is made. The glance *starts* the fire; the gaze *stokes* the fire.

2. She Took: The Desire Became a Decision

She was now in the throes of temptation. She held the forbidden fruit. She was deliberately playing with temptation, toying with the forbidden fruit.

3. She Did Eat: The Choice Became a Chain

Satan can pander to our desires. He is the "super-pimp" of the universe. He can procure, propose, and pander, but he cannot push. But the moment Eve ate, she became a slave. She committed sin, and as Jesus said, "Whosoever committeth sin is the servant of sin" (John 8:34).

4. She Gave: The Sinner Became a Seducer

It is a proven fact that people who are entangled in the snare of an evil habit, an enslaving lust, or an unquenchable craving, will try to get others to join them in their sinful actions. Eve was no different. It did not take weeks, months, or years for all her sin to develop. Sin sprang full-grown into her soul. She was no sooner a sinner than she was a seducer.

Nobody has to learn how to be a sinner. Nobody has to be taught how to tell lies, how to be self-willed, how to throw a temper tantrum, or how to indulge the lusts of the flesh. We are all very good at sinning—quite naturally.

Eve woke up that morning in fellowship with the angels of God, at peace with the world, and a daughter of Heaven. She went to bed that night a sinner, very much alive to the knowledge of good and evil. She became a slave to sin and a stranger to goodness.

III. EVE'S FAMILY

For the rest of her days, Eve's life revolved around two focal points.

A. A Messiah

Her dreaded confrontation with the holy God was not long in coming. But lo! God, true to His character, tempered government with grace, law with love, ruin with redemption, and punishment with promise. For even as He pronounced sentence, He pronounced salvation. He promised that a Messiah would come from the seed of the woman, no less. There would be a serpent seed, but God would also provide a special seed. One day from the woman (not from the man) One would come who would trample the serpent, give His precious blood to cleanse mankind, provide His righteousness as a robe for their souls, and restore the lost splendors of Eden.

Eve believed that. In fact, when her first son was born, she cried out with joy, "I have gotten the Man, even Jehovah!" She was wrong in her conclusion but right in her conviction. She thought Cain was the promised Christ. He turned out, though, to be more like the seed of the serpent than the promised Savior seed.

Cain was a clever little boy, but he was also very contrary, and cruel. Eve had to cope with his temper tantrums, with his pride and self-will, with his lies, and with his downright disobedience. We wonder how she managed to cope with all that.

By the time her second son was born, Eve knew her mistake. She called him *Abel*, which means "vanity." One thing she was sure of: Cain was not the promised Savior seed. She reacted to this disillusionment by registering her disappointment, doubt, and discouragement in selecting the name *Abel*.

B. A Murderer

The two boys grew up. Abel was a genuine believer; Cain was merely religious. Then one day Abel disappeared.

"Cain, have you seen Abel?" we can imagine Eve asking.

"No, I don't know anything about him," he responded. "Why should I? Am I my brother's keeper?"

Shortly after that the terrible truth came out. Cain had murdered Abel. Cain had murdered him in a fit of rage and resentment over Abel's faith in God. Branded and accursed of God, Cain packed his bags and left home—defiant to the last— to become the world's first city-builder and to found a great but utterly godless civilization. The civilization was so godless that before it ended, its evil called down the flood tides of God's wrath on the earth.

Who but a mother can measure the heartache and sorrow that Eve carried with her to the grave as a result of that terrible tragedy? She had reaped a bumper crop of the harvest of her sin.

But what a woman she was, after all. We can picture her one day, not long after the tragedy, listening when Adam said, "Well, Mother Eve, I guess that's about it. Two sons—one a martyr, the other a murderer!"

But Eve answered, "No, that's not it at all. I'm going to have another son. I'll call him *Seth*, which means 'the appointed one.' You see, dear husband, I was not wrong about the *truth* of the coming seed; I was just wrong about the *time*. I still believe in God. I challenged His Word once, and Cain and Abel were the result. I shall never challenge His Word again."

So in due time Seth was born and became the founder of the royal line to the Messiah. After the passing of many centuries, One came of whom we read:

> God, who at sundry times and in divers manners spake in
> time past unto the fathers by the prophets, Hath in these

last days spoken unto us by his Son, whom he hath
appointed heir of all things, by whom also he made the
worlds; Who being the brightness of his glory, and the
express image of his person, and upholding all things by
the word of his power, when he had by himself purged
our sins, sat down on the right hand of the Majesty on high
(Hebrews 1:1-3).

3
Elimelech, the Backslider

Ruth 1:1-5

The story of Elimelech is a Biblical classic on the high cost of backsliding. Despite all his professions of faith, Elimelech took the reins of his life into his own hands. He became a backslider in Moab and sowed the seeds of all the sadness and sorrow that followed in his life. Indeed, the first chapter of Ruth is dark with tragedy. Tears flow in rivers. All is chaos and darkness. And this all resulted because Elimelech was a backslider.

It has been well said that the first call from God to a person

is this question: *Heaven or Hell?* One has to decide how he
wants to spend eternity. He can spend it as a child of God and
joint-heir with Jesus Christ in the mansions of glory; he can be
saved by sovereign grace, washed in the soul-cleansing blood
of the Lamb, and regenerated by the Holy Spirit; his name can
be written in life's eternal book. Or he can spend eternity
forever lost in the blackness of darkness, cut off from God and
His grace in that terrible place where there is weeping, wailing,
and gnashing of teeth. That is the first question: Heaven or
Hell?

The second question is similar. Once a person decides
that at all costs he wants to go to Heaven, a second question
surfaces: Which world are you going to live for, Heaven or
earth? This question arises in the story of Abraham and Lot in
the Old Testament and in the sad case of Demas in the New
Testament. It is tragically possible for a person to have a saved
soul and a lost life, to see one's whole life as a Christian go up
in smoke as wood, hay, and stubble at the judgment seat of
Christ—to be saved "so as by fire" (1 Corinthians 3:15).

There seems to be little doubt that Elimelech was a
genuine Old Testament believer. But he lived for the wrong
world, and he paid a very high price for that in both his own
life and his family's lives.

Five things come into focus when we think of Elimelech.

I. A FALLEN MAN

Our first consideration has to do with his remarkable
name. Almost everyone familiar with the Bible knows that
Biblical names, particularly Old Testament names, are of great
significance. The name *Elimelech* was no exception. It means
"My God is King," and it tells us three important things.

A. A Confession

Look at the center of that definition. What do you see?
The words *God is.* Elimelech carried that truth around with him
to his dying day.

It is significant that the Holy Spirit begins the Bible with the grand assumption that God is: "In the beginning God created the heaven and the earth." There is no attempt to prove that there is a God, just the bare assertion: "God created."

We, of course, might have wanted to suggest half a dozen lines of reasoning to prove that there is a God. We might have started an argument using the clear evidence of law and order in the universe (law and order that seem more intricate and marvelous the more we study various scientific disciplines). Then we might have concluded that the universe could not have formed by chance.

For instance, millions of complex factors make up one living, functioning, human body; the idea that it could be the end product of chance is ludicrous. We could put the parts of a watch in a washing machine and slosh them around for a hundred billion years and they would never assemble themselves into a watch.

But the Holy Spirit makes no attempt to demonstrate the fact that God is. Like the writers of the American Declaration of Independence, the Holy Spirit deems that certain truths are self-evident.

So we have Elimelech's confession: God is. Elimelech was not an atheist or agnostic. He adopted the key position later enunciated by the Holy Spirit: "For he that cometh to God must believe that he is, and that he is a rewarder of them that diligently seek him" (Hebrews 11:6).

Elimelech's name also shows:

B. A Connection

The name embodies a personal pronoun. It does not just mean "God is"; it means "*My* God is." Somewhere along the line, the living, self-existing God of the universe had become Elimelech's personal God. His testimony was simple: "The God who is, is my God." For Elimelech, God was not a remote, infinite, impersonal being, who having created the universe simply tossed it into space and left it to its own devices. He was a God who permitted, encouraged, and even sought a personal relationship with members of the human race.

This is another marvelous truth about God. He has revealed Himself. He wants us to know Him. Even more important, He wants to belong to us and He wants us to belong to Him. This is the clear teaching of the Bible. In the opening part of John's Gospel we read this remarkable statement: "As many as received him, to them gave he power to become the sons of God, even to them that believe on his name: Which were born, not of blood, nor of the will of the flesh, nor of the will of man, but of God" (John 1:12-13).

In other words, the God who is, can become my God. I can accept God into my life by inviting the Lord Jesus to come and, by His Holy Spirit, take up permanent residence in my innermost being. Many people will affirm that God is; not many can say that they have established this vital connection with God.

C. A Coronation

"My God is King." That is also part of the revelation of God in the name *Elimelech*. Indeed, how could God be anything less?

According to what Elimelech professed through his name, there had been a time when he had crowned the true and living God—the Creator of the universe, Elohim-Jehovah, the God of creation and the God of covenant—as *Adonai*, the God of control. He had handed the legislative, executive, and judicial roles in his life over to God.

God cannot accept anything less. In Luke 6:46 Jesus said, "Why call ye me, Lord, Lord, and do not the things which I say?" He also told the story of the foolish virgins (Matthew 25). They came and knocked on the door of the house after they missed the coming of the bridegroom. "Lord, Lord, open to us," they said. He replied, "I know you not."

It is possible for a person to profess faith in Christ and not, at once, recognize that he must hand over all aspects of his life to Jesus. The believer may not learn at once that the Lord Jesus has the right to reign and rule in his heart. But if the professing believer never learns that and never makes any attempt to give Christ His proper place, possibly that person does not know Christ at all.

There is a great deal of theological debate about the place of the lordship of Christ in conversion. It is possible for a person, like Elimelech, to give Christ His proper place once and then take back, into his own hands, the governing reins of his life. Some people, however, say that Jesus is their Lord and yet have missed salvation completely. There can be no greater tragedy than to discover at last that Heaven's door has been shut and to hear the Lord say that He never knew you. The best thing to do is to make sure of our salvation.

As we look at Elimelech, we see a man who by his very name claimed to have made a confession, a connection, and a coronation in his life. "My God is King!" he seemed to be saying.

But even as the story opens, we see that he was a fallen man. He was saying all the right things and doing all the wrong things. And that can only spell disaster for any man.

II. A FALSE MOVE

"A certain man of Bethlehem-judah went to sojourn in the country of Moab, he, and his wife and his two sons" (Ruth 1:1). Notice the Holy Spirit's use of the *polysyndeton*—the repetition of the word *and*. It indicates a deliberate, significant, step-by-step happening. The journey was also a false move.

The name *Bethlehem-judah* means "house of bread and praise." Symbolically, Bethlehem is the place where God meets the needs of a starving world. To Bethlehem, indeed, He sent the Bread of Life from Heaven. Bethlehem is the house of bread, the house of praise. In other words, Bethlehem is a type[1] of the local church, the New Testament "house of bread and praise." Here God's people gather to feed on the bread of Heaven and offer praise to God.

Now we can recognize Elimelech's false move. He left Bethlehem-judah. He left the place where God had put His name, the place where God met the needs of His own, the place where God's people offered praise to Him. If Elimelech were living today, we would say that he left the local church, the gathering place of God's people.

Elimelech, of course, had good reasons for leaving Bethlehem-judah—at least they seemed like good reasons to him. There was a famine in the land, and even God's people were suffering.

Elimelech's solution to the problem was typical. He left. Probably he did not make a fuss about it. Very likely he simply said, "There's not much here for me. My family isn't getting fed. I'm leaving." That was his big mistake.

He should have stayed and allowed God to do something for him there and, indeed, something through him there. He should have allowed God to be God in his life. He should have said, "There has to be a reason for this dryness and barrenness. I want to be part of the solution." Instead, he quit.

How often have we met people like Elimelech? They leave a local fellowship after finding fault with the preacher, the elders, or some of the others. Everyone who wanders away from the local church thinks he has a good reason. Instead of saying, "There is a problem here, there is a famine of the Word of God among His people here, but I'm going to let God work through me to turn things around," they leave. As often as not, they end up in Moab. They finish the course of their lives by going nowhere, by joining a church with flawed doctrine, or by completely immersing themselves in the world.

Moreover, backsliding never takes place in a vacuum.

---

[1]Webster defines *type* as "a person or thing (as in the Old Testament) believed to foreshadow another (as in the New Testament)."

Backsliding always involves other members of the family. Elimelech's wife was involved, as were his two sons. Of the four who went to Moab only one was ever spiritually recovered.

Elimelech should be renamed. Instead of being called "my God is King," he should be called "I am king." We now see a man completely out of touch with God, His Word, His people, and His Spirit. He made a false move.

III. A FORBIDDEN MARRIAGE

We do not know how old the sons were when the family moved to Moab. Probably they were teenagers, at least. Here is the Holy Spirit's comment through Scripture: "They came into the country of Moab, and continued there" (Ruth 1:2). Perhaps there were more job opportunities in Moab. Perhaps someone offered Elimelech better pay in Moab. Doubtless he only planned to stay there until the situation improved in Bethlehem.

The sad fact was, however, that Elimelech continued living there. Likewise, it is far easier for us to continue a course of backsliding than it is to return to the house of bread and praise. To return involves making the verbal or unspoken confession: I made a mistake.

So Elimelech's sons grew up in Moab. During their most impressionable years, when they were forming their most important friendships, they were thrown into contact with an exotic, sinful world. They grew to manhood outside that protective boundary where God draws His own circle around His own.

One day Mahlon brought a girlfriend home. Her name was Ruth. She was lovely, but she was a Moabite—a stranger to God and His Word. Their friendship developed into marriage. So now one of Elimelech's children was thoroughly married to the world.

Before long the other son, Chilion, did the same. Now both of Elimelech's sons were "unequally yoked together" with unbelievers and committed to a Moabite way of life.

The names of these two young men are significant. The name *Mahlon* means "sickly"; the name *Chilion* means "pining." The Holy Spirit intended for these names to indicate their spiritual condition. One son was weak; the other was wistful. And no wonder. Neither grew up in the kind of spiritual atmosphere that would have developed a robust faith. Elimelech could talk about God's truths as much as he wished (and no doubt he did), but the example he set undid everything that he said. Why shouldn't the sons settle in Moab? Their father had. If they found *marital* compromise with the world acceptable, it was because their father had found *monetary* compromise with the world acceptable. Likewise, we cannot bring up our children in a worldly atmosphere and then complain because they have worldly appetites.

Elimelech must have known that God's Word was crystal clear on this matter. "Neither shalt thou make marriages with them. . . . For they will turn away thy son from following me . . . so will the anger of the Lord be kindled against you, and destroy thee suddenly" (Deuteronomy 7:3-4). And it happened—even more dramatically because God's special curse rested on Moab. "An Ammonite or Moabite shall not enter into the congregation of the Lord; even to their tenth generation" (Deuteronomy 23:3)

These marriages, then, were forbidden by the law of God, but Elimelech seems to have written that legislation off as so much narrow-mindedness. In the East parents arranged marriages and were quite involved in drawing up the contracts. By now Elimelech was so far backslidden, had lost control over his sons to such a degree, and was so much the victim of his circumstances that he actively helped to arrange these marriages. That was the final nail driven into the coffin of Elimelech's backsliding. He lost his family in Moab. It was bad enough that he became a backslider, but look well at what he did to his sons.

IV. A FAMILY MORGUE

"And Elimelech Naomi's husband died. . . . And Mahlon and Chilion died also both of them" (Ruth 1:3,5). The family was in Moab for a scant ten years, but the tragedy of unbelief and backsliding had struck long before death came in. God's displeasure was quickly demonstrated.

First we have the death of Elimelech, whose name meant "My God is King," but whose every breath in Moab was a repudiation of the testimony of his name. The life of the backslider is a lie. When God is no longer a person's king, his life has little meaning. The whole purpose for which he was created in Adam and recreated in Christ is annulled.

God left Elimelech alone for a while to see if, like the prodigal son, he would come to his senses and return to Him. This Old Testament prodigal never did that. Perhaps he liked Moab; probably he became too involved in Moab. It is amazing that in our day believers who will not become involved in the church are willing enough to become involved in the world's clubs, associations, leagues, and societies. Thus these believers advertise to their children exactly where their true values lie—in the world.

So God waited, but Elimelech showed no sign of repentance and return; he just continued his daily routines and settled down in Moab. He became a willing exile, far from the place where God had put His name, far from the place that, despite its drought and difficulties, was the one place in all the world where God met with His people. There in Moab Elimelech died—out of fellowship, a backslider.

That first funeral in Moab was a direct word from God. It was a terrible, tragic, and unmistakable word. God intends that every funeral we attend should cause us to search our hearts and examine our ways. The dead person lying in his coffin preaches his last sermon, for better or for worse, to those who have been left behind.

How dark it was. No one in Moab read a comforting Scripture to the sorrowing family. No one came in and prayed with the bereaved. Their neighbors doubtlessly dropped in to pass on a few pagan platitudes, but that was all.

The death of their father, however, did not speak to either Mahlon or Chilion. Mahlon should have said to his younger brother, "You know, Chilion, we need to get back into fellowship with God's people. Dad always said that he was not going to die in Moab. He often told us about Jacob and Joseph and how they wanted to be buried in Canaan. Let's take our father's body and go back to Bethlehem—back to the house of bread and of praise." But no, only silence reigned. Or maybe, if Mahlon did speak like that, Chilion replied, "My wife would not come, and even if yours would, what kind of reception would she receive from God's people?"

Both Mahlon and Chilion died in Moab too. They died young, as they had lived, with no interest in spiritual things. The family morgue was busy those days, as the death angel came again and again. God spoke once, again, and yet again, and always in the same stern voice.

V. A FINAL MISTAKE

We read of Naomi: "And the woman was left" (Ruth 1:5). This statement is so brief that we tend to hurry past it in our Scripture reading. But it is the last despairing signpost on the highway of the backslidden man. *Left.* In Moab. Left in the company of the ungodly, far from God's people. Left to shift for herself with two sons in a place where God had never intended them to be. That is the last blot on Elimelech's life, and a very black blot it is.

So he died and was buried and angels carried him to

Abraham's bosom. But we can well believe that, unlike Lazarus, poor Elimelech would not be comforted. Like the rich man in Hell who could only think of his brothers, Elimelech could only think of his boys. We can imagine a conversation between Abraham and Elimelech in Heaven.

Abraham might say, "Can't you be still, Elimelech?"

"Oh, Father Abraham," Elimelech might reply, "I have two sons. Send Caleb; send Joshua."

"They have Moses and the prophets, so let your sons hear them," Abraham would respond.

"But oh, Father Abraham, I neglected to nurture them spiritually and failed to ground them properly in the truth of Moses and the law. I was too concerned that they receive a good education in Moab, that they attend the best schools, and that they make the right business contacts. Maybe if someone rose from the dead, they would believe."

"If they don't believe Moses and the prophets," Abraham would say, "neither will they believe if someone rose from the dead. They have their Bible. God has no other word than that."

So poor Elimelech tossed and turned. His sons lived like pagans in Moab, and they died like pagans in Moab. Now poor Elimelech has nothing to look forward to but the coming judgment day when God will call him to account for the way that he lived and the influence that he wielded.

Again, we can almost reconstruct the scene at the judgment day: "Well, Elimelech, so you are here. Where are those two boys I trusted you with in Bethlehem-judah, in that house of bread and praise?"

"Alas, Master, like Abraham I commanded my children and my household. He commanded his children in Your ways; I commanded mine in the ways of the world. I took them to Moab, Lord, and I left them there. I lost them there."

4
Naomi,
a Backslider Restored

Ruth 1:8-22; 2:19-22; 3:1-5

I. HER PLIGHT
II. HER PLAN
III. HER PLEA
IV. HER PLACE

    A. Her Fellowship
    B. Her Fruitfulness
    C. Her Fragrance
    D. Her Future

limelech, the Old Testament's prodigal, died in Moab, far from the promised land. Unlike the New Testament prodigal, Elimelech was content to sit down and eat the husks that the swine ate.

Some backsliders are like that. They know the Lord. They are not dogs returned to their vomit or sows wallowing in the mire. They are sheep, but they are wandering sheep. We can be sure that Elimelech never did the evil things that the

Moabites did. He did not worship their terrible gods. But he made no attempt to get back to Bethlehem-judah, where God had put His name.

Naomi was different, and it is with her that we are concerned here. She received restoration with truly wonderful results.

I. HER PLIGHT

What a serious plight Naomi was in, to be a widow and a foreigner in Moab. Let's look at the inhabitants of that land to gain a clear picture of her environment.

The Moabites and the Ammonites were descendants of Lot. During two nights of drunkenness and incest mentioned in Genesis 19, Lot—the great backslider of his day—spawned two terrible foes of God's people, Ammon and Moab. The Ammonites were descended from Lot's younger daughter, the Moabites from Lot's older daughter.

The Ammonites represent in Scripture the sinful world's open and undisguised *hostility* to God's people. They were a wild, nomadic race, often in league with the enemies of God's people.

The Moabites, on the other hand, were more settled and civilized. They did not fight against Israel; they were more subtle. Moab hired a false prophet to curse God's people and sent women to seduce God's people. Balaam's advice was simple. In effect, he said, "You cannot *subdue* them, my lord king, so *seduce* them. Don't rely on the men of Moab; rely on the women of Moab." (See Revelation 2:14.)

In Scripture the Moabites represent the sinful world's *hospitality* to God's people. The world is always a dangerous place for believers, but never more so than when it offers us the right hand of friendship and fellowship. The world says, "Come and join us. Join our lodges, our clubs, and our fraternities. Come and enjoy our lifestyle. It is much more free and open than yours. Come and compromise with our gods. We do not demand that you worship them—just that you do not preach against them."

This was the Moab in which Naomi now lived, a lonely widow. It would be hard to imagine a more dangerous place to which a man could lead his wife and family or a more perilous place in which to leave them.

The chief god of the Moabites was Baal-peor, probably another name for Chemosh, who was worshiped on the summit of mount Peor. The god Chemosh was cruel, like Moloch, and people worshiped him with horrible rites. Little children, for example, were sacrificed in the fire to Chemosh. How a genuine believer could *not* preach against that kind of evil activity is hard to understand.

In the Mosaic law, God set up a special barrier against the Moabites. No Moabite, as we saw in Deuteronomy, was to be permitted to have a share in the worship of God until his tenth generation.

During the days of the judges, the Hebrews, because of their sin, were allowed a taste of Moabite rule. Eglon, the fat and repulsive king of Moab, oppressed them for eighteen long years. If nothing else, *that* should have warned Elimelech of Moab's true nature.

But Elimelech, as we have seen, was a backslider, and backsliders rarely pay much heed to the Word of God even when they know its facts and precepts by heart.

So we note *Naomi's plight.* She had been abandoned in Moab. Her plight was all the more difficult because her sons had cemented their backsliding by marrying into Moabite families.

Naomi's name means "pleasant," which suggests that she had an attractive disposition. She had been pleasant to know and be around, but backsliding changed all that. When she finally arrived back home in Bethlehem, people hardly recognized her. They said, "Is *this* Naomi?" (Ruth 1:19, italics added) Notice her reply: "Call me not Naomi, call me Mara: for the Almighty hath dealt very bitterly with me" (1:20).

Naomi used a rather interesting name for God—the name *Shaddai*, which means "the Almighty." *Shaddai* does not mean "the God of creation," or "the God of the covenant," but "the God of contentment." He is the God who will "supply all your needs according to his riches in glory by Christ Jesus" (Philippians 4:19). Elimelech had denied this aspect of God's character when he moved to Moab simply because there was a temporary famine among God's people. He thought that God had let him down and that the world would treat him better than God. And now Naomi blamed God for her sad state: "Shaddai, the God of contentment," she said in effect, "has let me down." It is extraordinary how people blame God for the troubles they bring on themselves. "Call me not Naomi, call me Mara." Backsliding had turned her into a bitter old woman.

II. HER PLAN

"She had heard in the country of Moab how that the Lord had visited his people in giving them bread" (Ruth 1:6).

This is an Old Testament way of saying that the people of Bethlehem-judah had experienced what today we would call a revival. God had made His presence felt, and Bethlehem-judah had again become "the house of bread and praise." God's people were feasting on both the living bread and actual, physical bread.

Yet Naomi was living in a far country, perishing with spiritual hunger. She was surrounded by starving millions who never so much as knew of a place like Bethlehem where God visited His people and gave them bread. All they had tasted was the bitter bread of Baal-peor.

A great longing sprang up in Naomi's heart, a deep desire to return to the house of bread and praise, to go back to the fellowship of God's people. She did not know how much longer she would live, but she did know that she did not want to die in Moab, out of touch with God and far from the place where He spread a table for His own. All Moab had ever given her was a place to bury her dead.

One day Naomi announced the news to her two daughters-in-law, her only real friends in Moab. "Orpah and Ruth," she said in effect, "I'm going to say goodbye. I'm going back home, back to Bethlehem-judah, back to the God of my youth." The two women decided to go with her.

III. HER PLEA

We observe that all three women took the first steps together: "Wherefore she went forth out of the place where she was, and her two daughters in law with her; and they went on the way to return unto the land of Judah" (Ruth 1:7). Often one person's decision to get right with God influences other people.

There was, however, a great deal of difference in the attitudes of these three women. Naomi was a backslider coming back to God. Ruth was a genuine convert who made a life-transforming decision. Orpah was an inquirer who started well but did not follow through; she came forward, so to speak, but that was all there was to it.

Orpah never did make it to the promised land. We are not going to develop that side of the story here, but we must note that she turned back and we must lay much of the blame for that tragedy on Naomi.

Picture these three women heading toward the Moabite frontier. We can see Naomi and Ruth in earnest conversation as Naomi told her about the God of Heaven, the God of the Hebrews; Naomi told the stories of Abraham, Isaac, Jacob, Moses, Joshua, and the conquest of Canaan; she told Ruth about the law, the offerings, and the feasts. Then suddenly they missed Orpah. They turned around and there she was, far behind, looking back toward her childhood home. She was thinking of all that she was giving up and leaving behind.

They went back to her and then Naomi, still in her backslidden condition, gave the two women terrible advice: "Maybe you'd better not come with me after all. You see, girls, you'll not have much chance of getting married again in my country. Indeed, I can't think of a single self-respecting Jew who would marry a woman from Moab. No Jew living within the boundaries that God has drawn around His people would marry you. You'd have a much better chance of getting remarried if you stayed down here in Moab."

Here two young women had shown initial interest in the truths of God and had taken the first steps toward life's most important decision. All Heaven and Hell swung in the balance for these Moabite women, and what did Naomi do? Did she try to engage Orpah's affections toward the living God? Did she urge Orpah not to look back but to go on? Did Naomi say, "Remember Lot's wife"? After all, the Moabites were descended from Lot.

No. She poured cold water on their incipient faith. She talked to them about getting married, as if that were the all-important goal in life. Indeed, she waxed eloquent on the subject. She said all the wrong things. Trust a backslider to do that.

Then Naomi's terrible eloquence bore fruit. The women hugged, shed tears, and the moment of decision came. We can picture Orpah straightening up and hear her saying, "You're right, Mom. I know some nice young men in Moab, and I do want to get married again. I can't stand the thought of remaining single all my life. I'm going back."

Back she went—back into spiritual darkness, back to the demon gods of her people, back to Moab. And we read of her no more. In later years Naomi may have awakened in the night and thought of Orpah down there in Moab. She may have touched her cheek and felt the place where Orpah had kissed her. She may have thought of Orpah going to a lost eternity—thanks to the advice she had given.

It is a terrible thing to have another's soul on one's

conscience. Yet how careless we are in a backslidden state. We say things, we do things, we influence other people, and we barely give a thought to the results. We help to push someone a little further down the broad road that leads to destruction and do not lose a moment's sleep.

Then, through God's grace, we may regain a right relationship with God. But there are still people whose feet are firmly fixed on the wrong road, who hurry on toward endless pain because of something that we have said or done. And what do we do? We yawn in the face of God and go on as though there were no great white throne for lost sinners and no judgment seat of Christ where He will review and judge the deeds that believers have done. What must God think of our adamant hearts and our cast-iron consciences?

The Holy Spirit does not record that Naomi was ever bothered about Orpah. We would like to think that she was. However, nothing is said. No prayer for Orpah is recorded. No wish is expressed that some traveler from Judah might make a bypass through Moab and look Orpah up. Nothing.

There are other examples. Think of Abraham and Lot. Through Abraham's backsliding in Egypt, Lot developed a taste for this world. Because the well-watered plains of Jordan looked "like the land of Egypt," Lot moved down there. Abraham never forgot that it was largely his fault that his weak nephew developed a taste for backsliding. Abraham rescued him once. And when Lot went back to Sodom a second time, Abraham pursued him with prayer. Indeed, the very night that Lot fled to the hills to escape the doom of Sodom and then fell into those terrible sins that produced an Ammon and a Moab, Abraham was praying for him, pleading with God for whatever righteous souls might be found in that city of sin.

IV. HER PLACE

The Holy Spirit does not tell us of all the adventures and discouragements that marked Naomi's journey home. But at

last, after considerable time, she began to see the fields and
farms of her native Bethlehem. She was a widow, she was
poor, and she had been away for a number of years. But she
had now come back home—back to the place where God
always intended her to be. We note four things about Naomi,
now living in the place of blessing instead of the place of
backsliding.

A. Her Fellowship

"And it came to pass, when they were come to Bethlehem,
that all the city was moved about them" (Ruth 1:19). The
restoration of this backslider caused quite a stir among God's
people. Everyone in Bethlehem was talking about it. "Naomi's
back. Have you seen her? She's looking terrible. She's glad
to be back, but she has paid a high price for backsliding." We
can imagine how the tongues wagged. They always do. That
is a part of the price of restoration to fellowship. There will
always be those who are thoughtful, considerate, and Christlike,
but there will always be others who gossip. The prodigal son,
for instance, had his elder brother to face. Unfortunately the
church has its share of such narrow-minded people. But the
important thing was, Naomi had returned.

This story points out great differences between the Old
Testament and the New Testament. In the Old Testament, all
blessings were connected with a *place;* in the New Testament,
they are connected with the *person* of Christ. In the Old
Testament, one had to be in *Canaan;* in the New Testament,
one has to be in *Christ.* In the Old Testament, everything had
to do with being in the *land;* in the New Testament, everything
has to do with being in the *Lord.* In the Old Testament, the Jew
who moved out of the land was out of the place of blessing and
fellowship—the place where God had put His name—because
all God's blessings were "yea and amen" in Canaan. (See 2
Corinthians 1:20.)

Thus in Ruth 1, all is sadness. The family expected to

profit from going to Moab; instead it reaped nothing but sorrow. But now Naomi was back in fellowship with God's people, back to where the songs of Zion were sung, back to where the Word of God was known, back to where God's people were daily reminded of Calvary, back to where the table was spread, and back to where God took up His place in their midst. What did Moab have to compare with all that? "I went out full," Naomi sadly admitted, "and the Lord hath brought me home again empty" (Ruth 1:21).

B. Her Fruitfulness

Naomi did not have any sons to carry on the family name. What sons she once had, she had lost in Moab—a terrible place to lose them. When will we ever learn the high cost of backsliding?

But although Naomi had no sons, she did have a daughter. Naomi had become a soul-winner. She had brought a poor, lost pagan under the shadow of the wings of the Lord God of Israel (Ruth 2:12).

How quickly Ruth—this new convert—grew in the things of God. We can be sure that at first many Jews viewed Ruth with suspicion. The people of God do not always welcome new converts with open arms, especially when they come from a wholly pagan background. Christians should welcome them, but sometimes they don't. There are cliques in many churches. It can be quite difficult for a newcomer, especially if he is from a "suspicious" background, to gain acceptance. All too often our churches are refrigerators rather than incubators. But Ruth persevered.

It wasn't long before the people were saying to Naomi, "Thy daughter in law, which loveth thee . . . is better to thee than seven sons" (Ruth 4:15). That was quite a testimony.

And Boaz took note of her too. He said, "All the city of my people doth know that thou art a virtuous woman" (Ruth 3:11). What better fruit could one want than that?

C. Her Fragrance

We remember that when Naomi first came back into the fellowship, she was a bitter old woman. "Call me Mara," she said. But it wasn't long before the quiet influence of the place of fellowship wrought a change in her. As a result the people again called her *Naomi*—"pleasant."

That is what a right relationship with the Lord and His people will do for us. It will change us, make us more Christlike, and make us pleasant to be around. If that is not happening, something must be very wrong with our relationship with the Lord and His people.

One fruit of the Spirit is joy. The world offers many things, including pleasure and all kinds of amusement, but it cannot offer joy. Joy is much greater than happiness. Happiness depends on what happens; joy transcends circumstances. The Lord Jesus—that great Man of Sorrows—constantly spoke of His joy in the upper room, with Calvary's shadow already dark upon His soul. The Bible says that a person who is filled with the Spirit will express it "in psalms and hymns and spiritual songs, singing and making melody in [his] heart to the Lord" (Ephesians 5:19).

Only sin can spoil a believer's joy. After his sin with Bathsheba, for example, David did not lose his salvation, but he lost the joy of his salvation.

So, then, Naomi had her fragrance restored to her. Instead of shedding gloom everywhere she went, she shed gladness. People began to notice her joy. They discovered that she was a pleasant person to be around. They gave her back her old name—Naomi. We must notice that in the Spirit-filled temperament, love, joy, and peace are predominant characteristics. May the Lord lend us His fragrance so that we may advertise an attractive brand of Christianity in this gloomy, sinful world.

D. Her Future

What future did Naomi have in Moab? Judging by the experience of her husband and her sons, the only future she had was a grave. Time was getting on, she was getting older, and misery was her constant companion. But once she was restored to God's people, once she returned to the place of blessing, her future was restored.

That is how the story of Naomi ends. Ruth gave birth to a baby boy, and the women of the village put their heads together and named the little fellow *Obed*, which means "worshiper." The Holy Spirit, however, did not stop there. He went back to Pharez, the son of Judah, and counted eight generations to Obed. And the Holy Spirit did not stop there either. He counted two more generations to David—ten generations altogether.

The Holy Spirit thus linked together grace and glory. He went back to the time of Pharez because it was then that God exhibited *grace* to the house of Judah—undeserved grace, overruling the circumstances of Pharez' birth. He went on to the time of David because it was then that God exhibited *glory* to the house of Judah. In Obed, Naomi's future was secured. We can trace that future as it runs from Obed to Jesse and on to David. Later the Holy Spirit added other names until the names springing from little Obed culminated in the name that is above every name—Jesus!

So Naomi's future was restored. God gave her a future beyond her wildest dreams when backsliding in Moab. Through her grandson Obed, God gave Naomi a living link to Jesus. What more could a person want?

The Lord restored to Naomi "the years which the locust [had] eaten" (Joel 2:25).

When we walk with the Lord in the light of His Word,
What a glory He sheds on our way!

While we do His good will He abides with us still,
And with all who will trust and obey.

Trust and obey, for there's no other way
To be happy in Jesus, but to trust and obey.
(John H. Sammis)

5
Ruth,
a Pagan Seeker

Ruth 1:4-22; 2:1-23; 3:1-18; 4:10-17

Ruth was a Moabitess, a member of an accursed race. She was born and bred in paganism. The gods of her people were fearful, filthy, demon gods. We can well imagine that when Ruth was little, she would sometimes catch her parents whispering together in fear: their tones hushed, their eyes watchful, their faces grave. She would catch a word or two to add to the little store of information that children collect about the adult world. We all know how children do it; we have done it often enough ourselves. They add two and two together until they know more than their parents give them credit for. Soon Ruth knew that her parents' fears centered on the priests.

The priests of Moab were powerful and cruel, and they served an assortment of gods. But the most feared god of all was Chemosh, or Moloch. Chemosh had his terrible place among the gentler gods on a platform of movable stones under which great fires could be kindled. Chemosh's lap was so constructed that little children placed on its red-hot surface would roll down an inclined plane into his fiery belly while slaves kept fresh fagots heaped on the hungry fires.

When disaster threatened Moab—plague, famine, the possibility of war—the priests called for another burning. They would come around the homes to inspect the children for possible victims, looking especially for firstborn sons. With a red dye obtained from the seashore, they would stain the wrists of designated victims. There was no court of appeal from the priests' decision. Children with stained wrists were doomed to horrible deaths.

Perhaps when Ruth was a child, she would hear her parents whispering about this and her heart would be filled with dreadful dreams that would be transformed into nightmares.

When Ruth was old enough to play with other girls, she heard about another god—actually a fertility goddess who offered the Moabites regeneration through the gratification of lust with harlot priestesses in the temple. The fertility of fields and farms, people believed, depended on the sex orgies in her temple.

Just as the priests always kept their eyes open for firstborn sons that could be fed to Chemosh, they kept their lustful eyes open for promising girls who could be conscripted for the foul trade of the temple. Ruth and her little friends doubtless shared the scraps of information they gleaned about these practices.

So Ruth grew up a pagan, in a land cursed by the foulness and ferocity of its gods. While growing up, Ruth would have been just as haunted by the rumored stories of what went on in the temple as by the hair-raising screams that came at times from the idol of Chemosh.

This is the woman around whom the story in the book of Ruth revolves. The account tells how Ruth came to know the living God of Israel and how she entered the family of God through a redemptive act of a kinsman-redeemer.

When we first meet her, Ruth is spiritually lost. According to the decree of the Mosaic law, no Moabite could have any part in the worship of the true and living God of Israel until his tenth generation. Translated into practical terms, that meant that Ruth could not be saved, her son could not be saved, her grandson could not be saved, and so on for ten generations. She was not only lost; she was hopelessly lost. Between her and any hope of salvation stood the entire weight of the law of Sinai. The law, with its implacable decrees and unbending demands, mandated against her. There was no way she could escape those edicts that had thundered forth from Sinai.

The book of Ruth, however, shows how God devised a means whereby "his banished be not expelled from him" (2 Samuel 14:14). It tells how a stranger to the commonwealth of Israel, dwelling far away in pagan darkness, was brought into a covenantal relationship with Israel's God. It tells how God not only adopted Ruth into the royal family of Judah, into the outworking of His glorious grace, but also put her in a direct line to David and Christ.

If any book in the Bible demonstrates God's matchless grace and illustrates the divine plan of redemption, it is the book of Ruth. In the Bible, redemption is set forth in two ways: redemption by power, and redemption by purchase. Ruth's story illustrates redemption by purchase.

We can divide the story of Ruth into two parts.

I. RUTH AND THE SOVEREIGNTY OF GOD

Long before Ruth knew anything about God, God knew everything about her: her name; where she lived; her marriage; the name of her husband Mahlon; and her secret thoughts. Long before Ruth knew anything about Him, God set in motion a series of events designed to bring her face to face with Boaz, the man who became her kinsman-redeemer. Boaz did for her in a beautiful, picture-book, Old-Testament-kind-of-way just what Jesus—our kinsman-redeemer—now does for us in a spiritual, eternal, New-Testament-kind-of-way.

A. Drought - A Famine

"It came to pass," we read in Ruth 1:1, "that there was a famine in the land." Thus the first link in the chain that was designed to bring Ruth to Boaz was a sovereign act of God over which she had no control. There was a famine in the foreign country of Judah—one of thirteen famines mentioned in the Bible. Quite possibly Ruth knew nothing about the famine, and if she did she was certainly glad that it was in Judah and not in Moab. The people of Moab would look with smug satisfaction on an outbreak of famine in the country of the Jews, for Moabites had little love for Jews. In any case the famine was far away and seemed unconnected to Ruth's life in Moab. She had no idea that the famine had any relevance to her.

It is like that with our redemption too. Long before we know Him, God works to initiate a chain of circumstances that in the end will bring us face to face with Christ. Often God arranges the circumstances even before we are born. When I think back on my own life, I can see that God was at work before I ever knew Him. This happened; that happened. At the time it never occurred to me that these unfolding circumstances had anything to do with my coming to Christ. But now, looking back, I can easily see God's hand.

B. Discovery - A Family

One day a family moved into Ruth's life, a family of
believers.   Ruth had never before met anyone quite like
Elimelech, his wife Naomi, and their two sons. She became
friendly with the family, especially with one of the sons.

We can well imagine that at first Elimelech and Naomi did
not like the idea of their older son becoming involved with a
Moabite woman. We can imagine Ruth asking, "Why don't
they like me, Mahlon?"

Probably he replied, "Oh, they like you well enough,
Ruth. The problem is their religion. They have no use for your
religion. They think it's a false religion. They're afraid I might
become involved in your religion if I marry you." But he
married her anyway.

As time passed, Ruth became well acquainted with this
family. At the supper table she heard many talks about the
things of God, for though Elimelech was a backslider, he was
still a believer. Things that Ruth would do, he would not do;
places where she would go, he would not go. As for the demon
gods of her people, he left her no doubt as to what he thought
of them.

She doubtless asked questions about the God of the
Hebrews, and Elimelech and Naomi told her about Abraham,
Isaac, and Jacob. They told her the wonderful story of Joseph.
They talked to her about the exodus, about Moses, and about
the Passover lamb. They recounted for her the wilderness
wanderings of the Hebrews. Ruth learned how Balak—king of
Moab—had hired Balaam to come from the Euphrates to curse
the Hebrew people and how, having failed to curse them,
Balaam had taught Balak how to corrupt them. Elimelech and
Naomi explained that this was why the law cursed Moab. They
told her about Joshua and the conquest of Canaan, and
recounted some of the stories of the judges. Then Naomi sang
Ruth some of the hymns of her people—the song of Deborah,
the song of Moses, or perhaps the noble stanzas of Psalm 90.
And Ruth drank it all in.

Ruth discovered a world of truth of which she had never dreamed. She learned about a true and living God, a kind God, a pure and holy God, a God wholly unlike the dreadful, lustful, and savage gods of her people. This discovery thrilled her soul. A great longing sprang up in her heart to know more about Him, and she never tired of asking questions. She was not yet ready to make a commitment to this God, but He attracted her just the same.

C. Death - A Funeral

A tragedy happened; death visited that home. There were three funerals, one after the other. Elimelech died. Mahlon died. His brother Chilion, the husband of Orpah (the other Moabite girl), died. We have the sad spectacle of three weeping widows standing around their graves in the land of Moab and mingling their tears.

We can almost picture Ruth standing there, looking down at the remains of her husband and watching as his casket was lowered into the ground. It was all so sad, so seemingly senseless. There was the ache of loss, the mystery of death, and the seeming unfairness of it all.

At this point Ruth could have become very resentful. She could have turned on Naomi and exclaimed, "If this is an example of what your God of love does, don't ever speak to me about Him again. God of love, indeed! Why did He have to take my husband? Why did He have to take yours? Why did He have to take Orpah's?" Ruth could have become bitter, as many people do when death invades a home. But she did not fall into that trap of the devil.

God is too loving to be unkind, too wise to make any mistakes, and too powerful to be thwarted in His plans. The death of Ruth's husband was part of His plan. Mahlon *had* to die because there was no other way Ruth could come to know Boaz as her kinsman-redeemer. In Israel, redemption by means of a kinsman-redeemer meant that Boaz had to marry

Ruth. Obviously he could not marry her if she were still married to Mahlon. So Mahlon's death was part of the overruling sovereignty of God, part of His sovereign grace to Ruth's soul. God planned Mahlon's funeral out of the kindness of His heart.

We can be sure that in later years Ruth looked back to these dark days in Moab. Circumstances had seemed to make no sense at the time, but she could see their meaning now—now that she was married to that mighty prince of the house of Judah and was living in the promised land. She could look back and say, as did Anne Ross Cousin:

> I'll bless the hand that guided,
> I'll bless the heart that planned,
> When throned where glory dwelleth,
> In Immanuel's land.

D. Dismay - A Fear

A crisis came for Ruth when Naomi announced that she was going back to Bethlehem because God had "visited his people." There had been a revival, and Naomi had made up her mind that there was to be no more backsliding in Moab for her. She was going home. She intended to return to the fellowship of God's people.

Ruth must have received this news with considerable dismay because the only light she had was going out. It was not much of a light, the somewhat garbled testimony of a backslider whose advice at this time was anything but spiritual. In her backslidden condition, Naomi was far more inclined to feed Ruth with doubt and discouragement than to sustain her tentative moves toward God with help and blessing. Indeed, Naomi did all she could to discourage Ruth and Orpah from coming with her.

All Ruth could see was a meaningless future in a Moab she no longer loved. All she knew of God was wrapped up at that moment in Naomi, and now Naomi was going away. Ruth now faced an emptiness even greater than that caused by her husband's death. A dark and dismal future stretched before her—a future dominated by Moabite gods, Moabite goals, and Moabite gloom, and ending in a Moabite grave. Ruth could not stand the thought. So the sovereignty of God brought her to her first great decision.

II. RUTH AND THE SALVATION OF GOD

Ruth and Orpah both made the same decision. They would go with Naomi.

A. A Roused Soul

Scripture says of Naomi, "Wherefore she went forth out of the place where she was, and her two daughters in law with her; and they went on the way to return unto the land of Judah" (Ruth 1:7). So far so good. It looks as though Ruth and Orpah became converts. When we get to the end of the story, however, we discover that this was not so. Two walked down the aisle, so to speak, but there was only one wedding. Here we need to pause.

It happens thousands of times: under the stress of an overwhelming circumstance, in the heat of a revival, or under the urging of a faithful evangelist, numbers of people come forward, but that does not mean that they are saved. Some may make a profession of faith and take initial steps toward the promised land, but that does not mean that they are saved. All we have in many instances are roused souls, intellectual responses to the gospel, or emotional responses to appeals.

We must not assume at this point that genuine conversion has taken place. The Lord warned about this in His parable of the sower, the seed, and the soil. The apostle warned about this again and again in the five great warning passages of the book of Hebrews. "Let us go on," he said (Hebrews 6:1). Going on is the acid test of whether or not an initial response to Christ is real. Look at what happened next in the book of Ruth, for it is both sobering and instructive.

As they walked along, Naomi began to doubt. She began to think about her reception in Bethlehem when she showed up with two pagan Moabite women, and she began to throw discouragement their way. She urged Ruth and Orpah to return to Moab. There, she said, they would stand a much better chance of getting married again.

We can see that presently Orpah began to lag behind, casting thoughtful glances back toward Moab. Finally she stopped. The other two, having walked on, missed her and turned around to look for her. There she was, far behind, gazing longingly toward Moab. When they came back to her, Orpah made her final decision: "I can't go on," she may have said. "You're right, Mother. My place is in Moab." We can imagine the emotional scene as Orpah kissed Naomi and said a heart-rending. tearful, eternal goodbye. Then Orpah went back to Moab, back to the demon gods of her people, back to her old way of life, and back to a lost eternity. Her name was henceforth blotted out of God's book. Orpah pictures for us all those whose souls have been roused, but who have never really been saved at all.

Most preachers have known people who have come forward, who have started out for Canaan, but who have had second thoughts. Like Orpah they have come to a stop, turned back, and returned to their old lives, their old gods, their old religions, and their old companions. Such people are as lost as pagans, only more so because once they were enlightened. They have tasted of the heavenly gift, have been made partakers of the Holy Spirit's work of conviction, and have tasted of the good Word of God and the powers of the world to come. Yet they have fallen away. By so doing they have shown that, as Peter said to Simon Magus, they have "neither part nor lot in this matter," for their hearts are "not right in the sight of God" (Acts 8:21). Moreover, the Holy Spirit solemnly says that it will be impossible for those people to be renewed to repentance because they have crucified the Son of God afresh and put Him to an open shame. (See Hebrews 6:4-6.) It is a sobering possibility. "Make your calling and election sure," God warns (2 Peter 1:10). "Let us go on," He urges.

So Orpah turned back toward Moab. Slowly she drew away from the other two women. Sadly but resolutely, she set her face toward the city of destruction—with many wistful looks back at her two dear friends standing there, with many pathetic waves of her hand. At last a dip in the road hid her from view and she was gone. Forever! Her soul had been roused; now it was lost.

As for Ruth, she clung to Naomi. Any thought of going back to Moab was distasteful to her. Still doubtful, Naomi said, "Behold, thy sister in law is gone back unto her people, and unto her gods: return thou after thy sister in law" (Ruth 1:15). Ruth replied:

> Intreat me not to leave thee, or to return from following after thee: for whither thou goest, I will go; and where thou lodgest, I will lodge: thy people shall be my people, and thy God my God: Where thou diest, will I die, and there will I be buried: the Lord do so to me, and more also, if ought but death part thee and me (Ruth 1:16-17).

Ruth was a roused soul indeed.

B. A Redeemed Soul

Not every roused soul is a redeemed soul. Many people turn back, their professions of faith unsupported by the evidence of their lives. But let us look at Ruth.

1. Ruth Meeting Boaz

The two widows arrived in Bethlehem and in their poverty took up their abode somewhere in town. We can imagine that one day Ruth said to Naomi, "Mother, we are very poor. I need to get a job."

Naomi answered, "We have social security in our country," and she explained how Ruth could glean in the harvest field behind the reapers. All that she gleaned she could have. The grain would be hers.

So we watch Ruth wend her way through the village in the dawn's early light. We see her standing irresolutely in the harvest fields, wondering which way to turn. We see her choose a portion of the field that belongs to Boaz. What a story this tells us of God's overruling sovereignty still at work to bring this seeking soul to the Savior. Of all the fields that surrounded Bethlehem, she chose the one that God had chosen for her—the field of Boaz.

Then Ruth met Boaz. He spoke to her kindly, welcomed her into his field, provided for her thirst, and gave to her of his bounty. "Then," we read, "she fell on her face and bowed herself to the ground, and said unto him, Why have I found grace in thine eyes, that thou shouldest take knowledge of me, seeing I am a stranger?" (Ruth 2:10) During this meeting with Boaz, she found grace in the eyes of a kinsman-redeemer whom she did not even know. All this long way God had sovereignly directed her steps. At last she was face to face with the one who could redeem her. Her situation changed quickly after that. In Ruth 2 she is in Boaz's field. In Ruth 3 she is at his feet. In Ruth 4 she is in his family!

2. Ruth Marrying Boaz

We can picture the scene after that first day of gleaning when Ruth arrived home with the great pile of grain Boaz had given her. Naomi must have wondered where Ruth had obtained so much. Naomi had seen gleaners many times in her life, but she had never known them to come home with an amount like that. She no doubt thought that Ruth's old Moabite habits had overcome her conscience and that she had been robbing the barn instead of gleaning in the field. We can imagine Naomi asking, "Where did you get all that?"

Then we can hear Ruth eagerly replying, "I met a man today who was so kind to me."

"What is his name?" Naomi may then have asked.

And we hear Ruth say, "I'll never forget his name, Mother. His name is Boaz."

Then the light dawned on Naomi; she saw instantly what the next step should be. "He is a near kinsman," she told Ruth. "He is the one person in the world who can redeem you and put you into the family of God. You must go to him. Put yourself at his feet. Ask him to redeem you. Ask him to marry you. Ask him to make you his own." Ruth made no excuses and immediately did just that.

She might have made all kinds of excuses that people still make for not coming to Christ, the heavenly kinsman-redeemer. She might have said, "I'm not worthy to come." "I'd be embarrassed." "What would people say?" "I think I've done enough." "Maybe, but some other time." But no, she went to Boaz and asked him to make her his own.

The sequel of this story shows that Boaz loved her enough to make her his own—at great cost.

So Orpah remained lost in dark, pagan Moab while Ruth married a prince of the house of Judah, became a joint-heir with her redeemer, and dwelled with him in bliss.

This story of Ruth can be repeated in the life of any lost child of Adam's ruined race who will come, as Ruth came, to the Redeemer.

6
Boaz, the Mighty Man

Ruth 2:1–4:13

> I. HIS RIGHT TO REDEEM
> II. HIS RESOLVE TO REDEEM
> III. HIS RESOURCES TO REDEEM
> A. Ruth's Person
> B. Ruth's Property

The first chapter of the book of Ruth is a sad chapter, for it contains nothing but backsliding, death, and unhappiness. And the chapter never so much as names Boaz, the mighty kinsman-redeemer. Likewise, any chapters in our life histories that we write without naming our heavenly Boaz are bound to be filled with fear, frustration, folly, and failure. The chapters of life written by unsaved people, who are total strangers to God's grace, are bound to end in ruin. And if they

67

persist in writing such chapters until the last, their lives will end in eternal night.

Boaz is finally introduced in Ruth 2. From then on the emphasis is on him. He is mentioned ten times in chapter 2 and ten more times in chapters 3 and 4, making a total of twenty times. Similarly, once we introduce the Redeemer into the story of a human life, He is bound to become the center of everything.

Notice also that in Revelation 4 there is no mention of the Lamb. There is only a terrible throne wrapped with thundering and lightning. God is portrayed as hard and adamant as a jasper and a sardius stone. His attendants, aflame with glory, herald the holiness of God. All is remote and unapproachable. But once the Lamb is introduced in Revelation 5, He becomes the center of everything. Indeed, we read about the Lamb no less than twenty-eight times thereafter in the book of Revelation. As hymnist Anne Ross Cousin wrote, "The Lamb is all the glory / Of Immanuel's land."

Once Boaz is introduced into the story of Ruth, he dominates it as the royal kinsman, the mighty man of wealth who is able and willing to redeem. He takes poor, alien Ruth and puts her in the family of God.

Boaz possessed the right to redeem, the resolve to redeem, and the resources to redeem.

I. HIS RIGHT TO REDEEM

The role of kinsman-redeemer was not open to everyone. When Ruth first came home from the harvest field of Bethlehem and told Naomi that she had met Boaz, Naomi exclaimed, "Blessed be he of the Lord, who hath not left off his kindness to the living and the dead . . . The man is near of kin unto us" (Ruth 2:20).

According to the Mosaic law, a kinsman had a threefold function, depending on the circumstances. In the case of *manslaughter*, he had to act as the avenger of blood. His task was to see to it that "whoso sheddeth man's blood, by man shall his blood be shed" (Genesis 9:6). Unless the manslayer fled with all speed to the nearest city of refuge, he had no hope of escape.

In the case of *misfortune*, a kinsman had to watch for the forced sale of the impoverished relative's property and purchase it so that it would remain in the family. Eventually the property had to be restored to its rightful owner.

In the case of *marriage*, a kinsman had a responsibility to his brother's wife. If she were left a childless widow, he had to marry her. Children born of this union were to be treated as the brother's children. Sons of such a Levitical marriage inherited the property of the one who would have been their father, had he lived.

So, not everyone could redeem. It had to be a kinsman, and a near kinsman at that. Here we touch on the genius of the gospel. The Lord Jesus entered the human family so that we might enter the heavenly family. He became near of kin to Adam's ruined race so that He might have the right to redeem. The Son of God became the Son of man so that the sons of men might become the sons of God. "Great is the mystery . . ." wrote Paul. "God was manifest in the flesh" (1 Timothy 3:16). The glory of the gospel lies in this magnificent truth: "The man is near of kin unto us."

At this very place—Bethlehem—nearly two thousand years ago, the second person of the godhead entered human life in order to become our next of kin and have the right to redeem us.

This decision was made in a past eternity. When God the Father, Son, and Holy Spirit decided to act in creation, they knew that they would also have to act in redemption. One of them would need to become a man. "Whom shall [we] send, and who will go for us?" was the great question. "Here am I; send me," was the glorious reply of the second person of the godhead.

In the fullness of time, "God sent forth his Son, made of a woman, made under the law" (Galatians 4:4). When the time was ripe the Holy Spirit went to work and fashioned a body in a virgin's womb. The Son said His fond farewells at home up there in the highest Heaven, stepped off the edge of eternity, and entered time. He stooped down, was contracted to the span of a virgin's womb, and was born in Bethlehem.

A handful of people on this planet heard about His birth. A few poor shepherds huddled against the cold of a winter's night heard the angels' tidings as they watched their flocks in the fields of Bethlehem near the Jerusalem highway. Some wise men from the East, a nobleman-carpenter from Nazareth, an aged woman named Anna, and an elderly man named Simeon were aware of what had happened. The second person of the godhead had become near of kin to Adam's ruined race.

So we meet Boaz. He is introduced into the Scripture text as "a mighty man" (Ruth 2:1). There are five Hebrew words for *man*. This one is *ish,* which signifies a great man in contrast to an ordinary man. It is the word used in Scripture when God is spoken of as a man, and when someone is called a man of God. When Eve said, "I have gotten the Man, even Jehovah," she used the word *ish*: "Ish eth Jehovah!" she said.

So Boaz was mighty, a fitting type of Him of whom Eve spoke when she said, "Ish eth Jehovah." The promised man-child, thus heralded by Eve, was not to be Cain. She was terribly mistaken in that, but we must give her credit because she believed that God would keep His word and send that man.

The father of Boaz was Salmon. That is of interest too, because Salmon was a direct descendant of Judah and a nephew of Aaron. So Boaz was a prince of the house of Judah and was also related to priests of the house of Aaron. In Salmon, the lines of prince and priest converged. This then is the uniqueness of Boaz; he was at once both prince and priest by right of birth. He was, therefore, in the image and likeness of Melchizedek (Hebrews 6:20–7:21).

But there is more. Boaz's first recorded words point us directly to the Christ of whom he was a type. "The Lord be with you," he said to the reapers (Ruth 2:4). One of the names for Christ is *Immanuel*, which means "God with us." In other words Boaz, the kinsman-redeemer, made it the first business of every day to remind his people that a true kinsman-redeemer was on the way. "God be with you," he said. In a parallel vein, the Holy Spirit says, "God with us, Immanuel," pointing us to Christ.

So Boaz had the right to redeem. He was near of kin. He was the mirror-image of both the priest-king and the kinsman-redeemer, the One whose coming means that God at last is with us as near of kin.

II. HIS RESOLVE TO REDEEM

It would have been bad news for Ruth if Boaz had not desired to redeem her. That would have been a greater tragedy than having no eligible redeemer at all.

That possibility certainly existed, as we learn from the story of the nearer kinsman. This man also had the right to redeem, but he did not have the resolve. We need to pause here and take a closer look at him. He presents us with a sorry spectacle. This unnamed individual looked at Ruth and decided that he wanted no part of her.

He had the right to redeem and was willing enough, up to a point, to exercise that right. But what he was interested in was the property. He wanted to get his hands on that. When he realized, however, that he could not have the property without the person, he backed off right away, saying, "Lest I mar mine inheritance" (Ruth 4:6).

Salmon had other sons besides Boaz. This "nearer kinsman" must have been one of them. Probably, too, he was a son by a different wife. He did not want to mar his inheritance by marrying a Moabite and putting Moabite blood into his bloodline. He was afraid of the curse of the law. He was afraid too that by contaminating the purity of his bloodline he might render it impossible for one of his sons to be the promised Messiah.

Boaz was not concerned about this threat to the purity of his pedigree. The reason is evident. His father Salmon was one of the two spies Joshua had sent into Jericho to spy out the land. There Salmon had met (and later married) Rahab the harlot, who became the mother of Boaz. So the pedigree of Boaz was already contaminated—or so men thought. Boaz was not concerned about adding Moabite blood to his pedigree; his line already had Canaanite blood in it anyway.

So the "nearer kinsman" backed off, horrified at the prospect of having to marry a woman from Moab. Perish the thought! "I cannot redeem," he said. He had the right but not the resolve. He had no love for Ruth in his heart, only cold calculations of property and pedigree.

A requirement of the Mosaic law should have been applied at this point. The man who had a right to redeem, but refused to do so, was to be brought before the elders. His widowed sister-in-law was then to pull off his shoe, spit in his face, and say, "So shall it be done unto that man that will not build up his brother's house" (Deuteronomy 25:9).

The plucking off of the shoe spoke of his *disinheritance*. When the prodigal son came home, the first thing the father did was put shoes on his son's feet and put him back into the family. Taking off the shoe reduced the man to the status of a disinherited slave. Spitting in his face spoke of his *dishonor*. No greater shame could have been brought on a man than to have a widow publicly spit in his face with the full approval of the community.

In the days of Ruth, this legal requirement of the Mosaic law had been modified in practice. When the nearer kinsman refused to redeem Ruth, he took off his own shoe and handed it to the one who would redeem—a sign that he relinquished all legal right to the property. Even so the action was quite symbolic.

Look at your shoe for a moment. What does it represent? One part of your shoe, the sole, comes in direct contact with the ground. A shoe is all that stands between a man and the world. The other side of the sole feels the full weight of the body, the full weight of the flesh. Removing that shoe symbolically suggests that there is nothing between the world and the flesh in that man's life. In other words, he is vulnerable.

Look again at Boaz. He had the right to redeem and the resolve to redeem. But underneath that resolve was something else—love. There can be no doubt that Boaz had fallen in love with that destitute, Moabite widow. He wanted her for himself just as much as she wanted to be his. Love led him on to make her his wife, in spite of the law's curse on Moab.

And we sing of *our* beloved Redeemer:

> Out of the ivory palaces
> Into a world of woe,
> Only His great eternal love
> Made my Savior go.
>   (Henry Barraclough)

Love brought Jesus down from Heaven's heights to tread these scenes of time. Love shone in all His ways. His was the love that many waters could not quench, the love that suffers long and is kind.

Boaz not only had the right to redeem and the resolve to redeem. There were also:

III. HIS RESOURCES TO REDEEM

It is no accident that the first time Boaz is introduced into the story, Scripture describes him as "a mighty man of wealth" (Ruth 2:1). That is because redemption was a costly business. It would have been of small comfort for a man to have had the right and the resolve, but not the resources. Suppose Boaz had been a beggar. That would not have helped Ruth at all. He had to be rich enough to buy the property that had fallen into default and was now in alien hands.

Now think how rich our Lord Jesus was. Paul wrote, "For ye know the grace of our Lord Jesus Christ, that, though he was rich, yet for your sakes he became poor, that ye through his poverty might be rich" (2 Corinthians 8:9).

We know that Jesus was rich, but we have no idea how rich He was. We shall have to wait until we get home to glory before we discover that. In His country they pave the streets with gold, build their walls of jasper, hang their gates of pearl, garnish their foundations with all kinds of precious stones, and build their palaces of ivory. Where He comes from, the streams are of purest crystal. The throne on which He sits is ablaze with the beauty of jasper and sardius stones and bathed in all the colors of the rainbow. The banks of the crystal stream are lined with the magnificent tree of life. So bright is the uncreated light of that world that its inhabitants have no need of the sun to shine by day or of the moon to shine by night. Jesus' ministers are a flame of fire. Ten thousand times ten thousand sons of light hang on His words and rush to do His bidding—to the utmost bounds of the everlasting hills and the remotest edges of the vast empires of space. (Revelation 6, 21–22) Oh yes! He was very rich.

As John W. Peterson's hymn declares:

> He owns the cattle on a thousand hills,
> The wealth in every mine;
> He owns the rivers and the rocks and rills,
> The sun and stars that shine.

We know too that for our sakes "he became poor," but we have no idea how poor Jesus became. We pick up clues here and there throughout the Gospels. He was born into the home of a laboring man. His mother was a Galilean peasant. She descended from David, but the fortunes of David's house had sunk so low by that time that the rightful heir was the wife of a village carpenter.

We can picture the kind of home in which Jesus lived, for travelers in Palestine before the era of modernization have described such dwelling places. Most likely the living room was located over a cave and contained no furniture. Mary might have been seen there sifting grain through a sieve. In the corner were matting beds that family members rolled up and tucked away out of sight during the day. A few waterpots and jars stood in another corner. The living room was probably separated from the animals' quarters by a pole and some sacking. The noise and smell of the animals were ever present. Outside was a bakestone for making pita bread. The downstairs cave was the carpenter's shop. The whole situation added up to poverty beyond anything most of us have experienced.

Oh yes, Jesus knew what it was like to be poor. He could say, "The foxes have holes, and the birds of the air have nests; but the Son of man hath not where to lay his head" (Matthew 8:20). To teach the multitudes, He had to borrow a boat. To feed them, He had to borrow a little lad's lunch. To confound His critics, He had to borrow a penny. To ride into Jerusalem, He had to borrow a donkey. To keep the last Passover, He had to borrow a room. He died on another man's cross, and He was buried in another man's tomb. All He had left, when soldiers cast dice for His few bits and pieces of worldly wealth, were the clothes He had on His back. We know that He became poor.

We also know that, because of Him, we will be rich! We are given some idea of *how* rich we will be by the fact that the *earnest*—the down payment of our inheritance, the sign that God is in earnest and means business about our redemption— is the Holy Spirit in our hearts. The Holy Spirit is the one member of the godhead who permanently abides in us and operates through us. Another indication of how rich we will be lies in the fact that as Christians we are now children of God and joint-heirs with Jesus Christ. God intends to dissolve the entire universe, which sin has so sadly marred and stained. Then He will put forth His creative genius and create a new heaven and a new earth that will be filled with wonders and delights beyond anything we can begin to imagine. Jesus Christ has been appointed heir of all things, and we are joint-heirs with Him.

But let us come back to Boaz and Ruth. He had the right, the resolve, and the resources to redeem her. And he did. First he redeemed:

A. Ruth's Person

Boaz bought Ruth. He began by meeting all the demands of the law. That was absolutely fundamental. He could not say, "I love you. I want you. You love me. You want me. So that's all that is necessary." He said, "The law of God has its righteous claims; these must be met. The law legislates against you as a Moabite and raises a barrier between you and God. There is no way that you, as a Moabite, can fulfill the law's demands. But I can, and I will." That is what he did. He set out, methodically and meticulously, to meet every demand of the law. The law of the kinsman-redeemer was a higher law than the law against a Moabite. So when Boaz paid the price of Ruth's redemption—bought her at great cost—he made her his very own.

But he not only redeemed her person. He also redeemed:

B. Ruth's Property

"Ye are witnesses this day, that I have bought all that was Elimelech's, and all that was Chilion's and Mahlon's, of the hand of Naomi. Moreover Ruth the Moabitess, the wife of Mahlon, have I purchased to be my wife" (Ruth 4:9-10).

We should underline that passage. Boaz would have redeemed poor Orpah too if she had not gone back to Moab.

He paid the price for her too. But she lost everything—her hope of redemption, her inheritance, her very soul—in Moab.

Redemption of our property is as much a part of Calvary as the redemption of our persons. That is why there has to be a millennial reign on this planet. God bought this world at infinite cost. In Heaven John has already seen the title deeds of earth pass into Jesus' capable, nail-pierced hand! (Revelation 4–5) One day Jesus will come back to take possession of the earth and run the world as God has always intended it to be run—as a paradise of beauty and bliss far beyond what any words could describe.

Take one last look at Boaz and Ruth. The purchase price has been paid. He has taken her into his arms and made her his very own. He has so satisfied the law's demands that there is now no barrier between her soul and her savior. Now Christ can be formed through her lineage; she can become one of those rare, special people in the Bible who stand in a direct line to Christ.

So it is with our heavenly Boaz, the Lord Jesus. He points to the life that He lived—a life that met all the demands of the moral law. He points to the death that He died—a death that met all the demands of the ceremonial law. He says, "Come!" And when we come, we can sing:

> Now I belong to Jesus,
> Jesus belongs to me,
> Not for the years of time alone,
> But for eternity.
>   (Norman J. Clayton)

7
Nicodemus, the Man Born Twice

John 3:1-15; 7:50; 19:39

S ome scholars think that the Nicodemus who came to Jesus by night was Nicodemus ben Gorion, the brother of Josephus the historian. If so, Nicodemus was one of the three richest men in Jerusalem. If so, he became one of the poorest men too, for his daughter was later seen gathering barley corns for food from under horses' hooves. If so, doubtlessly his poverty resulted from the persecution he suffered after becoming a Christian. If so, Nicodemus is certainly one of the richest men in Heaven today.

We learn three things about him. In the book of John, the only Gospel that mentions Nicodemus, we read about Nicodemus and the *Christ,* about Nicodemus and the *crowd,* and about Nicodemus and the *cross.* The first time John set before us the *conversion* of this man. The second time John told us about the *confession* of this man. The third time John recorded for us the *consecration* of this man.

I. NICODEMUS AND THE CHRIST

Nicodemus was "a man of the Pharisees," which tells us something about his *religion;* and he was "a ruler of the Jews," which tells us something about his *rank.* He was unquestionably very religious.

Normally we equate the Pharisees with hypocrisy because most of them were hypocrites. They acted a religious part on the stage of life. Most of the Pharisees, as the Gospels record, were avowed enemies of Jesus. But Nicodemus was not a hypocrite. He was sincerely religious. He fasted twice a week, tithed his income scrupulously right down to the mint and herbs in his garden, kept holidays as holy days, and knew much of the Bible by heart. He was a religious conservative who espoused traditional teaching of the Scriptures and engaged in private and public prayer.

A. His Plan

Nicodemus had heard about Jesus. Indeed, it would have been difficult in those days for him not to have heard about Jesus. The young preacher from the north had taken Jerusalem by storm—so much so that the Sanhedrin was considering what action to take against Him. Jesus had dared to call down God's wrath on those in the temple courts who were acting as money-changers and merchandisers, selling animals for sacrifice to visiting Jews. He had done even more. He had actually driven them out of the temple and had called it "my Father's house."

The temple was the Sanhedrin's special preserve, and temple concessions were very profitable to certain of its members. But the Sanhedrin was cautious about responding to Jesus because large numbers of people believed that He was a prophet.

So Nicodemus came up with a plan. He would privately meet with Jesus. He would talk with Him man to man, perhaps counsel Him to temper zeal with caution, and try to get Him to see that it would do Him no good to infuriate the establishment (of which Nicodemus was a part).

Nicodemus wasted no time in putting his plan into action. Having arranged for a night visit, he began in a condescending and confident way. "Rabbi," he said, giving Jesus the benefit of the doubt, "we know that thou art a teacher come from God: for no man can do these miracles that thou doest, except God be with him" (John 3:2). So the stage was set for a revolution to take place in Nicodemus's soul. He would learn in a hurry that Jesus was not just a man God had sent. Jesus was a man inhabited by God.[1] And He was not just a rabbi or a teacher. He spoke with authority, not as the scribes spoke. In one sentence, as we will see, Jesus swept away everything on which Nicodemus had been depending for salvation.

B. His Plight

The Lord quickly dismissed all the patronage of this influential, well-disposed, and devoutly religious senator. "Verily, verily, I say unto thee," Jesus said, "Except a man be born again, he cannot see the kingdom of God" (John 3:3).

---

[1]This is true as far as the Lord's humanity is concerned, but obviously an inadequate description when we consider His deity.

Jesus swept away all Nicodemus's scrupulous attention to the ritual requirements of the Mosaic law; all his punctilious observance of religious rules; all his fasting, tithing, and praying; all his almsgiving and good works; all his reliance on circumcision, keeping of the sabbath, and observance of the feasts; all his sacrifices and offerings; all his trust in racial pedigree, attainments, and status as a member of the Sanhedrin. Jesus said, in effect, "What you need, Nicodemus, is to be born again."

Nicodemus was so utterly dead in sins, not the least of which were religious sins, that there was only one remedy— a new birth!

Strange to say, Jesus' revolutionary, radical statement struck a responsive chord in this old man's soul. Nicodemus was already acutely aware that all his religious observances, all his morality, and all his good works and attention to ritual had not stilled the small voice of conscience that told him such practices were not enough. This thoughtful religious leader did not question Jesus' startling challenge. He did not ask, "Why?" He knew why. If *he* was not satisfied with himself, how could he expect God to be satisfied? If he was aware of unconfessed, uncleansed, and unconscionable sin deep, deep within—how much more was God aware of it?

Yes, that was what he needed. He needed to be born again. The most remarkable thing about a newborn baby is that he has no past; he only has a future. So the Lord not only revealed the plight; He gave a hint as to the remedy, and Nicodemus seized it. Instead of asking, "Why?" he asked, *"How?"* "How can a man be born when he is old?" (John 3:4)

The Lord then said, "Except a man be born of water and of the Spirit, he cannot enter into the kingdom of God" (John 3:5).

Doubtlessly that startled Nicodemus too. Indeed, the recent preaching of John the Baptist had shaken the whole land from Dan to Beersheba, including all Jerusalem and Judea. "I indeed baptize with water unto repentance," John cried, "but he that cometh after me . . . shall baptize you with the Holy Ghost" (Matthew 3:11). Note John's reference to water and the Spirit. John had been baptizing thousands of people in the Jordan river. He had been preaching *repentance;* his baptism was one of repentance. To be born of water simply meant repentance. To a man, the Sanhedrin, led by the Pharisees, had rejected John and all that he stood for—especially his baptism of repentance.

Jesus brought Nicodemus back to that teaching. No John, no Jesus. That was the formula. If there were no water, there could be no Spirit. Without repentance, there could be no regeneration.

In effect Jesus said, "What you need, Nicodemus, is to go down to John at the Jordan river—religious man that you are, respectable man that you are, rich man that you are, ruler that you are—and repent and be baptized. When you have received John's baptism after confessing your need of repentance, your heart will be ready to receive the next work of God, the work of the Holy Spirit—*regeneration.* Then you can be born again."

That was strong medicine for Nicodemus. It is strong medicine for every religious person to face the fact that religion will not save him, that only repentance and regeneration can effect the kind of new birth that puts a child of Adam's ruined race into the family of God.

C. His Plea

"How?" Nicodemus asked again. "How can these things be?" (John 3:9) He had studied the Bible since he was a boy. He had been a diligent student of the rabbis. He had absorbed the precepts of the great religious teachers of the age. One of his colleagues was the learned Gamaliel. Yet his studies had all been in vain. His Bible teachers had been blind leaders of the blind. Nicodemus too had become a blind leader of the blind. He was a walking Bible encyclopedia, but he had missed the most important lesson of all—he needed to be born again. Learned scholar that he was, biblically literate as he was in the schools and seminaries of men, Nicodemus confessed to Jesus that he did not know how to be born again. Is there a sadder page than this in all of the Bible? Here was a sincere, studious, and scholarly old man who was as lost as any pagan in spite of having spent his life in religious pursuits.

"How can these things be?" Nicodemus asked. We can thank God for this word *how* because most religious people ask *why* and want to challenge the statement that their personal morality, religious observances, and righteous behavior will not get them into the kingdom of God. Nicodemus's question led to his salvation.

Consider Jesus' reply. (If one wants to know "how," it's all here.) Jesus answered the question in two ways. We must look at the *illustration* Jesus gave right here in John 3, and we must look at the *illumination* Jesus gave back in John 1.

Let's begin with what Jesus said in John 1. "He came unto his own, and his own received him not. But as many as received him, to them gave he power to become the sons of God, even to them that believe on his name: Which were born, not of blood, nor of the will of the flesh, nor of the will of man, but of God" (1:11-13).

We will leave Nicodemus while we consider this statement.

These verses contain the nearest thing we have in the New Testament to a formula, the nearest thing to an equation of salvation. Notice the three *sudden stops* in verse 13 and the three *simple steps* in verse 12.

1. Three Sudden Stops

The following three negatives strike down all man's natural hopes for salvation: "Which were born, not of blood, nor of the will of the flesh, nor of the will of man."

Man's salvation is "not of blood"; that is, it is *not of human descent.* It has nothing to do with *the purity of one's pedigree.* The Jews, of course, thought that salvation had everything to do with blood. They thought that they had an automatic ticket to Heaven just because they were Jews and were "Abraham's seed."

Many people today believe the same thing. They think that they are Christians because they were born in a so-called Christian country or because they were born into Christian homes. Years ago our neighbor attended a church service and heard a message on the subject of being born again. Afterward I asked him, "What did you think of the message? Did you feel any need to be born again?"

His answer was ludicrous, especially from an otherwise intelligent man. "My wife," he said, "is a descendant of John Wesley." (That would be like asking a man if he were married and hearing him say, "I had an aunt once who went to a wedding.")

I replied, "That's interesting. Your wife is a descendant of John Wesley. Well, John Wesley certainly knew what it meant to be born again. He was a preacher for years before experiencing the new birth for himself. But being a descendant of John Wesley is not going to help you very much. I'm a descendant of Noah myself, and that didn't help me."

Being born into a Christian home does not make a person a Christian, any more than being born in a stable would have made him a horse. Our salvation is "not of blood." It is not of human descent. It has nothing to do with the purity of our religious pedigree. Jesus said so.

Then comes another sudden stop: "Nor of the will of the flesh." Salvation is *not of human desire.* It has nothing to do with *the fervor of one's feelings.* Few things in this world arouse the passions of men more than their religious beliefs. They will die for those beliefs; they will massacre and murder people over their religious beliefs. People feel strongly about their religious beliefs, and most people put a great deal of confidence in their feelings. But no amount of wishful thinking or degree of religious ecstasy will put a person into the family of God.

There is one more sudden stop: "Nor of the will of man." Salvation is *not of human design*. It has nothing to do with *the confession of one's creed*. Men have invented all kinds of creeds and a thousand ways to get to Heaven. To be saved, people are urged to do this, that, or the other. They must make this pilgrimage or engage in that fast. They must give to this cause or that one. They must subscribe to this set of rules or to that set. They must undergo this ritual or perform that rite. But the Holy Spirit rules out all such effort. Salvation is not of the will of man.

So God is saying to the religious person, "Stop!" To become a child of God and an heir of Heaven is not a matter of birth, breeding, or behavior. It is not a matter of desiring or doing. Salvation operates on an altogether different principle.

Here we should look at the Lord's illustration in John 3. He reminded Nicodemus of a historic day in Israel's history. The children of Israel, on their way from Egypt to Canaan, were murmuring, grumbling, criticizing, and complaining almost every step of the way. God sent a plague of fiery serpents among them as punishment. A serpent's bite meant certain death, and there was no human remedy. However, in His mercy God provided a way of escape, a means of salvation. Nicodemus knew the story well.

Moses made a serpent of brass and hung it on a pole. (The only way to do that, of course, was to affix a crosspiece to the pole and drape the serpent over the crosspiece and nail the serpent there. Thus the serpent was really nailed to a cross.)

To paraphrase Numbers 21:8-9, God said to the Israelites who had been bitten, "All you have to do is look and live. Look at that cross—and live!"

This remedy makes no sense at all to human reasoning. The scientist would say, "What nonsense. There is no correlation at all between serpent venom and a brass serpent on a pole. There is simply no way that looking at that thing can save anyone."

The psychologist would say, "We must look for the cause of our problem in some inhibition of childhood, some aberration of personality brought about by repressive parents. The thing for us to do is to express ourselves sexually. There is no way that looking at that thing will effect a proper personality adjustment and remove the psychological cause of these painful feelings."

The Christian Scientist would say, "Our problem is simply an error of mortal mind. There is no such thing as pain, and death is not real."

The liberal theologian would say, "There was no such person as Moses, and even if there were, he would not have been able to read and write. So we can discount the whole story as Hebrew mythology. In any case, there could not have been a miraculous cure because all miracles have a rational explanation."

The medical doctor would say, "Serpent venom is a highly complex chemical. We need to develop a serum and immunize the population. It is obvious to medical science that just looking at that serpent on the pole is no antidote to snake venom."

The legalist would say, "We need to get back to the law and do our best to keep it. We can only be saved by our good works."

The religionist would say, "What is needed is to offer a costly sacrifice."

The optimist would say, "I'm related to Moses. I'm sure that is going to help me."

But the solution to the Israelites' problem was "Look and live." That is still God's answer to the venom of sin that courses through our spiritual veins, bringing death in its wake. That serpent, nailed to that cross, pointed to Calvary and to the time when the Lord Jesus, who knew no sin, was to be made sin for us. All we have to do is look and live.

In John 1 there are not only those three sudden stops to consider; there are also:

2. Three Simple Steps

"As many as received him, to them gave he power to become the sons of God, even to them that believe on his name" (John 1:12). There is the formula: believe, receive, become. Of these three action words, two refer to our part in being born again and one refers to God's part in this process. Our part is to believe and receive.

The first thing we must do is to believe—but not just anything. We are to believe on something specific—His name. His name is Jesus! When Scripture tells us to "believe on his name," it simply means that we are to believe on that for which His name stands. His name has a special and significant meaning. When the Lord Jesus was born, the angel said to Joseph, "Thou shalt call his name Jesus: for he shall save his people from their sins" (Matthew 1:21). Therefore, to "believe on his name" means that we acknowledge our sins and need for a Savior. It means that we believe that the Lord Jesus Christ can and will save us from our sins. He is the One whom God has provided to save us from sin's penalty, power, and presence. The Lord Jesus can do this because of the cross. Remember, He told Nicodemus that He would deal with the problem of sin on the cross. He would bear the world's sins in His own body on the tree.

We must also receive. The salvation promise is given to as many as receive Him. We can believe something in our heads without believing it in our hearts; that is, we can give intellectual assent to a truth, yet never allow that truth to change our lives. I can believe that Jesus is *the* Savior yet not be able to say that He is *my* Savior. To make Him ours, we must receive Him.

Suppose someone were to offer you a book. You believe that he is sincere in offering it to you. You believe that the book is valuable, well worth owning, and that it would be a blessing to you. You really believe that the person intends for you to have it. Does that make the book yours? Of course not. You must receive it. The book is not yours until you take it.

Likewise, God offers us Jesus as our only possible Savior from sin, but we must receive Him. We must say words to this effect: "Lord Jesus, I believe You are the One who died to save me from my sin. I take You as my Savior. Thank You for loving me enough to die for me. Now come and live Your life in me."

That is man's part: believe and receive. When we do our part the miracle happens. God does His part. He gives us "power to become the sons of God"! Instantly the miracle of new life takes place in our souls. We are regenerated: born again; born from above; born of God. The Holy Spirit of the living God comes, takes up permanent residence in our lives, and imparts to us the very life of God. That is the way we are born again. Nicodemus asked, "How?" That's how.

II. NICODEMUS AND THE CROWD

The second time we read about Nicodemus, he is with his own crowd—the other members of the Sanhedrin. Everyone has his crowd, and any crowd can be intimidating. The Sanhedrin was a Christ-rejecting crowd. It was a jeering, scoffing crowd.

We see Nicodemus standing up for Christ against that crowd. He was not overly brave about it. He did not say much when they sneered at him and suggested that he was ignorant and out of touch. But at least he put in a favorable word for Jesus. It is always a good sign when a person who has been born again stands up for Christ—even when his old friends become new enemies because of Jesus.

III. NICODEMUS AND THE CROSS

Nicodemus did not really begin living for Jesus until the significance of Calvary dawned on his soul. When he finally saw what the world was like by what it did to Jesus, then he broke with the world once and for all. By means of Christ's crucifixion, Nicodemus was crucified to the world and the world was crucified to him. After Calvary he no longer cared what his crowd thought about his allegiance to Christ. Nicodemus lost all fear of what the world might do. The cross revolutionized his thinking about his evil world—all its values and vanities. He was through with it. He stood up to be counted for Christ, boldly and triumphantly.

He may have said to himself, *I may have been too big a coward to be anything but a secret disciple of the Lord Jesus during His life, but I certainly intend to identify with Him in His death and resurrection. Right now He needs a royal burial. Joseph of Arimathaea has a tomb. I have the treasure. I'll invest the price of a king's ransom in spices and see to it that Jesus' body is wrapped in the rarest ointments and the costliest linens. He may not need the tomb for long, but it will be His for as long as He needs it.*

That type of response is always a good sign of a genuine new birth. When a new believer looks at his world in light of the cross and thereafter dies to that world and lives for Jesus, it is proof enough that he has been born again.

The cross made the difference in Nicodemus's life. We have no evidence that he actually visited the cross, although the likelihood is high. Certainly the implications of the Sanhedrin's dreadful decision must have stabbed his conscience into full wakefulness at last. He knew that he should have taken a bolder stand for Christ years earlier. Now Christ was nailed to a Roman cross, and Nicodemus's cowardice and compromise had given silent consent to the deed.

Well, enough was enough. Nicodemus decided not to

compromise any longer. He sought out his colleague, Joseph of Arimathaea, and bared his soul. The two old men looked at each other, horror-struck at where the fast-paced events of the previous dreadful day had taken the nation. Jesus, the Christ, had been crucified! Well, it was too late now for them to undo whatever damage their silence had done in aiding and abetting Caiaphas and his crowd. We can picture the scene.

"Well, Joseph," Nicodemus might have said, "there's still something we can do. We can give His body an honorable burial."

"I've picked up a rumor," Joseph might have replied, "that our esteemed colleagues of the high priest's party are quite prepared to have the body thrown into Gehinnom."

"Never. Not so long as I have a breath in my body," we can almost hear Nicodemus exclaim. "Aren't you building a tomb here in Jerusalem, off the Damascus road?"

"Indeed I am," Joseph might have said, "and it's His. Moreover, I'm going to the governor the moment this terrible crime consummates in Jesus' death, to beg for the body. I have a feeling that he'll give it to me, if only to spite Caiaphas."

"Yes indeed," we can hear Nicodemus say, "and what's more, my friend, you and I will be fulfilling an ancient prophecy. Remember the words of Isaiah? 'With the rich in his death' (Isaiah 53:9). You supply the tomb, and I'll supply the spices."

And so Nicodemus did. He purchased one hundred pounds of costly aromatic spices with which to embalm Jesus' body.

It was the cross that did it. What happened at Calvary opened the eyes of Nicodemus, took away his fear of his fellows and put the cross between himself and the world. Had he known the deathless words of Isaac Watts, Nicodemus might well have said:

> When I survey the wondrous cross
> On which the Prince of glory died,

My richest gain I count but loss,
And pour contempt on all my pride.

Were the whole realm of nature mine,
That were a present far too small:
Love so amazing, so divine,
Demands my soul, my life, my all.

8
Peter
in the Spotlight

John 1:40-42; 6:16-21; Matthew 16:13-25;
John 18:15-27; 21:1-22; Acts 2:14-42; 1 Peter; 2 Peter

I. HIS EYE ON THE LORD

II. HIS MIND ON THE STORM

III. HIS FOOT IN HIS MOUTH

IV. HIS TEARS IN HIS EYES

V. HIS BOAT ON THE LAKE

VI. HIS LORD ON THE THRONE

VII. HIS PEN IN HIS HAND

There is a popular program on television called "Candid Camera." The producers of the show hide cameras in all sorts of unexpected places, set up all kinds of unusual situations, and then film people during their unguarded moments.

One of my favorite episodes involved a stevedore union in New York. The muscle-bound, hard-bitten stevedores were called into an office one by one and were told that they had to go to a bird sanctuary and spend their vacation time watching birds. I can still see the incredulous look on one tough stevedore's face as he pointed a gnarled finger at his hairy chest and growled, "Me? Watch boids? Not me!"

Some of the best photographs we take of children (or adults) are snapshots taken during unguarded moments. Such photographs are not posed; they are real-life pictures.

The Bible gives us a number of candid pictures of Simon Peter—impulsive, impolitic, impressionable Peter.

I. HIS EYE ON THE LORD

Peter had a brother, just about the best kind of brother a man like Peter could have had. He had none of Peter's fervor and fire. He was not nearly as flamboyant, impetuous, or outgoing as Peter.

Peter's brother Andrew had become a disciple of John the Baptist. Andrew spent as much time as he could spare from the family business listening to John and learning how to prepare people for the coming of Christ. Doubtless there were many lively discussions at home about John and his prophecies. Peter perhaps was inclined to be skeptical, while Andrew defended his hero. "He knows what he's talking about, Peter, believe me," we can hear Andrew saying. In the end, even bluff and businesslike Peter was impressed. Andrew described the crowds and the converts of John the Baptist. We can be sure he recounted John's confrontation with the authorities and talked about John's character. "He was raised a priest, Peter, but he is far more than a priest. I'll tell you who I think he is. I think he's Elijah, who has come back to prepare the way for the Messiah."

Then one day Andrew would have burst into that Galilean home. "Simon, where are you? I say, Simon, we've found *Him*. We've found the Messiah; we've found the Christ. I've just met Him—Jesus, the Son of God, the Savior of the world, the promised Messiah!" Andrew insisted that Peter come and meet Jesus too. At last Peter went, finally persuaded by his quietly persistent brother. That day Peter put his eye on Jesus, and he rarely took it off Him again. That day Peter changed. Jesus said to him, "Hello there, Simon. I'm going to call you *Peter*. I'm going to call you *a stone*. There is a rock-like quality about you that I can use." That's our first snapshot—Peter with his eye on the Lord.

II. HIS MIND ON THE STORM

It had been an exciting day. Jesus had preached to an enormous crowd. It had seemed to the disciples as though the prayer Jesus had taught them, "Thy kingdom come," was about to be answered. Jesus had crowned the day by feeding five thousand men plus women and children with a little lad's lunch. Peter, who had seen the boy give his five barley loaves and two small fish to Jesus, had himself been given bread and fish in abundance to distribute to the crowds. He had come back again and again for more. The boy's lunch had turned into a banquet with twelve baskets of food left over. Peter had thought it amazing, and the crowd had thought so too. The people were ready, then and there, to crown Jesus king. Far from accepting the proffered crown, however, Jesus had sent the disciples away and then the multitude.

Oh well, Peter might have thought, *I expect He wants to be acclaimed king in Jerusalem, not here in Galilee. Probably that would be better.*

Jesus had told the disciples to get into a boat and row across the lake, where He would meet them later. He would stay behind for a while to pray. We can imagine Peter, halfway across the lake, turning to the others and saying, "I say, you fellows, I don't like the look of those clouds. I think we're in for a storm." They all knew how dangerous a storm could be on that lake.

Sure enough, the winds howled, the waves heaved, and the disciples struggled against what now had become a terrible tempest, bringing with it what seemed to be certain death. Then one of the disciples saw it—a shape walking on the water toward them. They were terrified. It must be a ghost, some uncanny specter from the deep. Peter was petrified.

A loved voice called out above the shriek of the gale: "It is I; be not afraid" (Matthew 14:27).

Impulsively Peter called back, "If it be thou, bid me come unto thee on the water" (Matthew 14:28).

"Come," Jesus challenged (Matthew 14:29). And Peter did. First he probably put one leg over the side, then the other, holding on to James and John. Feeling the waves unexpectedly solid beneath his feet, Peter took a step, and another, and another, keeping his eye on Jesus.

Then the noise of the wind dinned in his ears, and the fearful sight of the waves caught hold of his eye. With his eye now on the storm, Peter began to sink. "Lord, save me," he screamed (Matthew 14:30).

What a picture. What a lesson. We all know what Peter learned that day. He learned that he must never focus his eye on the storm; he must keep his eye on the Lord. All too often we look at the waves and listen to the wind. We focus on our adverse circumstances when we should be looking to Jesus. When we look to Him, all will be well.

III. HIS FOOT IN HIS MOUTH

Peter always seemed to put his foot into his mouth, just like most of us. That of course is what is so downright lovable about him.

In this particular snapshot, we catch Peter in one of his more spectacular mistakes. The Lord asked the disciples, "Whom do men say that I the Son of man am?" (Matthew 16:13) They replied that some people said that He was Jeremiah, some said that He was Elijah, and some thought that He was John the Baptist raised from the dead. One and all, people were likening Jesus to the greatest men in their nation's history. But that would never do. So Jesus asked the disciples, "But whom say ye that I am?" (16:15)

Peter quickly replied, "Thou art the Christ, the Son of the living God" (Matthew 16:16).

"Blessed art thou, Simon Bar-jonah," the Lord responded to Peter's confession of faith, "for flesh and blood hath not revealed it unto thee, but my Father which is in heaven" (Matthew 16:17). Peter's heart swelled with pride, and Satan got hold of him in an instant. Very few of us can absorb large doses of praise.

Jesus at once began to speak to the disciples of His impending betrayal, crucifixion, death, burial, and resurrection. But all Peter heard was that one ominous word *crucified*. He blurted out, "Be it far from Thee, Lord" (Matthew 16:22).

Instantly Jesus replied, "Get thee behind me, Satan: thou art an offence unto me: for thou savourest not the things that be of God, but those that be of men" (Matthew 16:23). Peter had put his foot into his mouth.

We have another snapshot of Peter doing the same thing on the mount of transfiguration. Peter had been taking a little nap. It had been warm, strenuous work to climb up the rugged slopes of mount Hermon. Peter threw himself down with a sigh and, before he knew it, he fell asleep. When he woke up, he rubbed his eyes with astonishment. There were some visitors talking with Jesus on the mountaintop. And what visitors! Peter recognized them instantly as men from the past. They were two giants of the faith—Moses and Elijah—the great representative of the law and the great representative of the prophets. They were talking earnestly with Jesus, and Peter overheard as they spoke to the Lord about His "decease which he should accomplish at Jerusalem" (Luke 9:31).

Peter "rose" to the occasion with magnificent disregard of the proprieties of the situation. Ignoring the fact that nobody was talking to him and that the conversation did not concern him at all, he again put his foot into his mouth. "Lord," he blurted out, "it is good for us to be here. We've never held a meeting like this. Let's settle down a while. Let's set up three tents—one for You, one for Moses, and one for Elijah." What folly. Peter was putting the Lord on a level with mere men. God from Heaven broke up the meeting and told Peter to be quiet. "This is my beloved Son," He said. "Hear ye him" (Matthew 17:5).

IV. HIS TEARS IN HIS EYES

The shadow of the cross was now dark and impenetrable, and the Lord looked sadly at His somber disciples. A prophecy came to His mind, a prophecy of Zechariah that had long slumbered in the womb of time but was now stirring to life and fulfillment: "Smite the shepherd, and the sheep shall be scattered" (Zechariah 13:7). Already Gethsemane was looming up against the night shadows. Jesus said, "All ye shall be offended because of me this night: for it is written, I will smite the shepherd, and the sheep of the flock shall be scattered abroad" (Matthew 26:31).

Peter bristled. "Not me, Lord," he stated in so many words. "Others might be offended, but not me."

"You think so, Peter?" Jesus replied. "Well, listen for the crowing of the cock. Before the cock crows twice, you will deny me thrice."

And that is what happened. Shortly afterwards, as the Jews bullied and beat Jesus, Peter warmed his hands at the world's fire. Three times he denied the Lord, the last time with oaths and curses. Then the cock crowed, and at that very moment Peter intercepted Jesus' look (Luke 22:61). It was not an "I told you so" look, but a look of such love and forgiveness that it broke Peter's heart. Immediately he went outside and wept bitterly. Scripture does not tell us where Peter went, but we might not be far wrong if we suspect that he went to Gethsemane.

Never had Peter experienced a darker night. He was so ashamed, so sorry, so full of repentance and remorse. Had it not been for the Lord's kind and understanding look, Peter might have taken the terrible road that Judas was now taking and gone out and hanged himself.

What was it Jesus had said? "Satan hath desired to have you, that he may sift you as wheat: But I have prayed for thee" (Luke 22:31-32). That prayer of Jesus held Peter on the path of sanity and kept him from suicide during that terrible night, and the days and endless nights that followed, until he met the risen Christ and received full absolution from Jesus' pierced hands.

V. HIS BOAT ON THE LAKE

After the events at Gethsemane and Gabbatha (John 19:13) and Golgotha, Peter thought that he would never lift up his head again. For some time he seemed to be subdued. Perhaps it appeared to him that although Jesus had forgiven him, the other disciples had not. Likewise, we are not nearly so willing to forgive a brother's fall as Jesus is. We hold it against him, color every subsequent action with suspicion, and act as though we have never fallen ourselves.

Gradually, however, Peter's confidence in the Lord came back and along with it his self-reliance. Jesus had said after His resurrection that He would meet Peter and the other disciples in Galilee. So off to Galilee they went. Back at home in the familiar surroundings of his boyhood and business days, Peter soon began to feel like himself again. Time passed, and still Jesus did not come. Peter wandered around, hating this inactivity. He was essentially a doer, not a dreamer like John. Suddenly Peter came to a decision: he would go back into business. Living by faith was all right so far as it went, but now he was fed up with it. He determined to fix up his nets, clean out his boat, see to his lines, and go back to fishing.

We can imagine Peter resolutely setting out from the house for the beach. The other disciples saw what he was doing and followed him down to his boat. "Figuring on doing some fishing, Peter?"

"Yep, I've had enough," we can hear Peter say. "I'm going back into business, starting tonight. You coming?" No doubt there was some heated discussion. Finally, some of them made up their minds.

Doubting Thomas said, "I'm with you, Peter."

Nathanael, a man singularly free from guile, said, "I'm coming too."

James and John, Peter's fishing partners during the old business days, found the temptation too strong as well. "Count us in, Peter." Two others, for some reason not named, also sided with Peter.

So seven out of the remaining eleven disciples went on an expedition that night; but they caught nothing. Going back into business was not such a good idea after all. They were tired and frustrated. Then as the morning broke, they saw someone on the shore. "Cast the net on the right side of the ship," He called out (John 21:6). They did so, with astonishing results. Then John recognized Jesus. "It is the Lord," he said (21:7).

In a moment Peter, the headstrong and impulsive man, jumped over the side of the boat and waded with giant strides toward the shore. Breakfast was ready. Jesus had some fish sizzling on the fire and some bread. Without a word the disciples took their places and ate the welcome meal, glancing sideways at each other and at Peter, waiting for what might come next. Then it came. The Lord singled out Peter, the born leader of men.

"All right, Peter," we can hear Him saying. "Now tell Me, do you love Me more than these? More than these disciples? More than these fish? Do you love Me, Peter?"

We know with what choking hesitation Peter answered his Lord. He did not dare to use the Master's word for love— the all-embracing, all-compelling, all-conquering love that many waters cannot quench, the love that suffers long and is kind. "Lord! You know I am fond of You" was the best Peter could trust himself to say.

"Then feed my sheep, Peter. I called you out of this fishing business years ago. You are to be a shepherd, Peter—a shepherd, not a small-time businessman on this lake. You are to be a shepherd-pastor of My flock."

VI. HIS LORD ON THE THRONE

It was the day of Pentecost. For ten long days the disciples had waited in the upper room, not daring to leave lest they miss the promised coming of the Spirit of God. They had spent the time in preparation and prayer. Then had come the cloven tongues as of fire; the mighty, rushing wind; the promised baptism of the Spirit.

Down the stairs and into the streets the disciples rushed. Crowds came running. And now Peter was preaching— preaching as never in all his days he had thought it possible to preach—with passion, with persuasion, and with power. The Bible leaped to life, burning in his soul, and the crowd was hushed. Boldly, without fear or cultivating favor, Peter charged home to the crowd their guilt. They had crucified the Lord of glory; they had murdered the Messiah. Conviction settled down on hundreds and hundreds of hearts. Three thousand people were saved in a moment, in the twinkling of an eye. There and then, on the city streets, the church that had been born in the upper room expanded into a vast congregation of men and women and boys and girls—people who were ransomed, healed, restored, forgiven.

What a snapshot. If only we could take similar snapshots of the church today!

Here is another snapshot of Peter, taken quite a while later.

VII. HIS PEN IN HIS HAND

It is likely that Peter always regretted his slow start in the great world missions enterprise of the church. Others had taken the early initiatives. Stephen first saw that the days of Jerusalem, Judaism, and Judea were over. The Spirit had moved on. Israel's persistent rebellion and unbelief made judgment inevitable. Besides, the tearing of the veil had rendered the whole temple system obsolete. Most Jewish Christians, including Peter, were unable to see that truth, but Stephen did. It cost him his life.

Then Philip—not Philip the disciple, but Philip the deacon—was the first to take seriously the Lord's commission to evangelize Samaria. Peter only went there after the work was done.

It was Paul, not Peter, who blazed the trail to the regions beyond, who evangelized Galatia, Macedonia, Achaia, Cappadocia, and Bithynia. It was Paul who left a trail of churches in Pisidian Antioch, Iconium, Lystra, Derbe, Philippi, Corinth, and Ephesus. It was Paul who blazed the trail across Roman Asia and on into Europe.

Peter was a latecomer to the work of Gentile evangelism. Eventually he turned eastward, as Paul had turned westward, and settled in Babylon. There we see Peter with his pen in his hand. The storm clouds were gathering now; the climate was changing. Roman power had finally stirred itself in anger and rage against the church. Peter particularly thought of the Christians in Europe who were bearing the brunt of the persecution. He thought of the many people Paul had led to Christ. He thought of the Gentile churches far and wide, now dear to his heart. He thought particularly of Jewish Christians in those churches and took up his pen.

Peter wrote two letters. The first one dealt with troubles from *without*. The other, with the shadow of Peter's death becoming more and more defined, dealt with troubles from *within*. The first letter had to do with a *suffering church*. The second letter had to do with a *seduced church*. By this time persecution from without and apostasy from within were assaulting the church.

We can imagine with what warmth and enthusiasm Peter's letters were received. Peter had an enormous fund of goodwill in the Christian world. He was respected and revered as a disciple who had been with Jesus from the very first. Peter had walked with Him and talked with Him. Peter had heard all His parables and seen all His miracles. Peter had observed Jesus' flawless life and His fearless death. Peter had been present in the upper room and had attended the last Passover and first communion feast. He had been in Gethsemane and at Gabbatha. He knew all about Golgotha. He had been at the grave on the resurrection morning and on the mount of Olives when Jesus had ascended into Heaven. Peter had been in the upper room on the day of Pentecost when the Holy Spirit came and the church was born. Peter had led three thousand people to Christ with a single sermon. Peter had opened the door of the church to the Gentiles.

So he had an enormous fund of goodwill. His very faults and failings were endearing to people. Peter was "the big fisherman," the bluff, hearty, warm, and impulsive companion of Christ.

Peter's letters reveal his intimacy with Jesus. Peter used the same illustrative style—telling stories, painting word pictures—and made scores of allusions to his many months with the Master. People read and remembered Peter's words of encouragement and hope, his challenge to remain firm in the face of the foe, and his urgent pleas against the invasion of heresy and the vileness of apostasy. People cherished and preserved his letters until they found their way into the sacred canon of Holy Writ. Little did Peter think—as a boy in Galilee reading Job, Jeremiah, Moses, and Malachi—that one day his writings would appear as a divinely inspired addition to the Word of God.

9
Peter
in the Spotlight Again

Acts 3:1-16; 8:5-25; 10:1-48; 11:1-18; 9:32-43;
Galatians 2:11-16; 2 Peter 1:12-15

I. HIS HAND IN HIS POCKET

II. HIS LIFE ON THE LINE

III. HIS FINGER IN THE PIE

IV. HIS NOSE IN THE AIR

V. HIS BACK TO THE WALL

VI. HIS SHOULDER TO THE WHEEL

VII. HIS FACE IN THE MUD

VIII. HIS NAME ON THE LIST

Dear old Peter. We cannot help but love him. We still have Heaven's photograph album open before us. It is crammed with snapshots as well as formal portraits of all kinds of interesting people. We have seen Peter with his eye on the Lord, with his mind on the storm, with his foot in his mouth, with his tears in his eyes, with his boat on the lake, with his Lord on the throne, and with his pen in his hand. Let

105

us look at some more of those candid-camera snapshots of
Peter.

I. HIS HAND IN HIS POCKET

It was three o'clock in the afternoon. Peter and John were
on their way to the temple to pray. They had been good friends
for many years. In the old days they had been business
partners. Now they were partners in the gospel. Far from their
beloved lake-shore home in the north, they were living now in
the great, busy, impersonal city of Jerusalem. It was the city of
many boyhood dreams and many grown men's disillusions.
Even so, the temple never ceased to fascinate the two friends.
Peter could not as yet realize that the temple was obsolete and
no longer served any useful function. Habit drew him back to
the temple every time the call to prayer resounded through the
city. Perhaps that was not such a bad habit after all.

There were various courts in the temple. When Herod the
Great had embellished the temple, he had enlarged the outer
court. The Jews did not regard this enlarged court as part of
the temple's sacred area. Gentiles were allowed to walk
around in this court and it was therefore known as "the court
of the Gentiles." Steps led out of that public court into the
sacred temple area. After ascending these steps, the Jews (only
they were allowed to go beyond the court of the Gentiles) came
to a barrier known as "the middle wall of partition." On this
barrier was a notice warning Gentiles to go no farther.

Nine gates led through this barrier, and the gate Beautiful
appears to have been one of them. Once past the barrier, a Jew
entered the court of the women where the treasury was
located. Women could penetrate only this far into the temple.
Jewish laymen might go farther, into the court of Israel, and
there they had to stop. Beyond this was the court of the priests,
within which stood the temple itself with its holy place and holy
of holies.

According to Josephus, public sacrifices were offered

twice a day—in the early morning and "about the ninth hour" (about three o'clock in the afternoon). A service of public prayer accompanied each sacrifice and another service was conducted at sunset.

Thus we see Peter entering the court of the Gentiles, passing through the barrier by way of the gate Beautiful on his way into the court of Israel. Suddenly something he saw pulled him up short. At the gate Beautiful lay someone who was anything but beautiful—a lame man, a beggar. He had been there most of his life. He had been born lame, and now he was more than forty years old. He had become somewhat of a fixture there. Everyone knew him. Day after day his friends laid him at the gates of a powerless religion. The decades came and went, and that religion did nothing for him. Indeed, it could do nothing for him but let him beg.

With a keen eye for a prospective donor, the beggar sized up Peter and John. He could not hope for much, but they were evidently Galileans and perhaps more ready to part with a coin or two than were the Jews of Jerusalem. So he appealed to them for help.

We can see Peter now with his hand in his pocket. The beggar's eyes gleamed with expectation, but the hand came out empty. Then Peter spoke, and his first words dashed the beggar's hopes to the dust: "Silver and gold have I none; but such as I have give I thee." Peter's second statement raised the beggar's hopes as high as Heaven: "In the name of Jesus Christ of Nazareth rise up and walk" (Acts 3:6). What a snapshot. Peter's pocket was empty, but he was willing to give what he had, and he had something worth far more than a pocketful of gold.

II. HIS LIFE ON THE LINE

The lame man's healing and conversion caused a considerable stir in the temple area. People came running to see what had happened. No wonder. The fellow was leaping and jumping and shouting for joy, hanging on to Peter and John, proclaiming them as his benefactors. As the crowd gathered, Peter saw an opportunity to preach, and preach he did. Soon word reached the temple authorities that these Galilean peasants were preaching—and they weren't licensed to preach. How dare they preach—especially in that detested name of Jesus!

Soon Peter and John were arrested, hauled before the Sanhedrin, and told to give an account of themselves. Gone was the cowardly Galilean fisherman who had once been so ready to deny his Lord because of the casual comments of a serving girl. In his place stood a man as brave as a lion and as terrible as an army with banners. Peter wasted no time in telling the rulers of his people that they were guilty of murdering their Messiah. When asked what authority or name he had used to heal the lame man, Peter gladly told them it was the name of Jesus. Peter then boldly added, "Neither is there salvation in any other: for there is none other name under heaven given among men, whereby we must be saved" (Acts 4:12).

The Sanhedrin demanded that Peter and his fellows agree not to speak any more in the name of Jesus. Fearlessly Peter replied, "Whether it be right in the sight of God to hearken unto you more than unto God, judge ye. For we cannot but speak the things which we have seen and heard" (Acts 4:19-20).

Peter put his life on the line. By now the reality of Christ's redemption, resurrection, rapture, and promised return had taken such a hold on Peter's heart that no man or group of men, however powerful, could intimidate him.

III. HIS FINGER IN THE PIE

Since the ascension the twelve had largely ignored the Lord's great commission: "Ye shall be witnesses unto me both in Jerusalem, and in all Judea, and in Samaria, and unto the uttermost part of the earth" (Acts 1:8). That was all very well, but who would want to go to Samaria? Jews had no dealings with Samaritans. A deep-seated hatred of Samaria was born and bred in the breast of every Jew. No self-respecting Jew would go to Samaria. He would take the bypass road and go miles out of his way, rather than go through Samaria.

We can well imagine some of the heated discussions that took place in the upper room when the question of evangelizing Samaria came up.

Peter might have said, "John, you ought to go. You're the youngest. They might take more kindly to a young man."

John could have answered, "Not me."

Matthew may have chimed in, "You ought to go, Peter. You're the leader, after all. You should set the example. You took the limelight on the day of Pentecost. Take it now too."

Peter might have replied, "Not me."

Then Thomas would have had a word, and with a rare touch of sardonic humor he might have said, "I think Simon Zelotes ought to go—Simon the Zealot, Simon the Jewish patriot."

Simon Zelotes might have answered, "Not me."

Peter could have spoken up, "Andrew, you should go. You're good at bringing people to Christ. You and Philip brought those Greeks that time."

Andrew may have replied, "Not me. I have no leading at all along those lines."

So nobody went. Because none of the twelve would go, the Lord sent somebody else, Philip the evangelist. Revival soon broke out in Samaria, and at once Peter wanted a finger in the pie. He headed a two-man delegation to go down, see what was going on, and perhaps add his apostolic blessing. He found that a very good pie indeed was being baked down there in Samaria. It only had one rotten apple, which Peter soon detected and removed. That trip to Samaria turned out to be good for Peter. It helped to rid him of insular prejudice against the Samaritans. Moreover, Peter's endorsement of Philip's mission made the Samaritans full members, without barrier or bias, in the Christian community.

IV. HIS NOSE IN THE AIR

If visiting the Samaritans was distasteful to Peter, visiting the Gentiles was far worse. He certainly had no intention of doing that. He put his nose in the air with a gesture of arrogant, religious superiority and positively refused to have anything to do with such a visit. He drew the line with the Gentiles.

Then came the compelling, heavenly vision and Peter's resolute "Not so, Lord." The Lord instantly overruled Peter's objections and off Peter went to Cesarea, the detested Roman capital of Palestine, to meet a Gentile soldier named Cornelius. By now Peter's nose was not as high in the air, even though he still did not relish the idea of being forced to be hospitable to Gentiles, of entering a Gentile home, or of eating at what he had always considered to be an unclean table. *What if they serve me pork or ham?* he may have thought. *What if they give me bacon and eggs for breakfast?* He knew that any meal in a Gentile house would include meat that had been offered to idols and cooked with the blood still in it. Everything about this mission ran against Peter's Jewish grain.

However, once he met Cornelius and heard of God's dealings with him, all Peter's doubts were swept aside. His racial prejudice, as deep as the sea and as wide as the ages, was gone. The door of the church was flung open to the Gentiles. The Holy Spirit came down, and it was Pentecost all over again. Not many of us can overcome our prejudices as quickly as that.

V. HIS BACK TO THE WALL

Peter eventually returned to Jerusalem from his mission to Gentile Cesarea. What a reception committee awaited him there. The exclusive brethren, who made up a major part of the Jerusalem church, were waiting for him, ready to read him right out of the fellowship for breaking one of their religious taboos. Peter, they believed, had disgraced them. He had

visited a forbidden home and fellowshiped with religiously
unclean people. They had their case against him well in hand.

Peter, however, had anticipated their reaction and had
taken some Jewish witnesses with him on his mission. Now he
called on them to substantiate what had happened. In words
brief but pointed, he recounted the whole story and confronted
his critics with what God had done. "There you are, brethren,"
he said in effect. "You take up *that* matter with the Lord."

When we, like Peter, have our backs to the wall, it is good
to know that we have God on our side.

VI. HIS SHOULDER TO THE WHEEL

It finally dawned on the apostles in Jerusalem, and on
Peter in particular, that the Lord had been serious about
evangelizing not only Judea and Samaria but the uttermost
parts of the earth. After Philip opened up Samaria, Peter finally
put his shoulder to the wheel. He became active in the Lord's
work beyond the boundaries of Jerusalem.

His first venture was not very ambitious. He went down
to Lydda on the coastal plain of Sharon, about a day's journey
from Jerusalem. It was not much of an effort, but it was a start
and the Lord blessed him for making the move. In Lydda he
healed a man sick of the palsy. Then Peter was summoned to
nearby Joppa for the funeral of a gracious, generous lady
named Dorcas. He raised her from the dead, a truly spectacular
miracle.

These encouraging blessings on his widened ministry
greatly stiffened Peter's resolve to keep on reaching out to the
great world beyond Jerusalem's confining walls. The legalism
and narrowness of the Jerusalem church had trammeled him
too long. Then the Lord opened the door to the Gentiles (Acts
10) and Peter's horizons were further broadened. As time went
on, his travels widened and so did his interest in the mission
field. Eventually we find him writing to believers in faraway

places, in fields the apostle Paul had pioneered for the gospel:
Cappadocia; Pontus; Galatia; Bithynia; and Asia.

It is a great thing when we set our eyes on regions beyond,
when we catch the vision of a lost world and "the untold
millions still untold." It is a great thing when we put our
shoulders to the wheel. Peter never became the flaming
evangelist and tireless missionary that Paul became, but at least
Peter threw the weight of his influence and personality behind
such a man. We can do that too. We cannot all become
Hudson Taylors or David Livingstones, but we can all throw
our weight behind those people God has called in our
generation to make an impact for Him far and wide in this poor,
lost world.

VII. HIS FACE IN THE MUD

Revival had broken out among the Gentiles of Antioch, a
thriving metropolis in the nearby country of Syria. Barnabas
and Saul had labored there and tremendously expanded the
work. The news filtered back to Jerusalem where, for the most
part, it was merely a matter of passing interest. In the view of
the Jerusalem brethren, no work could be as important as their
own, and no church of Gentile believers deserved such high
regard in the sight of Heaven as a church of Jewish believers
in Jerusalem. Antioch! What a place for a revival to break out.
Even Peter was not particularly interested at the time.

Then Paul and Barnabas broke all precedent and boldly
carried the gospel to "the regions beyond." At last the Holy
Spirit made His move toward what Jesus had called "the
uttermost part of the earth." He had waited long enough for
Peter; from now on the limelight would be on Paul. Peter
probably did not care that much; evangelizing Gentiles did not
really appeal to him. True, he had opened the door, but he was
content to let someone else press through it. Paul was
welcome to assume the work of pioneering in Galatia among
wild, barbarous tribes and in other outlandish places.

In the meantime, however, Jewish believers had infiltrated the new church at Antioch and had brought with them typically Jewish sectarian views: Gentiles must be circumcised; they must keep the law of Moses; they must be zealous Jewish proselytes as well as Gentile Christians. It was all so much arrogant, high-sounding nonsense, but it made its impact. The Jewish believers seemed to have plenty of Scripture references to back up their views. Besides, something had to be done to keep the Gentile church from swamping the Jewish church, for ever-increasing numbers of Gentiles were already flooding into the church. Soon Jews would be a permanent minority in the church, and that in their minds would be a disaster.

What better way for us to keep the Gentiles in their place, the Jews thought, *than by putting them under the yoke of the law?* Such was the new Judaizing creed, and Peter did nothing to stop it. Perhaps he did not see anything wrong with it.

But Paul certainly did, and so did Barnabas. It was not long before a delegation came from Antioch to Jerusalem, asking that this effort to Judaize the Gentile church be stopped. Couldn't the Jews understand that there was only one church and that in that church there was neither Jew nor Gentile? A heated debate followed. To give Peter his due, he stood up for Paul. Then the Jerusalem church wrote a letter in which they admitted that Gentile emancipation from circumcision, from the sabbath, from the law, and from the traditions of the Jews was of God. Paul doubtlessly thanked Peter heartily for his share in getting this principle acknowledged in Jerusalem.

James, the Lord's brother, by now had assumed a dominant position in the Jerusalem church. James was a bit legalistic. He had agreed to Gentile emancipation from the law, but had insisted that some stipulations be included in the letter: Gentiles must abstain from fornication, from eating blood, and from eating animals killed by strangulation. Peter was intimidated by James.

Peter wanted to see for himself what was happening at Antioch, so he said goodbye to James and off he went. When Peter arrived in Antioch, he was thrilled at what he saw and grew to love the Gentile Christians. They lionized him. This

was Peter, who had spent over three years in the company of
Jesus. They pressed him for details. He spent many hours in
the homes of the generous and hospitable Gentile believers,
eating at their tables, sharing personal experiences of Jesus
with them. What happy times these were. What a grand church
this was! Peter did not miss for a moment the stuffy regulations
of the Jerusalem church. He felt marvelously free.

Then a delegation from Jerusalem arrived in Antioch.
They were sent by James to see what was going on. At once
Peter caved in. All of a sudden the same old Peter emerged
who had once shrunk from confessing his Lord before a serving
maid. Under the frowns of James' legalistic colleagues—
separatist and exclusive brethren—Peter retreated. He with-
drew from fellowship with the Gentiles and refused all further
invitations to their homes. He no longer ate meat with them.
Throughout the Antioch church confusion reigned. The
Gentile believers were dismayed. What had they done? Hadn't
this issue been settled? Did they not have in the church archives
the letter Peter and James had signed?

Then Paul came, filled with righteous indignation. He
took Peter aside and gave him a piece of his mind. Paul's eyes
flashed, and his eloquence ignited with holy anger, until Peter
became more afraid of Paul than he ever had been of James.
Besides, Peter knew in his heart that Paul was right and James
was wrong.

With that impulsiveness that made him so beloved, Peter
apologized, acknowledged that he had been wrong, and did
what he could to put things right. To his credit, Peter never held
Paul's actions against him. Peter felt that he had deserved
Paul's anger. Years later, when writing to churches Paul had
founded, Peter could speak of "our beloved brother Paul" (2
Peter 3:15).

VIII. HIS NAME ON THE LIST

We do not know where Peter was living when Nero
burned Rome and blamed the Christians. Roman tradition says

that Peter was in Rome, but that is doubtful. There is no concrete evidence that Peter ever visited Rome. Indeed Biblical evidence militates against the idea. Be that as it may, Peter's name was on the "persecution list." Nero, a dreadful tyrant in Rome, was disgracing the throne of the caesars as never before. His name has gone down in history as the arch-persecutor of the church and as a type of the antichrist. Nero so terrorized the early church that the idea was circulated that he would come back as the antichrist in the endtimes.

Nero was out to rid the world of Christians, so he had them rounded up and tortured to death. Some were thrown to lions in the arena or wrapped in animal skins and thrown to wild dogs. Some Christians were burned alive. Some were dipped in wax and burned as torches to light the orgies in Nero's palace grounds. We can well imagine that Nero said, "Get Peter. He's the ringleader. I want him dead . . . crucified, do you hear?"

Peter knew that he would be killed. He had escaped from death at the hands of Herod, but he knew that he would not escape from death at the hands of Nero. Jesus had told him years before that he would one day die for Him, and hinted strongly that he would die by crucifixion. Tradition has it that Peter's last request was to be crucified upside down, to make amends for the time he had denied his Lord.

Peter died a hero's death. When at last he drew his final, agonizing, painful breath and his great spirit departed for the courts of bliss, his beloved Lord welcomed him on the other side. "Welcome home, Peter," we can hear our Lord saying. "Come and see the mansion I've prepared for you on Hallelujah Avenue, just across from Victory Square. Well done, Peter! Ah, here's Gabriel. Gabriel, come and greet Peter, My dear friend."

And we can hear Gabriel saying, "Peter. Oh yes, I've met Peter. Do you remember me, Peter? The last time I saw you, you were sound asleep in prison and I opened the prison's doors for you. Welcome home, Peter."

"And now, Peter," we can hear the Savior saying, "Come and meet My Father." So Peter entered into the joy of his Lord.

10
Herod
the Great

Matthew 2:1-20

I. HIS DESCENT
II. HIS DOMINION
III. HIS DILEMMA
IV. HIS DEMAND
V. HIS DECISION
VI. HIS DEATH

H e was a monster in human form, a rapacious wild beast wearing the rich robes of a king. A typical afternoon's entertainment for this well-dressed savage was to get drunk with his concubines and invited guests and crucify seven or eight hundred of his subjects on a public platform in the middle of his capital city. Another one of his favorite tricks was to trap his unarmed enemies in a narrow place and send his legionnaires roaring through the doors in full battle dress,

117

armed with shields and short swords, to slaughter the defense-less captives.

One might wonder why the soldiers obeyed. One might also wonder why Himmler's executioners sat on the lips of death pits and mowed down boys and girls, women and old men—naked and starved wretches—by the countless thousands just because they were Jews.

While this vile man's legionnaires hacked away at their butchery and became soaked with blood, the monster himself would stand and watch, licking his lips, clasping his fat hands together in fury, and crying, "Death to them! Death to them all! They have opposed me."

His name was Herod. History, with its frequent myopia, has called him Herod the Great. During his reign Jesus of Nazareth—the Son of God, the Savior of the world—was born.

We will now ponder this evil king's descent, his dominion, his dilemma, his demand, his decision, and his death. We could subtitle this study "What happens when a thoroughly evil and unrepentant man meets Christ."

I. HIS DESCENT

Herod was an Idumean; that is, he came from Edom and was thus a remote descendant of Esau, the twin brother of Jacob. There had been little love lost between the two brothers way back in the beginning, and no love at all existed between the two nations they founded. Almost from the first, the nation of Israel and the nation of Edom were at war. Just as Esau and Jacob fought in the womb before they ever saw the light of day, so the two nations have fought ever since.

It is one of the great ironies of history that when God's Son stepped off His blazing throne of light and condescended to enter human life by way of the virgin's womb, He was greeted by a king of the Jews sprung from the Jewish people's most bitter foe. The great red dragon was waiting with open maw to devour the man-child as soon as He was born.

But we must go back a little way in Hebrew history. Between the last book of the Old Testament and the first book of the New Testament lie four hundred silent years during which God had nothing to say to His ancient people of Israel. He was preparing to speak once and for all through His Son.

During these long centuries, Palestine was the constant pawn in the struggles between Egypt to the south and Syria to the north. Not only was Palestine constantly ravaged by war, but the overlords, particularly the Syrians, sought to impose raw paganism on the people by brute force. As a result, a family of guerrilla fighters arose who not only trounced their mighty neighbor but won a measure of independence for their tortured land. These fighters were known as the Hasmoneans. For a while they governed brilliantly, but their family squabbles and power struggles eventually attracted the attention of Rome. Pompey made short work of the whole family, imposed a high priest of his choosing on Jerusalem, and hauled the rival priest off to Rome to grace a triumphal parade through the forum.

But Jerusalem and Judea were not as easy to control. Their constant uprisings were a headache to Rome. Consequently Rome decided the man to handle the Jews was Herod, the young Idumean. Herod had been born to command. At age fifteen he had fought Jewish rebels in Galilee. He was glamorous, daring, ruthless, and without conscience. His path to the Jewish throne became strewn with thousands upon thousands of Jewish dead. But Herod cared little for Jewish dead. He was an Idumean, and Edomites had always killed Jews. It was a national sport.

So it was that after various intrigues, after changing sides repeatedly to lick the boots of Pompey, Caesar, Mark Anthony, and Augustus—Herod, still in his twenties, was confirmed in his office as "king of the Jews." A proclamation by the senate, a sacrifice on the Capitol, a royal banquet—and Herod was "king of the Jews."

So much then for his rise to power. The Jews, who were about to crown all their other apostasies and iniquities by murdering their Messiah, and who would then at home and abroad ratify their decision by persistently and pugnaciously persecuting the infant church, had now been saddled with an Idumean for a king. It nearly drove them mad. It certainly did not lead them to repentance.

II. HIS DOMINION

Herod's dominion turned out to be terrible. He filled Jerusalem and his domains with foreign troops and councilors; he filled his cities with spies. No man or woman was safe during his reign. One by one he murdered every rival claimant to the throne. He stamped out the Hasmoneans. He murdered his wife's brother, a lad of seventeen summers and the darling of the Jews. He murdered his favorite wife and both her sons. Only five days before his own death, he murdered his son and heir. No wonder Caesar Augustus declared, "I'd sooner be Herod's swine than Herod's son." Herod hacked and hewed his way through life, murdering and slaughtering six to eight thousand of the best people in his realm.

"The army hates your cruelty," a tough old veteran of many of Herod's wars once dared to tell him. "Have a care, my lord. There isn't a private who doesn't side with your sons. And many of the officers openly curse you."

Herod threw the old soldier on the rack and tortured him beyond all power to endure. He screamed out worthless confessions and accused officers of treason to the crown. Still Herod did not spare him. The soldier's body was twisted and turned on the rack, jerked and pulled until his joints came apart and his bones cracked. The accused officers were then haled before Herod. He harangued the mob and turned it loose; they tore the men Herod suspected into pieces while the king danced up and down screaming for their deaths.

Herod's fiendish cruelties affected his brain. After the murder of his favorite wife he ran raving around his palace and pleaded for mercy from the ghosts that haunted him. "I killed the fairest Jewish princess the world has ever known," he would scream. "I am condemned!"

Herod would storm among his female slaves, point to this girl and that girl, and shout, "You are not Mariamne." Then one day, walking along the quays at Cesarea, he saw a girl who reminded him of his murdered love. Obsessed with her regal beauty, he seized her, ignoring that she was a woman of the streets. Later, when struck with a filthy disease, he screamed, "I knew it was Mariamne. She has come back to curse me!" Thereafter a new fire ran through his veins, a fire of madness begotten of the foul infection he had contracted in his besotted state.

The Romans stood back and laughed. Judea was a long, long way from Rome, and the tyrant knew how to butter up Rome. So long as Herod kept discipline among the Jews, Caesar cared little if a few thousand more or less of the hated Hebrews were slain. Besides, any charges against Herod were made against a king of the scarlet before an emperor of the purple, so Augustus always sided with Herod. What did it really matter if the most brilliant Jews were killed? That only made it easier for Rome to rule the world.

Herod rebuilt the temple for the Jews to conciliate his hated subjects and to indulge his passion for building. He spared neither men nor money to make the temple the wonder of the world. A thousand vehicles carried up the stone; ten thousand men slaved night and day. The work went on almost until the time the Romans burned it to the ground. To build Cesarea in honor of Caesar absorbed the revenues of Herod's kingdom for ten whole years, and to rebuild the temple cost him as much again. But Herod cared little about cost. The Jews could simply pay more taxes. Whole armies spent their lives cutting away the edges of rocks so that the diamond-hard stones could be fitted into perfect walls—each stone uneven and projecting in the center but perfectly aligned along the beveled edge. How many such stones? A million? Twenty million? What cared Herod so long as his visions of grandeur were realized? It took two hundred men to move each stone from the quarries great distances away, but each one fitted like a glove into its appointed place. Yet all would be burned down soon after the final overlay of gold was poured.

So the royal maniac drove his people to do his iron will. They detested him because he was an Edomite. They loved their temple, but they loathed its architect. They hated him.

Everywhere Herod left his mark. He built temples to the gods and to the caesar. He built and rebuilt towns. In Jerusalem, newly built theaters and amphitheaters proclaimed his Hellenistic tastes, the mighty fortress of Antonia proclaimed his debt to Rome, and the temple served as a means to pacify the Jews and come to terms with their faith. At the northwest angle of the upper city he built the noblest of palaces in which to live.

Herod's marked contempt for the Jews was always present. He was fully aware that the Jewish law declared, "Thou shalt not make unto thee any graven image, or any likeness of any thing that is in the heaven above, or that is in the earth beneath, or that is in the waters under the earth" (Exodus 20:4). Yet he placed a wooden image of a Roman eagle over the main gate of the temple. Herod knew too that no such image had affronted Jewish sensibilities since the dreadful days of Antiochus Epiphanes. When the Jews tore the eagle down, as Herod knew they would, he had them chopped into pieces. In its place he put a larger eagle and then, in a letter to Augustus, Herod said that he would kill a million Jews to keep the imperial image there.

So the hated Herod reigned over his domain. He was uneducated and ruled by sheer force of will. The longer he ruled, the worse he became. He filled the country with fortresses directed not against a foreign foe but against the people he ruled. He constructed huge buildings in foreign cities. He paved the streets of Antioch with marble blocks— two and a half miles of them, adorned along their length with colonnades—and paid for them with taxes wrung from the detested Jews.

Into this man's kingdom came the Son of God—born of the virgin Mary, born in a cattle shed, cradled in a manger, and bedded down in hay and straw. What an unlikely place for God's Son to be born—a stinking stable attached to a wayside inn. What an unlikely time for Him to be born—when a detested Edomite sat on the throne of His father David and ruled like a wild beast over the lost sheep of the house of Israel. But born Jesus was, during such a period and in such a place.

III. HIS DILEMMA

One day wise men came from the East saying, "Where is he that is born King of the Jews?" (Matthew 2:2) The question must have thrown the palace into pandemonium. If ever a suspicious, bloodthirsty, ruthless tyrant sat on a throne, it was Herod. If ever a man stained the pages of history with innocent blood after the merest hint or vaguest whisper of a rival claimant to his throne, that man was Herod the so-called Great.

These imposing-looking nobles from the East had arrived in Jerusalem riding on magnificent camels, bearing regal gifts, and telling a strange story about a sovereign and a star. The news must have taken Jerusalem by the ears. Herod's servants must have trod about the mad king's palace softly that day, trembling in every limb at each successive screech of rage that issued from the tyrant's lips.

We can hear him as he raged, "Where are they? Fetch them to me. A king of the Jews! I'll teach them who's king of the Jews. Wise men? Fools to come here publishing such tidings. Where are the guards? Ho, guards. Arrest those men. Where's the inquisitor? We'll roast them alive until they speak."

Herod faced the greatest dilemma of his evil life. He was now confronted with the birth of a babe, with the coming of a greater king than Caesar. This newborn king, as Herod well knew, was the rightful claimant to his throne. This baby was the Son of David, the Son of the living God, the Christ, the long-expected Messiah of Israel. This challenge to Herod's sovereignty came from the highest court of all. So Herod had a dilemma: should he crown this One, or curse Him? It was as simple as that.

Jesus' coming into this world has altered everything. He now challenges every man's throne, hammers at the door of every man's castle, and demands everyone's submission. He comes in seeming weakness—but woe to the man or woman who despises His claims. He comes to us. He demands that we instantly submit to His claims. He is our Maker, God's Son, and the Savior of the world. He knocks at our hearts, putting us into the place of decision. Neutral we cannot be. Will we crown Him or crucify Him? That is still the question.

Most people want nothing to do with Jesus. They wish that He had never come into the world, wish He would go away, and wish to have no part in such a choice. But the dilemma is inescapable. Christ has come. We *have* heard about Him. We must decide whether to crown or crucify the Son of God. There is no middle ground.

Herod's wicked life could all have been changed in a moment by his simple acceptance of Christ and submission to His claims. But Herod, like so many others, did not want his life to be changed. He wanted to hang onto life as it was. All he wanted was to get rid of this choice and to treat Christ the same way he treated everyone else who crossed his will.

So his greatest dilemma had come. Would Herod accept the claim of Christ? That would mean abdicating his throne, surrendering his sovereignty, and yielding his will. It would mean a new way of life and a new center. By yielding to Christ's claims, Herod could be saved. His whole life could promote the interests of God's Son. Herod certainly did not want that any more than most people living today do. Not to yield to Christ's claims, however, was to become even more of an open and avowed enemy of God than he had been before and to court the vengeance of eternal fire. To reject Christ would mean to go on living in wickedness and sin until God finally settled accounts.

IV. HIS DEMAND

"When he had gathered all the chief priests and scribes of the people together, he demanded of them where Christ should be born" (Matthew 2:4). Herod did not know the Bible. He detested the Bible and made fun of it. During this crisis, however, he tacitly confessed that the Bible was the Word of God and that it contained prophecies of great personal relevance.

After World War II when for a brief time Sir Winston Churchill was back in office as prime minister of England, he became troubled by events on the international scene. He remembered Yalta, that fateful conference in February 1945 when he, Stalin, and Roosevelt had met to decide the wartime fate of Europe. Churchill remembered how Stalin had insisted on a second front and had urged Roosevelt to open it soon to take the pressure off Russia. Churchill remembered Roosevelt's plans for opening a second front across the English channel on the shores of France, remembered the gleam in Stalin's eye as he heartily endorsed the plan, and remembered the flattery of that wicked old fox.

Churchill remembered too how he had promoted a different plan. The Allies were already in Europe, fighting their way up the long boot of Italy. He urged that the western powers beat the Russians into the Balkans and into Germany, so that these countries might be truly set free. He pointed out the folly of allowing Russia to get there first.

Churchill remembered Roosevelt's barely-concealed jealousy and how the American president fell for Stalin's flattery. Churchill remembered how he had been given the cold shoulder and how his superior statecraft had been ignored. He remembered Yalta.

Churchill remembered how events had all happened the way he had feared. Half of Europe was now enslaved again, only this time to a far more terrible foe than Germany had ever been. He saw that the West had won the war and lost the peace. He saw Russia astride the world and gaining new strength every day. And that farsighted old warrior-statesman was troubled.

Where could he find light on the things now happening in the world? Ah, there was the Bible. Didn't it say something about these things? He had never lived by the Bible, but maybe it could help him now. Maybe it could cast light on the shadows that lay across the world. Perhaps it could speak with authority to the fears that troubled his heart. Like Herod of old, Churchill began to look for someone who could chart a course for him through the unfamiliar seas of Holy Writ. An appointment was made for him with a well-taught English Christian, Harold St. John.

After greeting his guest, Churchill said, "Mr. St. John, I am a very busy man. You have half an hour; make the most of it. Tell me what the Bible has to say about Russia, about the problems confronting me in this dangerous postwar world." So Mr. St. John opened to him the Scriptures. At the end of the half hour Churchill called his secretary. "What other engagements do I have today?" he demanded.

"Sir," she answered, "at ten o'clock you have an appointment with the ambassador from India. At ten-thirty the foreign secretary wants to see you concerning affairs in South Africa. At eleven o'clock the chancellor of the exchequer is to see you about the budget. At twelve you are to have lunch with the chief lord of the admiralty. At one o'clock . . ."

Churchill cut in, "Cancel them all. Make any excuse you like. Set up new appointments. Anything! I'm spending the rest of the day with Mr. St. John and on no account do I wish to be disturbed."

At the end of that day, the great statesman looked at the humble Christian gentleman who had given him a view of the

Bible such as he had never had before. Churchill saw before him a poor man who had spent much of his life as a missionary in Argentina. He saw a white-haired man with a merry twinkle in his eye. "Mr. St. John," he said, and there was a surprising note of humility in his voice, "I would give half the world for your knowledge of the Bible."

"Sir," replied the courtly old missionary, "for my knowledge of the Bible I gave all the world."

The story does not record how Churchill used the Biblical information he received from God's servant, but history does record what Herod did with the knowledge he gained from the priests and scribes of Jerusalem. They told him that Christ would be born in Bethlehem. Thus Herod was confronted for the last time with factual knowledge of Christ, with the fact that God's Son had come into the world and that his own life would never again be the same.

V. HIS DECISION

Herod's decision was automatic and instinctive. It seems that he never gave the alternative so much as a passing thought. He categorically, totally, and unequivocally rejected the claims of Christ. Then he gave force to his bitter hatred of God's Son, who had dared to challenge his life, by ordering the coldblooded massacre of the babes of Bethlehem. It says a lot about Herod's wickedness that Josephus and other historians do not even record the deed. Herod had already massacred so many people. What difference did a few hundred more make? But God recorded it; God records everything.

Herod failed to kill Christ, but he would have done so if he could. People who reject Christ today may not be able physically to assault God's Son, but if they continue to reject Him as Savior they record their hearts' intentions just the same. God writes down their decisions in His book against the coming day when He will settle accounts at the great white throne. In His tender love and mercy, God sent His Son into this world. To reject Him is an unpardonable sin. That was Herod's decision; may it not be ours.

VI. HIS DEATH

The Bible scarcely gives Herod's death a footnote, but he died horribly. Gone were his sleek good looks. Once lean, he had become obese. He had lost nearly all his hair. Three of his front teeth had broken off. His legs had become great stumps, nine inches thick at the ankles. He could not eat without great pain. A dreadful sickness had spread throughout his body, attacking parts of his flesh and producing ugly, mortifying wounds. He had sores everywhere. His stomach had become so rotten that the guards had to be changed frequently lest they faint from the stench. He was a man of seventy on whose body had been visited all the crimes of his former years. He was foul beyond imagination. His breath was an abomination.

Even as he groveled on his deathbed in mortal agony, his mind ran to murder. He ordered the death of his fifth son. He also remained obsessed with the hatred of Jews. "When I die, I will see to it that they mourn me," he shouted.

He called for his mercenaries—Africans, Cilicians, Egyptians, Persians—the men who had coldly killed off the leaders of Judaism at his command through the years. He yelled at them in a few jumbled sentences: "Go to every city in Judea, arrest the leading citizens, put them in jail, and guard them well. Feed them luxuriously and let them have all comforts. But on the day I die, kill them—kill them all! Go to every city and village; none is too small." He strode about, hacking and thrusting with his right arm, and then fell back exhausted on his bed. Then he gathered himself together again and screamed, "When I die, the Jews may not mourn me, but by the gods they will mourn!"

Herod died as he had lived, a wicked, ungodly man. Laden down with his sins, he died and went to meet his Maker.

Death marks the end of human sovereignty. Napoleon once said of the hated English, "Britain loses every battle except the last." It sometimes seems, in His dealings with men, that God loses every battle, but He does not lose the last one. In the end He sends the angel of death to put an end to an individual's puny sovereignty. From then on God's will is enforced in judgment forever. We need to ask not only, What will we do with Jesus? but also, What will He do with us?

At the time of His birth Herod chose to reject Jesus. At the same time wise men from the East came and worshiped Him. The great question is, Do we take our stand with Herod or with the wise men?

11
The
Prodigal Son

Luke 15:11-24

What is the finest short story ever told? Should we search the works of Rudyard Kipling, Jack London, or Edgar Allan Poe? The finest short story ever told was written nearly two thousand years ago. It is the story of the prodigal son. Not counting the appendix that deals with his older brother, the story of the prodigal is all told in fewer than 350 words. Yet this story never grows old, never fails to charm, and never ceases to hammer home the greatness of our God.

This story is one of Jesus' deathless parables. Every one of His parables is a miracle in words. Every parable is an earthly story with a heavenly meaning; each is a matchless, priceless pearl of wisdom. The story of the prodigal son is essentially the story of a father's love.

Jesus came to teach us a new name for God. God had often revealed Himself in the Old Testament by means of His names. He was *Elohim, Jehovah, Adonai, El Elyon,* and *El Shaddai.* He was *Jehovah Jireh, Jehovah Shalom,* and *Jehovah Nissi.* He was the great I AM. He was the Creator, God Almighty, the Lord who provides, the Lord who is our peace, and the Lord who is our banner. The ages rolled by, and God lived up to the names by which He had progressively revealed Himself. Then Jesus came. He taught men a new name for God. He taught them that God is *Father*—and nowhere more so than in the story of the prodigal son. This story, together with the companion story of the older brother, is simply the story of God as Father. Jesus speaks of God the Father twelve times in twenty-two short verses. If we miss God the Father, we miss the whole point of the parable.

Yet this parable is not without its detractors. Some carping critics have found fault with this, the sweetest story ever told, along two lines. They say first of all that there is no element of *search* in the parable. The father did not run after his wayward boy. He did not scour the brothels, the bars, and the bawdy houses of the far-off country. He did not search through the dives and dens of sin. He did not haunt the gambling joints, the pleasure palaces, the back alleys, and the slums of the far country in search of his son.

Critics say too that the parable has no element of *sacrifice.* God does not smile, nod, and lightly forgive. His holiness demands sacrifice. As we read in Hebrews 9:22, "Without shedding of blood is no remission."

As usual, the critics are wrong. There *is* an element of search. When the prodigal son was far, far away, not a day passed that the father's heart did not follow the son into the distant country. The father did not run after his son because that never does any good.

Every day the father searched the horizon for the first sign of the prodigal's return. Not a day passed when the father did not take up his watch on some vantage point and stare with tear-filled eyes down the dusty road that led away from home. We know that because when the prodigal decided to come home, "when he was yet a great way off, the father saw him, and had compassion, and ran, and fell on his neck, and kissed him" (Luke 15:20). Oh yes, the element of search is there. It is not overly emphasized in this story because the search has already been fully treated in the sister story of the lost sheep.

The parable of the prodigal also contains an element of sacrifice. It is astonishing how critics could have missed the fact that the feast was founded on sacrifice. The father said, "Bring hither the fatted calf, and kill it; and let us eat, and be merry" (Luke 15:23). Of course there is an element of sacrifice. Jesus would not overlook that.

The story of the prodigal son revolves around two focal points: *the far horizons* and *the father's house.*

I. THE FAR HORIZONS

How do we measure the distance to the far country? Do we measure it in terms of *miles* or in terms of *morals?* Or do we measure it in terms of both? In the end the prodigal discovered that the far country was distant from the father's house both in terms of miles and morals.

We could measure how far the prodigal traveled in terms of miles if we knew his starting point (Jerusalem or Capernaum or Nazareth) and where he ended up (Antioch or Corinth or Rome). It would be simply a matter of mathematics or geography.

Suppose the prodigal headed north to Cesarea from

Jerusalem. That would be about sixty-five miles. If he then
sailed to Myra on the seacoast of the Roman province of Lycia,
that would be another five hundred miles. Suppose he
changed ships there and headed on to Malta; that would be
another nine hundred miles. If he went on from there to Rome,
landed where Paul had landed at Puteoli, and headed north up
the Appian way, that would be another five hundred miles or
so. By that time he would have traveled some two thousand
miles from home. In those days, given the terrible road
conditions and the even worse sea conditions, that would have
been a far country indeed.

It would be possible, then, to calculate how far the
prodigal went if we measure the distance in terms of miles—
no matter whether he headed north to Antioch, east to
Babylon, west to Rome, or south to Egypt. We have no way,
however, to measure how far he went in terms of morals.

When he came back from Corinth or Carthage, from
Galatia or Gaul, the road had a beginning point and an ending
point. But when the prodigal came back from his immoralities
and indecencies, from his debaucheries and drunkenness,
there is a sense in which part of him remained in the far
country. There he left behind unhappy young women whom
he had helped to ruin, and addicted young men whom he had
helped to destroy with drugs and alcohol. In the far country
remained men and women who were much worse now than
they had been before the prodigal had come their way.

In that far country, mothers wept because this young man
had come their way with his good looks and daredevil ways,
with his fine clothes and bulging wallet. These mothers cried
their hearts out because he had swept their daughters off their
feet, seduced them, and then laughingly gone on his way,
leaving them forever soiled and shamed. In that far country
fathers were bowed and bent because this young man had met
their sons and taught them how to use drugs and debauch
themselves.

So the prodigal had come back, but others had continued

in the wild ways in which he had encouraged them. How far was the far country in terms of morals? His sin was "a rebellion against the entire universe, an anarchy against society, an outrage on everything, a crime against everybody." His sin had contaminated the planet. Even the far country had become worse as a result of the prodigal's pleasures.

We can measure our waywardness if it is only to be measured in terms of miles, but we can never measure our waywardness in terms of example, influence, and cause and effect.

A. What the Prodigal Figured

We can picture this young man, who grew up in that good home, becoming increasingly impatient with his father's devotions, his father's duties, and his father's discipline. The father had lofty principles and high moral standards. He was kindly, but he was firm.

The prodigal decided at last that he had had enough. He was tired of family devotions, tired of the daily tedium of sitting through a reading of the Scriptures, and tired of listening to his father's pious prayers. He was tired of hearing his father say no whenever he wanted to go to this shady place or that questionable house. *If I leave home*, he thought, *I will be free*.

That is always the devil's first lie. "Be free," he says. "Please yourself. Get out from under these restrictions and restraints. Do your own thing." The prodigal followed the devil's lead when he decided he had had about enough of the rules that were part of living at home.

B. What the Prodigal Forgot

The prodigal forgot that the path of sin is expensive. He demanded his share of the family fortune and wasted no time in converting it into cash. Then he packed his bags, lined his purse, and went out—thoughtless young fool that he was—to live on his capital. Of course it soon ran out. Easy come, easy go. The money poured through his wasteful hands. Into taverns he went as the big shot calling for drinks all around. Into gambling joints he went crying, "Increase the stakes." Into fairgrounds he rushed announcing, "Come on, fellows. Everything's on me." The far country was expensive. It took everything and gave nothing.

C. What the Prodigal Found

1. Fair-weather Friends

In the far country the prodigal found fair-weather friends. "When he had spent all . . . he began to be in want" (Luke 15:14). His friends soon left him when he had no more money to throw around.

We can see the prodigal as he looks ruefully at his empty purse and searches his pockets for a forgotten dollar or two. We can see him as he approaches a friend on the street before the news is out that his funds are all gone. "Say, Marcus, could you loan me some money?"

"Sorry, old fellow. Wish I could, you know, but I'm short myself. Why don't you get your old man to send you some more? See you around."

2. Far-reaching Famine

In the far country the prodigal also found far-reaching famine. It was the worst possible time to run out of funds because a famine was on the way. Hard times were coming. Even those who might have been disposed to help him were too occupied with their own needs to care about him. "He began to be in want."

There are thirteen famines in the Bible and they are all significant. This one was providential both in its timing and in its terror. It was "a mighty famine," the Lord says (Luke 15:14), and it came just when the prodigal was most vulnerable. God sends circumstances like this into our lives to drive us to Himself. All too often we forget about Him when things are going well.

Earth's pleasures dried up for the prodigal. His resources failed. There was no more fun, no more food, and no more future. He had come to the end of the line. He had been having so much fun a few months earlier, but now he was stranded in a hostile environment. He had no resources left and no respect left. He had come to the end—but not quite the end. He had to sink lower still before he would give in.

Jesus says that "he went and joined himself to a citizen of that country; and he sent him into his fields to feed swine" (Luke 15:15). Remember, this young man was a Jew. For a Jew to have anything to do with swine was against the Mosaic law, which classified hogs as unclean. No Jew was to contaminate himself with such creatures. Swine-herding was a dirty business in Israel. For this well-bred young Jew to sink so low as to take a job feeding swine was an indication of how low he had sunk and how desperate his need had become. For him to take a filthy job like that then, would be like a man today making a living by peddling pornography.

He "joined himself," Jesus says, to the man who owned this unclean business. The word translated "joined himself" is interesting, for it means "he cleaved to" and comes from a word that means "to glue together." The prodigal found a man who had a job opening, even though it was a detestable kind of job, and he glued himself to this man. The prodigal stuck to him. Surely he could sink no lower.

But he did. "He would fain have filled his belly with the husks that the swine did eat" (Luke 15:16). He sat there by the pig swill. He watched the animals rooting in the garbage. He sank so low that he began to devour the foul food that the pigs were eating. We can see him with a lean and hungry look, his rags and tatters reeking of the swine trough, and his face and hands grimy with filth. We can see him scrape out the bottom of the pig pail and stuff into his mouth the scraps that even the pigs had left behind. He not only engaged in a filthy business; he stuffed himself with the garbage he handled. The prodigal truly had hit bottom. He had discovered that the devil is a cruel master and that the end of the road in this world is a cold place to be.

II. THE FATHER'S HOUSE

As long as the prodigal's money, his friends, and his good times lasted, he did not think at all. He was having too much fun. That is why God allowed him to become friendless and forsaken, homeless and hungry, beggared and abandoned. Now, in extreme need, he began to think.

A. His Decision

1. His Situation

"How many hired servants of my father's have bread enough and to spare, and I perish with hunger!" (Luke 15:17) It was the first kind thought the prodigal had had concerning his father since the seeds of rebellion took root in his soul. His father was good, generous, and gracious. His father would not allow even one of his hired hands to starve to death on his doorstep. *Yet here I am*, he thought, *miles from home, grubbing around in the garbage pails of sin, sitting with swine, trying to stave off my hunger pangs with slops from a pig pail*. He began to feel sorry for himself. *What am I doing here?*

2. His Sin

"I will arise and go to my father, and will say unto him, Father, I have sinned against heaven, and before thee, And am no more worthy to be called thy son: make me as one of thy hired servants" (Luke 15:18-19). That was a giant step forward. There can be no conversion without conviction. Not until the prodigal came to himself could he come to his father.

Not until we see our own desperate need of a heavenly Father's love, compassion, and grace can we make the first move toward home. We must first confess that we are poor, lost sinners. It would have done no good for this young man to return home as rebellious and as riotous in soul as when he left.

We can see the prodigal as he went up to the big house on the hill. The swine were still rooting in the field. The pig trough was almost empty of slops. Holding the pig pail, he banged on the farmhouse door. "Here, Mister," he called, "here's your pig pail. I won't be needing it any longer. I'm going home."

We can see the farmer as he eyed the young man up and down. He looked at the prodigal's tattered finery, his emaciated form, his straggly beard, his unkempt hair, his filthy face, his dirty hands, and his bare, mud-covered feet. He held his nose at the stench of the pigsty that reeked through the ruins of the young man's robes. "You're going home? Looking like that? After what you've done to your father's fine name? If you were my son, I'd turn the dogs on you. That's what I'd do."

"Mister," we can hear the prodigal reply, "I daresay you would. But you don't know my father."

B. His Discovery

The poor young fellow with a new look in his eyes strode out of the gate and headed along the highway for home. He had a long, long way to go. The outward trip had been so easy; it had been all downhill, all fun and frolic. The way back was steep and hard.

His heart must have failed him at times. What if he were too late? What if he had sinned away the day of grace? What if his father, tired of the long wait, had barred and bolted the door?

On and on he went, footsore, weary, and hungry. One fixed hope guided him: his father would be gracious and forgiving. At last the prodigal topped the last rise. There it was on yonder distant hill—the family home. We suspect that at this point his feet must have faltered. He had caught the neighbors' scornful looks as he went past their doors, and he had heard the crowd's caustic comments. Moreover, he had caught a fresh look at himself in the reflecting waters of a pool.

We can see him sit down on a worn stump and put his head in his hands. We can hear him groan in the bitterness of his soul. Coming home had all sounded so easy in the far country, but now . . . He dare not go on.

Then he heard a call; the prodigal heard his name. He lifted up his head and saw an old man running toward him at top speed. It was his father! For "when he was yet a great way off, his father saw him, and had compassion, and ran, and fell on his neck, and kissed him" (Luke 15:20). Yes, his father kissed him. He kissed him despite the filth, the stench, the vermin, the disgrace, and the shame. He kissed him.

"Father," the prodigal said, "I have sinned against heaven, and in thy sight, and am no more worthy to be called thy son" (Luke 15:21).

1. A Gracious Father

The father called for the best robe and a ring. He would not even hear the part about his son being made a hired servant. Likewise, our heavenly Father forgives us. He does not say, "Well, we'll see. We'll put you to work for a while. We'll need some good works out of you before we can receive you back into the family." Salvation is not of works. We come just as we are, wearing all the rags and tatters of our lost estate, and He receives us just as we are. He clothes us and crowns us, gives us the robe and the ring, arrays us with the righteousness of Christ. He gives us a position in the family— a position of love and trust, of sonship and responsibility. We have a gracious Father.

2. A Glorious Feast

"My boy is starving," said his dear father. "Where's the fatted calf?" What a feast there was—what music, what dancing! What a gathering there was in that home to welcome back the prodigal son.

That is just like God. First He saves us, then He satisfies us. Probably the prodigal had not had such a feast since he left home. It was good, wholesome food. It was not the fine, fancy food on which he had squandered his wealth, nor rare, exotic wines of distant lands. It was the good, plain, wholesome food of his father's house. Likewise, God will feed us. He will feed us on His Word and on all the good things that grace can provide.

3. A Great Forgiveness

"*My son*," said the father. "This my son was dead, and is alive again; he was lost, and is found" (Luke 15:24). The son experienced full and free restoration to the family.

Dead, alive, lost, found—in those four words we have the whole story of redeeming, regenerating grace. God is willing to pick up poor, lost sinners who are dead in trespasses and sins, and breathe into their souls eternal life. God will take rebels and reinstate them into His family. All we have to do is come—just as we are.

12
The
Elder Brother

When Jesus told the parables found in Luke 15, He had a threefold audience in mind. First there were His disciples. They needed teaching; they needed instruction in the truths of God, in the great facts of the faith. To the disciples, these parables were parables of *faith*. The stories of the lost sheep, the lost silver, and the lost sons were intended to instruct the disciples in the great principles and precepts of the Christian faith.

Jesus also had the publicans and sinners in mind. "All the publicans and sinners" were there, Luke said. The statement is a hyperbole. Luke wanted us to know that there were many of them. They were crowding to Christ. To them, these parables were parables of *hope*. These men and women—the outcasts of society, the dregs of humanity, the wretched flotsam and jetsam of the human tide—heard these parables with dawning hope. Although these people were probably outside the pale of Judaism, Jesus loved them. Theirs could be the kingdom of Heaven.

Finally, but perhaps most of all, Jesus had in mind the scribes and Pharisees. They were there too. They were Christ's constant, carping critics. "This man receiveth sinners, and eateth with them," they sneered (Luke 15:2). So Jesus focused these parables on lost ones. To the scribes and Pharisees, these were stories of *love*. God loves lost people. The scribes and Pharisees found this truth hard to understand.

Jesus added an appendix to the last parable. Having told of the wayward prodigal, He painted a portrait of a Pharisee, for that is who the elder brother was. In spirit, in soul, in scorn, and in all his acid sourness, the elder brother was a Pharisee. He was a smug Pharisee, keeping to the letter of the law, and never plunging into open, shameful sin. Yet he was lost. Sin is sin. It is repulsive and hateful to God. He loathes and detests sin for what it is in itself and for what it does in us. Somehow or other, we feel that the foul, filthy sins of the prodigal were almost attractive compared to the sins of the elder brother.

In the elder brother, we have a standing Biblical portrait of people who, while they never stray into the far country, manage to shed a shadow of gloom over everything and everybody. They never go to excess, they commit no crimes, and they violate none of society's laws. Yet they succeed in depressing everyone and in making everyone feel uncomfortable and unhappy. Their sins are not sins of debauchery; they are sins of the disposition. These people are self-righteous, complacent, moody, touchy, spiteful, niggardly, and bad-tempered.

We can picture the two brothers being sent out to play when they were boys. Mother would say, "Now don't play in that stream. And mind you, don't climb those trees. And stay away from the road." The younger brother would always come home soaking wet, having fallen into the stream. Or having fallen out of a tree, he would come home with a torn coat. "Well, I was only bird nesting, Mom," we can hear him saying. "I saw a super nest on one of the branches. It had three little birds in it. And anyway, what about him? He didn't climb the tree, but he threw stones at the birds." The elder brother, on the other hand, never came home with his shoes soaked or with his shirt torn off his back.

Mark Twain captured the spirit of these two boys when he created the characters of Tom Sawyer and Sid. We all like madcap Tom much better than his prim and proper stepbrother Sid. We feel smug when Tom punches the tar out of Sid for some sneaky act of betrayal. But of course the reason is that (as Paul wrote to the Corinthians) we are yet carnal and walk as men.

The parable of this unpleasant elder brother can be broken into parts: his *simple discovery*, his *swift displeasure*, his *surly disposition*, and his *seeming decision*.

I. HIS SIMPLE DISCOVERY

It had been a hard day in the field. The elder brother had been plowing, or weeding, or gathering in a harvest, or herding cattle, or making hay, or picking fruit, or mending fences, or tending sheep. Whatever he was doing, we can be sure that he was doing it conscientiously and competently. Now tired, hot, and bad-tempered, he was coming home for his supper and looking forward to a quiet meal, his easy chair, and an early bedtime.

As he approached the house, however, he heard music and dancing, so he hailed a servant and demanded an explanation. "Thy brother is come; and thy father hath killed the fatted calf, because he hath received him safe and sound" (Luke 15:27).

At that moment the elder brother made a simple discovery. He discovered how much he hated his brother. He hated him for his easy laughter, for his carefree ways, and for leaving him with all the work to do. He hated him for running away from home with half the working capital of the business and for wasting his substance with riotous living. He hated him for dragging the good, respected, family name in the muck and mire, and he hated him most of all for coming back again.

And if the elder brother did not actually hate his father at that moment, he came very close to it. He hated the thought of his father showing any kind of welcome to the prodigal. *The prodigal,* he thought, *should be confined to the servants' hall or, better still, be driven from home. He made his bed, so let him lie on it. It is foolish of my father to make this kind of fuss just because the wretched wastrel has come home.*

The younger son might have gone to the devil in the far country, but the elder brother entertained a thousand devils right in his own heart. There were devils of injured pride, self-love, self-righteousness, bad temper, malicious spite, and all their kin. The elder brother heartily welcomed each and every one of those demons and gave them the full run of his soul as he stood there, stock-still in the field, glowering at the servant who had brought him the news.

II. HIS SINFUL DISPLEASURE

"And," we read, "he was angry, and would not go in" (Luke 15:28). *What?* he was thinking. *Go in there? Go in there and shake that young criminal's hand? Go in there and sit down with him as though nothing has happened? Go in there and sing and dance like a village fool? Not me.*

Harold Begbie spent much of his life investigating amaz-

ing spiritual miracles wrought by God in The Salvation Army
in the early days when its soldiers marched into the slums of
London to seek out the lost. In his book, *Twice Born Men*, he
told the stories of the Puncher, Old Born Drunk, the Plumber,
and half a dozen more. Wonderful stories they are of prodigal
men and women who were won from the far country and
brought back to the Father's house. Begbie wrote about similar
miracles wrought through The Salvation Army in India. Few
books have ever done more to show the contrast between
callous Hinduism and compassionate Christianity.

Having delved deeply into stories taken from real life,
Begbie turned his hand to writing a novel called *The Vigil*. It
is a story of a young minister's spiritual struggle. The minister
is earnest about his parish duties, but knows nothing at all
about saving grace in his own soul.

The crisis of the story revolves around the death of Dr.
Blund, reputed to be the most wicked man in Bartown. This
was quite a reputation, for Bartown prided itself on being "the
wickedest little hole in England." Dr. Blund spent most of his
time drinking gin and playing billiards at the local tavern. The
only person who believed in him was his broken, bedraggled
wife, whose life had been spent in the shadow of his
debaucheries. Halfway through the book, the minister received an urgent call to come to the doctor's bedside. Dr.
Blund was dying and needed spiritual help.

The modernistic minister had little patience with the case.
He went with utmost reluctance to the doctor's bedside. He
could not see why a man who had lived so hideously should
be allowed to avert his just punishment in another world by
availing himself, in the eleventh hour, of whatever discharges
Christianity might offer. In any case, what could he say? If the
truth were to be told, the minister was not saved himself.
Religion, to him, was just a comfortable profession, the one at
which he made his living.

He bent over Dr. Blund and spoke to him professionally
of repentance and forgiveness, but the words did not come

from his heart and did nothing to comfort the dying man. It did not take the doctor long to see through the minister's facade. "Isn't there something in the Bible about being born again?" Blund asked desperately. "What is it to be born again?" Out of his depth, the minister floundered hopelessly. At last the doctor, to whom each moment was precious, fixed his eye on the wretched vicar. "Tell me," Blund said, "have you been born again?" The minister hung his head in silence. "You don't know," cried the doctor. "You're pretending. You can't help me! You don't know." Covered with confusion and shame, the unconverted minister fled from the room to seek another preacher, one who knew what being born again was all about.

The focus of the story now passed from the soul of the doctor to the soul of the minister. The doctor was saved and passed peacefully into eternity, and to the minister this did not seem fair. *Why should a man who lived so abominably*, he thought, *be absolved of all blame at the last?*

The minister was engaged to a young woman who was born again. "Do you think," he asked her, "that a deathbed repentance atones for a whole life of evil?" Her answer is one of the noblest in all literature. "No," she replied, "but Calvary does!"

> It is not thy tears of repentance nor prayers
> But the blood that atones for the soul;
> On Him then, Who shed it, thou mayest at once
> Thy weight of iniquity roll.
>
> (A. M. Hull)

Now the minister's problem was exactly the same as the elder brother's problem. He was angry and would not go into the house because he could not see, for the life of him, why the prodigal should be pardoned and receive forgiveness so full and so free. This was the reason for the elder brother's sinful displeasure. His trouble was that he knew about *religion,* but he knew nothing about *redemption*. He had a creed, but he did not have the Christ. He had dead works, but he did not have living faith. He knew nothing of Calvary love.

III. HIS SURLY DISPOSITION

The elder brother's sins were all dispositional sins. The Lord Jesus exposed him. Like a surgeon exposing an inner cancer, the great physician opens up to our gaze the meanness and malignancy of this man's soul. The elder brother had not committed a single crime for which society could ever arrest him, but his utter lostness was as real, as terrible, and as Satanic as that of the prodigal in his most abandoned state.

A. His Self-righteousness

"Lo, these many years do I serve thee, neither transgressed I at any time thy commandment" (Luke 15:29). In effect, he said, "I do this, and I do that, and I do the other." This was his religion. His whole religious outlook was one of self-sufficient, moral rectitude.

That is exactly why God cannot take anyone to Heaven on the basis of his imagined good works. In the first place, the elder brother's proud and petulant spirit offset his good works. When God exposes any person's works to the fierce light of His burning holiness, the sins, flaws, and imperfections of those works will be glaring, ugly, and utterly condemning. God *judges* men on the principle of *works*; He *saves* men on the principle of *faith*.

Suppose God were to take people to Heaven on the basis of their good works. They would do just what this elder brother did—begin to boast: "I am here because I did this, because I did that, or because I did the other. I am here because I did not do this, that, or the other. I am thankful that I was not a sinner like other people." Boasting is a manifestation of pride, and pride was the original sin. It was the sin of Lucifer—the morning star, the anointed cherub, the highest archangel of glory. It was pride that inflated him until he was filled with a sense of his own importance. It was pride that changed him from an angel into the devil.

If God were to take people to Heaven on the basis of their good works, moral rectitude, or imagined self-righteousness, they would have to be cast out again for the same reason Lucifer was cast out. The elder brother is proof of this. He took pride in his own imagined goodness. He congratulated himself on how much better he had been than his brother. That attitude kept the elder brother out of his father's house.

B. His Secret Regrets

"Thou never gavest me a kid," he said to his father, "that I might make merry with my friends" (Luke 15:29). The elder brother had the far country in the depths of his heart all the time. In his innermost soul, he was not a bit better than his brother, for both brothers wanted exactly the same thing. The elder brother had also wanted to take the father's resources and spend them on himself, to take all he could and squander it in sinful self-indulgence. The only real difference between the brothers was that the younger brother was more honest. He did not nourish and cherish his lusts secretly in his soul, but had the courage to bring them out into the open.

God knows our secrets. He searches our hearts. He knows where our secret fires burn. He knows the motives that control us, knows "those places where polluted things hold empire o'er the soul."

The elder brother's crowd might not have been the same crowd as that of the prodigal. Their idea of "making merry" might not have been the same as his. The elder brother's crowd probably would not have become drunk. They probably would not have hired women off the streets to share their lusts. They probably would not have caroused, rioted, taken drugs, and brawled. They would have sat around and gossiped, tearing to shreds the characters and reputations of people they disliked. They would have been spiteful, malicious, hateful, and cheap.

C. His Sinful Resentments

"Thou never gavest me a kid," complained the elder son, "that I might make merry with my friends: But as soon as this thy son was come, which hath devoured thy living with harlots, thou hast killed for him the fatted calf" (Luke 15:29-30).

"Thy *brother* is come," said the servant. "This thy *son*," said the elder brother to his father. The brother wanted nothing to do with a fellowship that included such a reprobate as the prodigal. "Thy *brother* was dead, and is alive again," replied the father. The elder brother was totally out of spirit with his father. He was as utterly lost as the prodigal during his worst and wildest days. He lived in his father's house and worked within a stone's throw from it, but he was a million miles away from it in spirit.

This elder brother was moral and religious, but he had nothing in common with his father. Nothing. God's people convene various meetings from time to time so that they can commune with their Father in Heaven. For all his respectability and religion, this elder brother would have participated in none of them.

For instance, we convene the prayer meeting so that we can talk to *the Father* about those of our lost loved ones who are far from God. At the prayer meeting, we plead Calvary love for family members who are away from the fold. The elder brother, on the other hand, never once talked to his father about the lost prodigal. The elder brother knew nothing of Calvary love.

Then too we convene the evangelistic meeting so that we can tell a lost world the news that "Calvary covers it all," that God is a God of infinite grace. At the evangelistic meeting, we tell *others* about Calvary love. The elder brother, however, made no attempt to bring his brother back. He knew nothing of Calvary love.

We also convene the worship meeting so that we can remind *ourselves* of the cost of Calvary love. At this meeting, we think through the nature of Christ's great sacrifice for sin. This meeting is a feast of remembrance, a time when the Father spreads the table for us as a tangible token of His grace. We gather to enjoy His love and tell Him how much we appreciate Him. The elder brother, on the other hand, refused to come to just such a feast. He knew nothing of Calvary love. He had no appreciation of his father or his father's love.

We also convene the ministry meeting so that we can learn more and more about the Father's grace, goodness, government, and glory. There we are exhorted to become more like Him so that we also might radiate Calvary love. The elder brother knew nothing of that love.

We convene the testimony meeting so that we can tell others how we ourselves came to respond to Calvary love. But the elder brother had never responded to his father's love and, of course, had no testimony.

We convene the missionary meeting to commission others to go to the world's remotest boundaries and seek the lost ones to tell them of Calvary love. At the missionary meeting, we pay heed to our Father's heartthrob for a lost and dying world. We each say, "Here am I; send me." The missionary meeting touches our hearts so that those of us who cannot go, can learn to give. As far as the elder brother was concerned, however, the prodigal was in the far country. The elder brother had not the slightest exercise of conscience over his brother's lost condition. He knew nothing of Calvary love.

Instead of participating in these meetings, or at least in what they represent, the elder brother's soul was full of sinful resentments, secret regrets, and self-righteousness. His surly disposition was an ugly reminder that his soul knew nothing of the father's love and grace. His only regret was that he had not had his share of this world's fun.

IV. HIS SEEMING DECISION

A. How He Was Loved

This, perhaps, is the most wonderful part of the parable. The father loved that mean-spirited, self-centered, canting, hypocritical elder brother just as much as he loved the prodigal. "Son," he pleaded, "thou art ever with me, and all that I have is thine" (Luke 15:31). What a picture—the father standing out there in the field, pleading with the elder brother, and urging him to respond to his grace.

B. How He Was Left

We do not know how the story ends. All we know is that at last sight, the elder brother remained outside, still making the wretched choice, still showing that he would rather starve than come inside.

There is nobody too bad for Jesus Christ to save, but some people think that they are too good. The elder brother was just such a person. He saw no need in his soul for his father's grace; he had done no wrong. So he stayed outside—unsaved—but the father still pleaded. In time, however, the father's patience probably was exhausted. Most likely he went inside and shut the door, leaving the elder brother to think malicious, evil thoughts. But Jesus ended the story before it reached that point. This is still the age of grace.

13
Barnabas, a Christian Gentleman

Acts 4:34-37; 9:26-27; 11:20-26; 13:1-13; 15:1-2,36-40

I. A SINCERE MAN

II. A SYMPATHETIC MAN

III. A SPIRITUAL MAN

IV. A SENSIBLE MAN

V. A SURRENDERED MAN

VI. A SOUND MAN

VII. A SEPARATED MAN

The Holy Spirit says that Barnabas was a good man. That is the clue to his character. The Holy Spirit also says in Romans 5:7, "Scarcely for a righteous man will one die: yet peradventure for a good man some would even dare to die." In other words, Barnabas was the kind of man for whom a person would die. We should carefully note that feature in Barnabas. He was *lovable*. Show me a man that other men would die for, and I'll show you a man well worth following.

Then, too, the Holy Spirit says in Psalm 37:23 that "the steps of a good man are ordered by the Lord." In other words, Barnabas was *leadable*. He was a man well worth following because he was a devoted follower.

With these two clues in hand, let us piece together the story of this lovable, leadable man and note seven of his characteristics.

I. A SINCERE MAN

We first meet Barnabas in the very early days of the church, when it was in the full fire and fervor of its first love for Christ. Barnabas appears at that time in the church's history when men were setting up what G. Campbell Morgan once called "a fanatical communism," governed "not by rule and regulation but by the wild impulse of love." (See Acts 4:34-37.) It was a glorious experiment, and failed, not because the impulse to share was wrong, but because the blazing fires of love died down.

Barnabas, a Levite, had estates on the island of Cyprus. That in itself is of interest because the Levites, in God's Old Testament economy, were not supposed to own land. When God divided up Canaan among the tribes, Levi received no province of his own. Instead, the Levites were scattered throughout the various tribes in the land—some here, some there—to become fulltime workers for the Lord, supported by freewill offerings of the Lord's people in the other tribes.

Barnabas, good man that he was, exemplifies for us the disastrous failure of the Jewish faith. He was a Levite and he owned land. Moreover, he owned it in a foreign country, not in the promised land.

In ancient times Cyprus was famous for its vineyards, wheat fields, oil, and figs. It was a secular Canaan, a land flowing with milk and honey. Anyone who possessed land in Cyprus was rich and influential.

During those early days of the church, many men sold their possessions and put them at the feet of the apostles, but Barnabas outdid them all. He evidently decided that he would become a Levite in deed—a Christian Levite, a landless man dedicated to the social and spiritual good of the church.

He was a sincere man. Such were his great wealth, generosity, noble character, and splendid services to the family of God that the disciples gave him a new name. To his old name *Joseph* they added the new name *Barnabas*, which means "son of consolation, son of exhortation, and son of prophecy." *Barnabas* is a significant name, cut from the same piece of verbal cloth as the name the Lord Jesus used for the Holy Spirit. Jesus called the Holy Spirit the *Paraclete*—"the Comforter, the One called alongside to help." The apostles called Joseph, the Cypriot Levite, *Paraklesis*. His character was such that they identified him with God's Spirit as a comforter and as a man gifted to communicate the Word of God.

This, then, is our introduction to Barnabas. He was a sincere man.

II. A SYMPATHETIC MAN

Barnabas introduced Saul of Tarsus to the apostles. Three years had passed since Saul's conversion. Nobody knew where he had gone. The church had heard rumors that he was saved, but he had vanished. God's saints had thoroughly enjoyed a blessed rest from persecution.

But now Saul was back. Worse yet, he was back in Jerusalem. Worse still, he was seeking to join the fellowship of the church. Naturally, everyone was frightened to death of him. Join the church indeed! Worm out its secrets! Compile lists of its members! Saul of Tarsus was the most dangerous man of the age. Nobody would speak to him. In Jerusalem he was the most hated, most feared, and most friendless man of all. With the blood of so many Christians still red on his hands, it is no wonder that every door in Jerusalem was bolted and barred against him. Christians considered him to be a sinister, Sanhedrin spy.

Against the first rays of that fast-rising sun, Saul of Tarsus, we get our first real glimpse of Barnabas's true stature. Barnabas alone, of all the disciples and apostles in Jerusalem, opened his door to Saul. James the Just—brother of the Lord, chief elder of the Jerusalem church—wanted nothing to do with Saul. Peter, with the keys of the kingdom in his hands, wanted nothing to do with Saul. John the beloved, the apostle of love, wanted nothing to do with Saul. Andrew, who always introduced people to Christ and had a rare gift for seeking out those who needed to know the Savior, wanted nothing to do with Saul. As for doubting Thomas, the scenes in the upper room may have washed all doubts about the deity of Christ out of his skeptical soul; but unless he could have tangible, positive, irrefutable, solid, material proofs of Saul's salvation, Thomas wanted nothing to do with him.

Barnabas, however, opened his door to Saul. He took him in, sat him at his table, and listened to his story. And he believed Saul. We can picture Barnabas taking him around to Peter's place and saying, "Peter, I want you to meet brother Saul." And Peter became so convinced that he entertained Saul in his home for two whole weeks.

What an eventful two weeks that must have been. Perhaps the two men were up early in the morning to pray together and then went to the house of Martha, Mary, and Lazarus. Or they went to Gethsemane. "Here, brother Saul," we can hear Peter saying, "here I fell asleep while Jesus prayed. I can still remember the bloodlike sweat on that matchless brow and the tone of His voice as He said, 'What, could ye not watch with me one hour?' (Matthew 26:40) And here, Saul, right here Judas kissed Him. Here I cut off Malchus's ear. Here the Lord stooped down and picked the ear up, turned it over in His hands, and put it back on again. And here my nerves broke, as did the nerves of us all. We fled like so many frightened sheep, pursued by nothing but our craven fears."

Or perhaps the two men traveled to Gabbatha. "Here, brother Saul, here is where they lit the fire. Here is where three times I denied our Lord. Over there He stood being bullied . . . well, you know the kinds of things they do. I stood here, warming my hands, denying Him, and cursing Him until at last the cock crowed. Then He turned and looked at me, and I went out—back to Gethsemane—to weep like He wept, only in sorrow, shame, remorse, and regret."

Perhaps they traveled up that rugged hill of shame and in silence gazed at the spot where the cross had stood and where the ground had soaked up His blood. Perhaps Peter and Saul went to the tomb of Joseph of Arimathaea, now empty, forsaken, silent, and deserted in its garden of flowers. "And Saul," we can hear Peter saying, "John and I came running, but he outran me. He's younger than I am, you know. But I blundered in first. There lay the graveclothes, just as they had been wrapped around His form. Here, right here, lay the napkin that had been bound about His face."

So Peter woke up early in the morning to give Saul of Tarsus the benefit of his memories. On into the night, beneath the fig tree in Peter's garden, Saul of Tarsus expounded the true meaning of the Jewish Bible as the Holy Spirit had taught it to him during those silent years in Arabia. Doubtless Peter gasped, amazed at this man's gigantic grasp of truth. Only one man—Jesus—had spoken like Saul, who also spoke with authority, and not as the scribes.

The day would come when it would be the greatest honor in thousands of homes across the wide Roman world to entertain the apostle Paul. But Barnabas was the first—the very first man of influence and responsibility—to open his heart and house to Saul. Barnabas was a sympathetic man.

And Barnabas was not the least bit jealous to see Peter making such a fuss over Saul. Barnabas was glad—heartily, humbly glad—that such a pillar of the church would make so much of Saul.

III. A SPIRITUAL MAN

The scene shifts to Antioch. Antioch was wealthy and magnificent, the third greatest city of the world of that time, after Rome and Alexandria. A four-mile-long street ran through the heart of Antioch. It was the home of a Roman prefect and his court. It was a thoroughly Greek city, but also had a large Jewish colony. It was also the seat of idolatry. Here in the world-famous grove of Daphne, heathenism flaunted itself in its most alluring and filthy forms.

Here at Antioch, quite apart from the officialdom of Jerusalem, the Holy Spirit began a new work. Here in sumptuous, voluptuous, sinful Antioch began a wholesale work of evangelism among the Gentiles. This work had no apostolic support or authority, but the preaching of the gospel was an instant success and large numbers of Gentiles were saved.

When reports filtered down to Jerusalem, the apostles decided to investigate this new and startling beginning. The heads of the Jerusalem church chose Barnabas to go and see what was going on. It was a wise choice because Cypriots and Cyrenians were spearheading the work in Antioch, and Barnabas was a Cypriot Jew.

Barnabas was a spiritual man. In connection with his visit to Antioch the Holy Spirit tells us that Barnabas was "a good man, and full of the Holy Ghost and of faith" (Acts 11:24). Because he was spiritual, he did not lecture the new believers. He did not say, "There are no authorized teachers here. No provision has been made for the proper administration of the sacrament."

He did not say, "We need a manual of theology so that these new believers can be systematically trained in sound Christian doctrine."

He did not say, "There is too much emotionalism in this work. This work needs a stronger emphasis on the moral side of the Christian faith, especially in such a vile city as Antioch."

No. Barnabas was spiritual. We read that "when he came, and had seen the grace of God, [he] was glad, and exhorted them all, that with purpose of heart they would cleave unto the Lord . . . and much people was added to the Lord" (Acts 11:23-24). He preached Christ, and the revival fires spread.

IV. A SENSIBLE MAN

It did not take Barnabas long to realize that the work in Antioch was growing so fast that it needed a stronger hand than his to guide it correctly. What should he do? To whom should he turn? Should he go back to Jerusalem and recruit help there? His mind ran down the list of the apostles. *What about Peter? No. Peter is too impulsive. What about James, the Lord's brother? No. He is too rigid. What about Thomas? No. Thomas is too skeptical. What about John? John is too emotional. What about Philip the evangelist? No. He is no longer in Jerusalem; he is in Cesarea and is too busy.* Indeed, Barnabas could not think of anyone in Jerusalem who could guide what was going on at Antioch. *What a pity Stephen is dead. Stephen would have been the man . . . What about Saul of Tarsus?*

"Then departed Barnabas to Tarsus, for to seek Saul: And when he had found him, he brought him unto Antioch" (Acts 11:25-26). It was a bold move. Instead of going to Jerusalem, he went to Tarsus. The word rendered "to seek" suggests that Barnabas did not really know where to find Saul. He went to "hunt him up." He took on himself the risk and immense responsibility of bringing Saul of Tarsus to Antioch without first submitting Saul's name to church authorities in Jerusalem. The Spirit of God led Barnabas to this decision.

Saul and Barnabas worked together in Antioch for at least a year to enlarge the church, to encourage the believers, and to evangelize the city. At Antioch pagans coined the term *Christians* as a nickname of contempt for believers. A sensible man, Barnabas had been absolutely right in his judgment. Saul was indeed the man for the job at Antioch.

Barnabas must have known that by bringing in Saul of Tarsus, he was bringing in a bigger man than he was—bigger in talent and genius, bigger in his grasp of truth, bigger in breadth of vision and boldness of action. But, as Alexander Whyte said, "To have the heart to discover a more talented man than yourself, and then to have the heart to go to Tarsus for him, and to make way for him in Antioch, is far better than to have all Saul's talents to yourself. . . . Speaking for myself," said that fiery Scottish preacher, "I would far rather have a little of Barnabas' grace than have all of Saul's genius."[1] Or, to quote Spurgeon's unforgettable verse:

> It takes more grace than I can tell,
> To play the second fiddle well.

It is rare indeed to find an older man, held high in the opinions of his brethren, who will allow himself to be eclipsed by a younger man. Barnabas was sensible enough to recognize his limitations.

V. A SURRENDERED MAN

"Separate me Barnabas and Saul," said the Holy Spirit to the elders of the Gentile church at Antioch (Acts 13:2). The Holy Spirit had called Barnabas and Saul, their two best men, their two ablest preachers and personal workers. It was the missionary call, the call of God to the regions beyond. It was a mighty mandate from on high, a mandate to reach out now to "the uttermost part of the earth," to take the glad tidings of the gospel to untold millions. Barnabas and Saul had been chosen.

---

[1] *Bible Characters from the Old Testament and the New Testament* (Grand Rapids: Zondervan, 1967), 139.

Barnabas was a surrendered man. He could have said, "I'm needed here. I want to stay here. I like it here. I feel much more suited to this kind of work than to pioneering work on the foreign field. I think I have done my share. Let another, younger man go. I'll stay here and mobilize the church to give, pray, and support others on the front-lines of Galatia and Gaul. What about John Mark? He's willing enough. I'll give him a crash course in evangelism and soul-winning. Paul can take him."

But Barnabas did not say these things. He had surrendered all to God. For months now he had been aware—as he and Paul had pioneered together at Antioch, as they had prayed together about the great, lost Gentile world—that the Spirit of God was burdening him, calling him, and separating him to carry out a work of worldwide evangelism.

Then, when the same Holy Spirit began to exercise the godly elders in the Antioch church regarding the great world of lost people and about sending Barnabas and Saul out as missionaries, that was it. Barnabas, the surrendered man, simply said in effect, "Here am I; send me." We remember the Holy Spirit's assessment of Barnabas: he was a good man, full of the Holy Spirit, and full of faith. These are the three great qualifications for a missionary. Education, zeal, or financial support does not make a missionary. A good man, full of the Holy Spirit, and full of faith—these are the marks of a missionary. These qualifications are what we should look for in missionaries we send forth.

Barnabas's goodness gave him the *compassion* that he needed. He no doubt was touched by the feelings of others' infirmities. He wanted to see other men discover the goodness that is of God.

Barnabas was full of the Holy Spirit. That gave him the *competence* he needed—competence to make a thousand decisions, to deal with spiritual needs, and to know when and where to go.

Barnabas was full of faith. That gave him the *compulsion*

he needed—the willingness to do and dare, the ability to trust God for provision, protection, and progress.

VI. A SOUND MAN

When the Jerusalem church wanted to send a man to Antioch to investigate the new work among the Gentiles, what sounder man could they have found than Barnabas? Now that a crisis had arisen in the Antioch church because of false instruction sponsored by teachers from Jerusalem, now that there was a need to send a man from Antioch to Jerusalem to settle the matter, what sounder man could be found than Barnabas? And so Barnabas (along with Paul and others) was sent.

The issues at stake were enormous. False teachers maintained that Gentile Christians should be circumcised and that unless they were circumcised they could not possibly be saved. That made sense to these legalists. The Christian Jew looked upon his Christianity as the natural outcome of his Judaism. He had come up through circumcision, the law, and the entire ritual and tradition of Judaism to faith in Christ. How could Gentiles be saved by starting halfway?

Apart from Barnabas, Paul would probably have broken with the Jerusalem church and the other apostles altogether and gone off on his own in the interests of truth. That would have permanently divided the church into two parts: a Gentile church and a Jewish (Hebrew Christian) church. The conference to settle the dispute needed a sound man who would mediate between the fiery zeal of the apostle Paul and the false zeal of the legalists. Who could be more conciliatory than Barnabas?

VII. A SEPARATED MAN

The question about the Gentiles and Judaism was settled at the Jerusalem conference. There would not be two churches (a Gentile church and a Hebrew Christian church), but one united church.

The good news was brought back to Antioch. The work flourished, and Peter came up to see it for himself. Then, when certain legalistic Jewish brethren from Jerusalem came to Antioch to persist in teaching their divisive doctrine, Peter—to keep in the good graces of James—went along with them. And, alas, so did Barnabas.

The first crack in an otherwise flawless character surfaced. Barnabas came within sight of being an altogether perfect man. But, after all, he was made of the same clay as ourselves.

Fiery Paul gave Peter the greatest dressing down of his life for his cowardice. It seems, however, that Paul said nothing to Barnabas. On the contrary, shortly afterward, Paul proposed to Barnabas that they set out on a second missionary journey.

Barnabas agreed. But then the separation came; the hairline crack in Barnabas's character split wide open during a lamentable quarrel with Paul over John Mark. Barnabas wanted to take his young nephew along again, despite John Mark's failure on the first missionary journey. Paul, however, adamantly refused even to consider this option.

The Holy Spirit draws our attention to "the contention" between them (Acts 15:39). The Greek word translated *contention* is one of Luke's medical terms. It is the word from which is derived our English word *paroxysm*, which means "fit" or "sudden attack" or "outburst of rage." This was not a small disagreement. Its thunder reverberated throughout the whole church. No doubt people took sides—as they have ever since.

G. Campbell Morgan said, "My own sympathy is entirely with Barnabas."

Alexander Whyte said, "Barnabas' ship strikes the rocks till one of the noblest characters in the New Testament is shattered and all but sunk under our very eyes."[2]

Who, then, was right? Let us consider the arguments that

---

[2]Ibid.

Paul and Barnabas might have offered during their more lucid moments when discussion took the place of dissension.

First listen to Barnabas:

"Mark," he says, "is my nephew, and I feel personally responsible for his spiritual well-being. What a travesty it would be if I, having risked my life for the heathen in foreign fields, had no concern about my own relatives. I admit that Mark failed, that he turned back after putting his hand to the plow. But I could point out many of my own failures too. Can we not at least credit Mark with enthusiasm for the cause of Christ? At least he started on the journey, when thousands of others stayed comfortably at home. And now, fully alive to the perils and pitfalls of the way, he wants to go again. He is thoroughly ashamed of himself and thoroughly repentant of his past disgraceful actions. Can we afford to break this bruised reed and quench this smoking flax? Shall we act in a way that is contrary to the Spirit of the Lord Jesus Christ, who picked up even Peter when—not once, not twice, but three times—he denied his Lord? Yes, indeed, Jesus picked Peter up and gave him an honored place in the forefront of the apostolic band."

Now listen to Paul:

"Barnabas, I must confess that I am deeply moved by all that you have to say. My heart is fully alive to a similar debt I owe you. Were it not for your influence in the face of opposition, perhaps I would not be where I am today. Because Mark is your nephew, I fervently wish that I could bow to your desire. But there are larger considerations than those of family and friendship. The cause and claims of Christ dwarf all lesser relationships.

"Mark might render excellent service to the Lord in other fields. For instance, he has a way with words. Let him write an account of the life of Christ for the blessing of all mankind. But for this particular enterprise—for a mission that calls for a cool head, an iron nerve, a steady hand—Mark is totally unequipped. He deserted the cause right when he was needed the most, right when difficulties and dangers loomed largest.

We cannot afford to run that risk again. To have a missionary play the coward before pagan converts who are faced with the world's bitter hostility would be disastrous. It would put Christ to open shame. It would bring mockery on the mission and the message. People would say that we did not practice what we preached. They would say that we expected them to face perils from which we ourselves shrank.

"I have long ago forgiven Mark, freely and with all my heart. I pray for him and long to see him greatly used of God. He has a gentle spirit. Everyone loves him for his sincerity, for his sweetness of disposition, and for his willingness to work for God. It would not be fair to Mark to expose him to situations that might be beyond him and that the Spirit of God never intended him to face. One plows and plants, another waters and weeds, and another garners and gleans. Let Mark recognize his limitations. It would be unkind to expose Mark to the kind of situation we faced at Lystra, for instance, where we were first worshiped and then stoned. I foresee rods and shipwreck. I foresee many journeys. I foresee perils of waters, perils of robbers, perils of our own countrymen, perils of heathen, perils in the city, perils in the wilderness, and perils among false brethren. I foresee weariness, pain, hunger, thirst, fastings, cold, and nakedness. I will not expose John Mark to these things—and that's that."

Who was right? Well, as in so many quarrels, both men were right and both were wrong. Barnabas parted company with Paul and the Holy Spirit left him to his choice and marched on with Paul.

VOLUME 2

CONTENTS

1

Enoch,
the Holiest Saint

Genesis 5:18-24; Hebrews 11:5-6; Jude 14-15

I. SURROUNDING GLOOM
   A. Socially It Was an Age of Permissiveness
   B. Scientifically It Was an Age of Progressiveness
   C. Spiritually It Was an Age of Presumptuousness
II. SAVING GRACE
III. SIMPLE GOODNESS
IV. SUDDEN GLORY

E noch appears only three times on the sacred page. The brief summary we have of his history, however, is freighted with significance. We read of him in Genesis 5:18-24, where we are told of his birth, his children, his walk with God, and his rapture to Heaven. We read of Enoch in Hebrews 11:5, where we are told that he pleased God and was translated to Heaven. We read of him in Jude 14-15, where we learn that he preached to the ungodly of his day, warning them of the Lord's coming in judgment. And that is all. But in these fleeting references, we have in a thumbnail biographical sketch the essence of the rapture.

Enoch and Noah stand out in the book of Genesis as archetypes of the last days. Enoch typifies the saints who will be caught away bodily to Heaven before the end-time judgments begin. That is, he symbolizes the church. Noah typifies those who will go through the storm but be preserved by God and emerge safely on the other side of judgment to inaugurate a new dispensation. In other words, Noah symbolizes Israel and the tribulation saints, who will be protected by the power of God and land safely on the millennial shore.

There were two kinds of people on the earth in the days of Enoch: the descendants of Cain and the descendants of Seth. The Bible records Cain's kind in Genesis 4 and Seth's kind in Genesis 5. Cain's kind lived for this world; Seth's kind lived for the world to come. To give us a record of Cain's kind of people, the Holy Spirit takes us into the market. He gives us a glimpse of great cities filled with the fruits of art, science, and industry— cities bursting with activity, excitement, and the everyday business of life. To give us a record of Seth's kind, the Holy Spirit takes us, of all places, into the morgue. All the way through Genesis 5 we hear the tolling of the bell: "And he died. . . . and he died. . . . and he died." It is God proving the devil a liar. The devil had said, "Ye shall not surely die" (3:4). God says, "He died. . . . he died. . . . he died."

The Holy Spirit says *twice* of each of the godly people in the line of Seth that he *lived:* "He lived. . . . he lived. . . . he died." He does not say the same of the Cainites. Each Sethite experienced a birth and another birth. Each lived and lived on, living again on the farther side of a new birth. From the standpoint of Heaven, it was the Sethites who lived, not the Cainites.

In recording the line of the Cainites, the Holy Spirit notes their worldly accomplishments but does not say that they lived. No doubt the Cainites, with their burgeoning civilization, their hot-beat music, their business enterprises, and their scientific discoveries, thought they were living, but God does not say so. He says it was the quiet, unassuming Sethites—those who contributed nothing to the world's pleasure, prosperity, or power—who really lived.

The Holy Spirit also says that the Sethites died. One would have expected Him to record the deaths of the godless Cainites, since "the wages of sin is death" (Romans 6:23). But He ignores their deaths and records instead the deaths of the children of Seth. The reason is that "precious in the sight of the Lord is the death of his saints" (Psalm 116:15). For the child of God, death is not the end. All death does is swing wide the gates of glory. Death lifted the Sethites above the sordid sins and the sadness of the cities of men. Death placed them in that great city where the streets are paved with gold, where time is not counted by years, and where Christ sits at the right hand of God.

The roll call of the dead in Genesis 5 continues until the introduction of Enoch, the seventh from Adam (Jude 14) in the godly line of Seth. In Genesis 5:24 we read about something quite different from death. Instead of a tomb there is a translation! God did something new on earth, something He had never done before but most certainly intends to do again. He reached down and took a man bodily into Heaven. Enoch went home, body and all, without having to pass through death.

In this first character study we will be considering this man Enoch and the lessons of his life. Enoch was a candidate for rapture, and as such is of surpassing interest to us who live in the closing moments of the church age. When we think of Enoch, we think of four things. We think of *surrounding gloom,* for he lived in a dark day. We think of *saving grace,* for there came a time when God met Enoch and saved him. We think of *simple goodness* because he walked with God in the midst of a pornographic society. And we think of *sudden glory,* for one moment Enoch was here on earth and the next moment he was there in the glory land, walking in his own body down the streets of gold.

I. SURROUNDING GLOOM

Enoch lived at the beginning of the climactic events that precipitated the flood. When Enoch was born, Adam was 622 years old. Adam had lived long enough to see what "one man's disobedience" (Romans 5:19) had done to the human race. He must have been the saddest man who ever lived. When Enoch was born, Seth—the founder of the godly line—was 492. Enoch's father Jared was 162, a young man according to the standard of the times. In other words, Enoch lived alongside Adam for 308 years and alongside the other patriarchs all his life. Yet even the presence of such notable "salt" was not sufficient to arrest the corruption of the age.

One place on the Niagara river is called "the point of no return." Someone who falls into the river below that point will go right over the precipice of the falls into the boiling caldron at the bottom. Enoch was born at a point of no return. The rising tides of wickedness were such that nothing could stop the world from falling into the judgment waters of the flood. God's Spirit was about to cease His striving with men; judgment was on the way. Enoch was raptured to Heaven just seventy years before Noah was born. Every sign would seem to suggest that today we stand where Enoch stood in his day—on the verge of rapture.

Enoch lived in an age of permissiveness, progressiveness, and presumptuousness.

A. Socially It Was an Age of Permissiveness

In Enoch's day people did "their own thing." Society imposed no restraints on crime and lawlessness flourished. Immorality was an accepted way of life, marriage a mere matter of convenience. Polygamy was an acceptable lifestyle.

The Holy Spirit says that the thoughts of men's hearts were "only evil continually" (Genesis 6:5). Lamech, seventh from Adam in the line of Cain, openly espoused the doctrine of permissiveness. He shook his fist in the face of God and told

Him to stay out of his life. Just as godliness had climaxed in Enoch, seventh from Adam in the godly line of Seth, so godlessness had climaxed in Lamech, seventh from Adam in the godless line of Cain. The wheat and the tares ripened together. As saintliness ripened for rapture, so sinfulness ripened for wrath.

B. Scientifically It Was an Age of Progressiveness

In Enoch's day people were wresting secrets from nature and making tremendous strides in science, engineering, and technology. Men had discovered the art of smelting, and the world had come through the antediluvian equivalent of an industrial revolution. Driven out of Eden, men were creating an artificial paradise based on science and technology. Great cities were flourishing, the exploding world population was becoming increasingly urban, and social sophistication was replacing the simplicity of earlier times.

C. Spiritually It Was an Age of Presumptuousness

Cain had corrupted the faith that God had delivered to Adam—the faith for which the martyr Abel had been prepared to shed his blood—into a social gospel. Believers made little or no impact on society. Truth still lingered in the Sethite family; fathers handed down the torch of testimony to their sons. Cainite civilization, however, largely ignored the Sethites.

Secularism and spiritism marked the spiritual climate of the age. Society was utterly *secularistic,* totally preoccupied with the good things of this life. The world was materialistic. People were absorbed with the necessities of life (eating and drinking) and the niceties of life (marrying and giving in marriage) and were blind to spiritual realities. As Jesus put it, they "knew not until the flood came, and took them all away" (Matthew 24:39). It never occurred to them that God might have something to say to them.

Along with secularism, *spiritism* flourished. People were tampering with the forbidden secrets of the occult. There seems to have been a diabolical breakthrough. Men had learned the deep things of Satan. Fallen angelic beings were mingling with the daughters of men and producing a hybrid demon progeny on the earth (Genesis 6:4). The mythology of the ancient world derived from this period of time. The love stories of the gods, so prominent in Greek religion, had their roots in this age. Satanism, the ultimate feature of the apostasy of Enoch's day, necessitated the holocaust of the flood. The race was corrupted beyond recall.[1]

Such was the gloom surrounding Enoch's generation. He lived in an age that was ripening fast for judgment, very much like the age in which we live.

Some years ago journalist Ed Sanders wrote a book about his investigation of the murders committed by the Manson "family." Charles Manson was a hippie, a Satanist, a car thief, a cult leader, and a sex maniac. He gathered around him a group of about twenty girls and a few young men who became so committed to him that they were willing to do anything, anywhere, any time for him. They became extensions of his personality and will.

In the introduction to his book Sanders described the lengths to which he was prepared to go to obtain accurate information on the "family."[2] He posed as a pornography dealer, a Satanist, and a psychopathic maniac. He investigated occult societies in Los Angeles, paying special attention to Satanists, to people who practice pain magic, and to occult groups who drink dog's blood, hang up rotting goats' heads in their kitchens, and rent corpses for their parties. He met people who commit human sacrifice and who told him ghastly tales of sacrificial rituals performed on the mountains and beaches of California. He abandoned some of his plans because the areas he set out to investigate were too dangerous.

While reading that introduction, I had to remind myself constantly that Sanders was not describing David Livingstone's Africa. He was not describing the upper reaches of the Amazon. He was describing twentieth-century America. Truly we live amid surrounding gloom. We live where Enoch lived, in a world that is plunging into the same seething caldron of sin that in all ages calls down God's judgment on society.

II. SAVING GRACE

Enoch, we are told, "walked with God after he begat Methuselah" (Genesis 5:22). Methuselah was born when Enoch was sixty-five years old. During his first sixty-five years Enoch lived an ordinary life. He may not have committed the same kinds of sin that the Cainites committed, but he was just as lost as the wildest and worst of them. He was born of Adam's ruined race. His father was a godly man and his grandfather was a godly man. Enoch stood in succession to a long line of godly men, but that did not make Enoch godly. He was lost and needed to experience saving grace.

When Enoch was sixty-five years old, he had an encounter with the living God that changed his life. From that moment on he began to walk with God. Since God does not walk the paths of sin, we know that Enoch came to a turning point in his life. He had what we would call a conversion experience. It changed the whole direction of his life. That is what genuine conversion is—a meeting with Christ that gives a new direction to life. Instead of going our own way, we begin to go His way.

Many centuries after Enoch's day the prophet Amos, speaking to another apostate age, threw down the challenge: "Can two walk together, except they be agreed?" (Amos 3:3) When the Bible says that Enoch walked with God, it means that he and God were in agreement—in agreement about the way he spent his time, about the way he spent his money, about the way he ran his business, about the way he treated his family, about the way he supported his place of worship. Enoch stumbled at first, no doubt, but then walked in this new life with ever-increasing confidence until he strode out along the upward way. Enoch walked with God.

III. SIMPLE GOODNESS

Walking with God resulted in a twofold testimony. First Enoch had *a testimony Godward.* According to Hebrews 11:5 Enoch "had this testimony, that he pleased God." Crossing the great divide that separates the Old Testament from the New, we meet another man who had the testimony that He pleased God. His name was Jesus. As God watched His Son tread these scenes of time, He opened Heaven and declared, "This is my beloved Son, in whom I am well pleased" (Matthew 3:17). So when we read that Enoch and Jesus had the selfsame testimony, we can only conclude that Enoch—in the pornographic society of his day—lived like Jesus lived.

Enoch had *a testimony manward* too. Jude 14-15 tells us that he preached to the wicked people among whom he lived about the coming of Christ in judgment: "Behold, the Lord cometh with ten thousands of his saints, To execute judgment upon all." Enoch's vision of the Lord's coming leaped over a thousand years to the flood, over another two-and-a-half millennia to Bethlehem and the first coming of Christ, and over another two thousand years of the age of grace to our day when we are looking for the rapture and the second coming of Christ.

Enoch saw the Lord coming "with ten thousands of his saints." Before the Lord comes *with* His saints, He has to come *for* His saints. The rapture of the church has to take place before Christ returns to reign. Enoch did not envision the coming of Christ for His saints; he participated in it! He was caught away before the catastrophe of the flood, just as we will be caught away prior to the judgments of the last days. Each day that Enoch lived he came closer to that surprise event, just as each day we live we come closer to the rapture of the church. Whole books have been written about events that must take place before the Lord comes with His saints. Not a chapter, page, paragraph, or single line can be written about events that must happen before the Lord comes for His saints. The rapture is imminent. It is the next item on the prophetic program. It could take place at any moment.

IV. SUDDEN GLORY

One moment Enoch was here; the next moment he was gone. Adam died. Abel died. Seth died. One by one each of the saints of God listed in Genesis 5 died—except Enoch. He "was translated that he should not see death" (Hebrews 11:5).

Genesis 5:24 says of Enoch that "he was not." Hebrews 11:5 says he "was not *found*" (italics added). In other words, people missed him and went looking for him. They suddenly realized the capital value of a man who knew how to walk with God. Now Enoch was gone and a tremendous sense of loss swept through his home, his community, his business, and the place where he met with the people of God. Enoch was sought in vain. God had called him home to Heaven by way of the rapture. Judgment was now inevitable and was already bearing down on the world.

One of these days God is going to reach down and take home to Heaven not just a champion, but a church! Millions of people are going to be missing—mysteriously and unmistakably gone from this planet. Parents will look for their children who have vanished without a trace. Young people will look for their parents. Husbands will look for their wives. Wives will look for their husbands in vain. But after the initial shock the world will continue on its way, and a new surge of every form of wickedness will instantly become evident.

Two kinds of people will be called home when the Lord appears in the air. Some will still be alive when He comes. As they go up, clothed instantly with immortality, they will sing, "O death, where is thy sting?" Others who through the ages have died trusting in Jesus—those whose mortal remains have been buried and returned to the dust—will also rise. Changed, transformed, and immortal, they will come bounding out of their graves singing, "O grave, where is thy victory?" (1 Corinthians 15:55) What a chorus that will be.

Some time ago, while driving through Atlanta, I listened to a man preaching on the radio. He had been talking about the second coming of Christ and had been recounting some signs

of the times. He then turned his attention to Paul's assurance
that the Lord will descend from Heaven with a shout, with the
voice of the archangel, and with the trump of God. "Brethren,"
he said, "the coming of Christ for His own is so close today that
I have *stopped looking for the signs* and I have *started listening
for the sounds."* We can say a hearty amen to that!

---

1. See John Phillips, *Exploring Genesis* (Neptune, NJ: Loizeaux, 1980) 78-80.
2. Ed Sanders, *The Family* (New York: Avon, 1972)

2
Caleb,
the Staunchest Fighter

Joshua 14:6-15

I. THE GREAT DECISION
   IN THE WAKING YEARS OF LIFE
II. THE GREAT DEDICATION
   IN THE WORKING YEARS OF LIFE
III. THE GREAT DETERMINATION
   IN THE WEAKER YEARS OF LIFE

Caleb was a very old man. The Jews divided old age into three stages: from sixty to seventy was "the commencement of old age"; from seventy to eighty was "hoary-headed age"; and a man over eighty was said to be "well stricken in years." Caleb was eighty-five. About the time most of us have been on Social Security for twenty years and are thinking of going into a nursing home, Caleb was thinking of conquering a mountain. "Give me this mountain," he said (Joshua 14:12).

We are going to study the story of Caleb, a man who finished well. We will divide his story into three parts: *the great decision* that marked the waking years of his life; *the great dedication* that marked the working years of his life; and *the great determination* that marked the weaker years of his life.

It is a great thing to finish well. The apostle Paul told us that he had a constant fear of finishing up his life as a wicked old man on one of God's rubbish heaps, of being "a castaway" (1 Corinthians 9:27). That is a healthy fear. Many people have started well but not finished well. Solomon started well, King Saul started well, Lot started well, and Demas started well. The Bible is strewn with the wreckage of men like them who started well but ended as failures.

We may become weak in body, but the important thing is to be strong in spirit, strong enough to say to God, "Give me this mountain." Let the novice and the tenderfoot be content with an easy path. Let us take on a mountain before we die. Let us determine to tackle giants.

When he was seventy-five, Abraham left Ur of the Chaldees to become the father of all believers and to become known in Heaven as the friend of God. At the age of eighty Moses left shepherding Jethro's flocks to become the "Abraham Lincoln" of his day and the greatest lawgiver of all time. And when Caleb was eighty-five, he set out to take on the sons of Anak, to give the devil and his brood a thrashing such as they had never experienced, and to leave the world a much cleaner place.

I. THE GREAT DECISION
IN THE WAKING YEARS OF LIFE

It is never too late to start tackling giants, but it is better to start young. Caleb started young, persevered in the perilous middle-age years, and finished well. At a comparatively young age he was filled with the vision of *a new Lord, a new life,* and *a new land.*

Caleb was born a slave in the land of Egypt. He knew the wretchedness, the defeat, and the constant humiliation of bondage. He knew the bite of the taskmaster's lash and the ever-present threat of death. He longed for a savior, for someone to come and lead him into a new dimension of living. He was tired of being kicked, cursed, beaten, and bullied. He was tired of being treated like an animal.

Then one day he made a great discovery. He did not have a Bible, but he did have the book of Genesis burned into his conscience by the verbal tradition of his people. He knew the stories of Abraham and Isaac and Jacob and Joseph. He knew the Abrahamic covenant by heart. Suddenly he remembered something God said to Abraham.

We can imagine Caleb perspiring profusely, toiling under a load of fresh-dried bricks, and stopping abruptly in his tracks when the great idea occurs to him. Oblivious of the task-master's whip and heedless of the savage curses of his particular Egyptian bully, Caleb is working something out in his mind. The idea is little short of an inspiration from Heaven. He is remembering that many centuries ago God said that Abraham's seed would be strangers in a foreign land; they would be oppressed for four hundred years but would find their freedom in the fourth generation.

There had been a stir among the Hebrew slaves in Goshen about the time Caleb was born. He remembered his parents talking about it. A man named Moses, the adopted son of pharaoh's daughter, had thrown in his lot with the Hebrew slaves. He had come as their kinsman-redeemer, but they had rejected him. But it was the fourth generation—Levi, Kohath, Amram, Moses—and Moses had to be coming back! Caleb's generation had to be the generation that would witness the return of the kinsman-redeemer. Hallelujah! From now on a new Lord filled his vision.

II. THE GREAT DEDICATION
IN THE WORKING YEARS OF LIFE

Moses did return, armed with might and miracle. Water turned into blood. Dust turned into lice. Hail and fire fell from the sky. Egypt swarmed with frogs, flies, and locusts. Darkness and death visited the land. Caleb learned what it meant to be put under the shelter of the blood (Exodus 12:12-13). He was baptized unto Moses in the cloud and in the sea (1 Corinthians 10:1-2). Caleb gathered with God's redeemed people around the table in the wilderness. He went to Sinai and learned how to order his life. He drank from the riven rock and feasted on bread from heaven (10:3-4).

Then Caleb came to Kadesh-barnea where, as one of the twelve spies, he had a taste of the promised land, a taste of all that awaited him in Canaan. One taste of the fruits of Canaan spoiled his appetite for the onions, leeks, and garlic of Egypt. After that foretaste, the vision of *a new land* and *a new life* in Canaan drew him onward.

In the majority report the ten carnal spies told terrifying tales of great fenced cities. In Canaan the ten spies had seen the sons of Anak—a race of giants—and had seen themselves as grasshoppers. But not Caleb! When others saw giants, Caleb saw God. When others saw cities walled up to heaven, Caleb saw cities reduced to rubble. When others saw a dangerous, dreadful, diabolical foe, Caleb saw only a defeated foe. When others only saw foes, Caleb saw fruit.

When others looked at the problems, Caleb looked at the promises. Had not Joseph said, "God will surely visit you, and bring you out of this land unto the land which he sware to Abraham, to Isaac, and to Jacob" (Genesis 50:24)? When so many of his fellow believers grumbled, complained, fretted, found fault, and fought among themselves, Caleb followed the Lord.

When he was eighty-five years old, Caleb could look back over the years and give this testimony to Joshua: "I have wholly followed the Lord."

Caleb had had to learn the lesson of positively trusting God early in life. The name *Caleb* means "dog"! His father Jephunneh seems to have had a bitter sense of humor. Having heard that a son had been born to him in that ghetto in Goshen, he may have jibed: "A son? What's the use of a son? Call him "dog" for all I care. It's a dog's life he'll have down here in Egypt."

The story is told of a man who went to a psychiatrist and said, "I have this terrible feeling that I'm a dog." The psychiatrist said, "How long has this been going on?" The man said, "Ever since I was a puppy."

That is how long the identification had been going on for Caleb—except he made up his mind that he was going to glory in that insulting name and make it a badge of honor. *If I'm going to be called "dog,"* he decided, *then I'll be the best dog around.*

When my son was quite young he decided he wanted a dog. He heard about a neighbor whose cocker spaniel had just had pups, and my son wanted to know if he could have one. "They are only fifty dollars each," he said. His mother, who didn't want a dog, said, "You can have a dog when you can afford to buy one." She thought she had settled the matter. However, another neighbor had a little business making flea collars, and our boy got friendly with his boy. The two of them went to work making flea collars, and within two weeks my son came home with a cocker spaniel pup.

There was something special about that dog. My son bought it, my wife fed it, my daughters exercised it, and yet that dog was crazy about me! When I'd get home late at night after preaching out of town, I'd often find the house dark and silent. Everyone else was in bed, but that dog would wait up for me. He'd wag his tail, bounce around, and show every sign of enthusiasm because the master of the house was home.

Caleb decided if he was going to be a dog, he'd be that kind of dog. He'd let his Master in Heaven know how much he loved Him.

A good dog knows who its master is. It follows hard at its master's heels and doesn't run off on expeditions of its own. It goes where the master goes and does what it is told to do. It follows in the master's steps all the time.

Caleb decided that if he was going to be called "dog," he'd be the Lord's dog. He would wholly follow the Lord. He'd be the best dog the Master ever had. Later, looking back over some sixty years, he could say that the controlling principle of his life had been absolute loyalty to the living God and to the kinsman-redeemer He had sent.

Caleb followed the Lord fully, faithfully, and fearlessly—even when people took up stones to throw at him for his stand. No foe could daunt him. No fear could haunt him. Nobody could turn him aside. He was going where God was going, and he would be hard at His heels wherever that might be. As it turned out, following the Lord involved forty years of wandering here, there, and everywhere, up and down a howling wasteland. No matter! If God was going there, that was where Caleb was going. All the time he was wandering in the wilderness he was living by faith in Canaan.

III. THE GREAT DETERMINATION IN THE WEAKER YEARS OF LIFE

Caleb was determined to end his life well. When we think of Caleb we should think of the mighty Amazon. Boisterous in its youth, this river is a settled, invincible, and steady flow in its old age.

The Amazon starts three miles high in the snow-swept Andes of Peru. At the source the river is only seventy miles from the Pacific ocean, but it travels nearly four thousand miles across the width of a continent toward the Atlantic. In the beginning a tiny trickle tumbles down a mountain and begins a long, eventful journey to the ocean. The stream takes its time and as it wends its way, it draws the water of two hundred other streams and brooks into its embrace until it is a full-fledged river. The Amazon churns through mountain passes, bursts with explosive force into the green wall of the jungle below, and becomes an inland sea, draining nearly half of South America—an area equal to two-thirds of the United States. At the mouth the banks stand ninety miles apart. When the Amazon reaches the end of its adventurous journey, it refuses to die. The power and drive of the river are so great that it floods the ocean with fresh water up to one hundred miles offshore. Indeed the current can still be seen two hundred miles out to sea.

Caleb was like the Amazon. At the ripe age of eighty-five he refused to consider for a moment that he had reached beyond hoary-headed age and was now well stricken in years. "Well stricken in nothing," Caleb would say. "Me? I'm ready to tackle a mountain. Me retire? Go to Florida and play golf? Not me! Give me an untamed mountain. Up to now I've just been in training. Now I'm ready to start."

By the time George Muller reached seventy he had already accomplished more than a half dozen ordinary men could accomplish in their combined lifetimes. His work with orphans had begun with a tiny trickle—some small change, three dishes, twenty-eight plates, three basins, one jug, four mugs, three saltstands, one grater, four knives, and five forks. But the work had grown and grown. Eventually there were five large buildings and a considerable staff and 2,050 boys and girls in his orphanages.

Through the years some ten thousand homeless boys and girls had been housed, fed, clothed, educated, and settled in gainful employment. Muller had given away large sums of money to help Sunday schools and day schools at home and abroad. He had circulated nearly two million Bibles and Testaments. He had distributed over three million books and tracts. It would be a hopeless task to try to calculate the cost of all this. The figures given in pounds sterling would have to be multiplied by the rate of exchange and then by an inflation factor representing the difference between the purchasing power of a dollar 150 years ago and a dollar today. The dollar amount would be astronomical; yet Muller, a poor man, obtained every penny by asking God for it. He did not ask anyone else for money.

At the age of seventy Muller decided the time had come for a change. When most of us would be thinking of a retirement home, he looked for a global parish. During the first eight years after his conversion he had offered himself as a candidate for the mission field five times, but he had always been turned down. (One wonders about the spiritual insight of the mission boards that rejected such a man.) Now Muller decided he had no need for a mission board and started out on his own. He traveled some two hundred thousand miles (long before the age of the airplane), visited forty-two countries, and preached at least six thousand times. For over seventeen years he was a living demonstration to hundreds of thousands of people that "God . . . is, and that he is a rewarder of them that diligently seek him" (Hebrews 11:6).

At ninety-one Muller said: "I am very near the end of my earthly pilgrimage. Still, I am able to work every day, and all day too. I preach five or six times a week besides. I am unspeakably happy."

That was George Muller—a veritable Amazon of a man. And that, too, was Caleb. At eighty-five he could say: "I am as strong this day as I was in the day that Moses sent me: as my strength was then, even so is my strength now, for war. . . . Now therefore give me this mountain" (Joshua 14:11-12).

Caleb knew the fight ahead would be arduous, for that mountain would have to be stormed. It would be an uphill fight all the way. He knew it would be tedious, for the great fenced cities were walled up to heaven. They would have to be taken by long and stubborn siege. He knew the fight would be dangerous, for the sons of Anak lived there. But Caleb was not deterred. He had his eye on the land. He had been thinking of the new land ever since he was a slave in Egypt, in the house of bondage. What he wanted was an abundant entrance into that land. As Johnson Oatman, Jr., put it:

I want to live above the world,
Tho Satan's darts at me are hurled;
For faith has caught the joyful sound,
The song of saints on higher ground.

That was Caleb's battle cry. "If so be the Lord will be with me, then I shall be able to drive them out as the Lord said" (Joshua 14:12). That was Caleb's victorious philosophy of life. He was counting on the Lord's *presence.* He was counting on the Lord's *power.* He was counting on the Lord's *promise.* He was an old dog now. He looked into the face of his Master and said, "If You're going up this mountain, I'm coming too." Faithful. Reliable. Steady. That was Caleb all the way through.

Years ago Alan Redpath, a former pastor of Moody Church, was crossing the Atlantic on the *Queen Elizabeth,* the world's largest liner. A smudge of smoke on the far horizon eventually resolved itself into the SS *United States,* the world's fastest liner. As the fast ship drew alongside and passed Redpath's ship, the skipper of the *United States* flashed a message to the skipper of the *Queen Elizabeth:* "You're very beautiful but you're very slow." Back came the answer: "It is not meet for the royal lady to keep fast company!"

Alan got to know the *Queen Elizabeth's* chief engineer, who took him down to see the engines, the four giant boilers, and the two enormous propeller shafts going out to the blades. The shafts were 450 feet long (150 yards of solid steel). Alan and the engineer could hear the thrash of four giant propellers driving all 82,000 tons of that mighty floating hotel across the Atlantic.

Alan said, "I suppose those propellers must be going round at an enormous rate."

"It's evident that you are no engineer," said the chief. "I could get those propellers going around so fast they'd simply dig a hole in the water. The ship would slow down and stop— with the propellers going at full speed." He paused. "I have forty-eight engineers on this ship, and they are continually calculating the ratio between revolutions per minute in the engine room and steadiness at the point of drive."

That was the secret of that great ship—steadiness at the point of drive. That was the secret of Caleb's life. He wholly followed the Lord. That is also the secret of a productive Christian life.

3
Saul,
the Worst Fool

1 Samuel 26:21

I. HOW DESPERATELY HE REQUIRED DAVID

II. HOW DISDAINFULLY HE RIDICULED DAVID

III. HOW DEEPLY HE RESENTED DAVID

IV. HOW DELIBERATELY HE REJECTED DAVID

V. HOW DREADFULLY HE REPUDIATED DAVID

King Saul is an enigma. He was called of God, anointed with holy oil, given another heart, and numbered among the prophets, but he was as lost as a pagan. The explanation of his life becomes clear, however, the moment we look at him in his relationship with David. What did Saul do with David? What did David do with Saul? Those are searching questions.

We can understand other puzzling people too if we ask questions about their relationship with Christ. What did this man or that woman do with Jesus? What will Jesus do with them? Such questions put each of us into final focus.

191

As we look at King Saul in his relationship with David, we will consider how Saul required, ridiculed, resented, rejected, and repudiated David.

I. HOW DESPERATELY HE REQUIRED DAVID

Something was missing in Saul's life from the very start. The problem really began with Kish, the father of Saul. First Samuel 3:20 tells us that "all Israel from Dan even to Beersheba knew that Samuel was established to be a prophet of the Lord"—all Israel, that is, except Kish and Saul, or so it seems.

Saul was an impressive man. He was the kind of man at whom people would take a second and a longer look. But he was ignorant concerning spiritual things. His own servant knew the things of God better than he (1 Samuel 9:6). The servant, said Alexander Whyte, would rush off to sit at Samuel's feet whenever he had a holiday.

Samuel had grown gray in the service of God. He had traveled regularly from place to place for many long years, earnestly teaching people about God. Everybody knew Samuel. Saul's servant knew Samuel, but Saul did not recognize the prophet even when face to face with the man of God. "Then Saul drew near to Samuel in the gate, and said, Tell me, I pray thee, where the seer's house is. And Samuel answered Saul, and said, I am the seer" (1 Samuel 9:18-19). This unfamiliarity with the old prophet indicates an area of desperate need in Saul's life.

After he became king, Saul remained ignorant of spiritual things. First Samuel 10:9 says that God gave Saul another heart, but we must read that verse in context. We can only judge a man's heart by what comes out of it. God did not give Saul a *regenerated* heart. That is obvious from the whole tenor of his life. God gave Saul a *royal* heart. God never calls a man to do a task without giving him what he needs to do it. If Saul was to be king, even though he was the choice of a rebellious people (1 Samuel 8:7,19), God would give him the heart of a king. God would give him the ability to think and act like a king. (Not that Saul availed himself of the ability very often—but he had it.)

As for Saul's gift of prophecy (1 Samuel 10:10), that had all the marks of excess that characterize many who claim to have the sign gifts today. Speaking with ecstatic utterance does not prove one to be a true child of God. Pagans can speak in tongues. African witch doctors can speak in tongues and prophesy. People can speak in tongues and prophesy to the satisfaction of the charismatic community without being born-again.

Prophecy is only sounding brass and tinkling cymbal if it is divorced from love (1 Corinthians 13:1-2). Saul had little love for anyone and no love at all for David. Possessing the gift of prophecy does not prove anything. The pagan psychic Balaam prophesied—and truly (Numbers 22–24). The godless self-seeking opportunist, Caiaphas, prophesied—and truly (John 11:49-53). We must not evaluate Saul's spiritual experience (or anyone else's for that matter) on the grounds that he prophesied.

Our conclusions regarding Saul's spiritual status lead to the fact that Saul needed David. Saul's need was obvious when one or two of his worldly escapades required the stern reproof of Samuel, a true prophet of God.

King Saul had to face three enemies: the Philistines, Amalek, and Goliath of Gath. The Philistines represent the *world,* Amalek represents the *flesh,* and Goliath represents the *devil.* Saul fell before each of them. He was unable to deal with his enemies and he needed someone who could. That is why Saul needed David. We need Christ for the same reason.

King Saul represents the kind of person evangelists and soul-winners often meet. This kind of person has an aroused soul, responds somewhat to spiritual things, and even seems to be a Christian, but he really is not saved. He has a questing soul but not a quickened spirit. Many people who come forward during evangelistic services are like that. They make empty professions of faith. They are sincere enough and may even show some of the initial marks of being saved, but they are not truly born again. Some of them go on to their dying day trusting in an experience that fell short of a soul-saving, life-transforming, spirit-regenerating new birth. Soul-winners need to be aware that a "convert" may say the right things and do the right things for a while although a personal love for Christ is lacking. Simon in Acts 8:5-24 is the classic New Testament example.

Saul lacked spiritual life. That became quite evident in his relationship with David. Samuel, great preacher that he was, could awaken Saul's soul to God, but he could never bring Saul into a heart-relationship with either God or David, the Lord's true anointed. There is all the difference in the world between being aroused to a personal need for God and being brought into a personal, quickening relationship with Christ.

Face to face with the Philistines, Amalek, and Goliath, Saul should have known at once that he had no power to deal with his enemies. He should have realized he needed David.

II. HOW DISDAINFULLY HE RIDICULED DAVID

The next step in King Saul's disastrous spiritual odyssey came when he encountered David face to face. What the king did with David, the Lord's true anointed, revealed the shallow nature of Saul's previous religious experiences.

It was during the episode with Goliath that the king reacted to David. Saul was afraid of the one and not willing to accept the other. Every day the giant of Gath scorned and ridiculed the Israelites and their God. King Saul was tall, but he was no match for Goliath. Size and reputation mean nothing to the devil. He is not the least bit afraid of any of us.

When the very thought of going down into the valley of Elah alone to fight Goliath froze Saul's blood, David came. He came in his shepherd character to be Israel's savior.

Saul already knew David. One of Saul's servants had given him a magnificent description: "Behold, I have seen a son of Jesse the Bethlehemite, that is cunning in playing [a testimony to his *competence*], and a mighty valiant man [a testimony to his *courage*], and a man of war [a testimony to his *conquests*], and prudent in matters [a testimony to his *caution*], and a comely person [a testimony to his *charisma*], and the Lord is with him [a testimony to his *character*]" (1 Samuel 16:18). So Saul sent for David, but at that time saw none of the traits so obvious to the servant. Or, if Saul saw them, he resisted them.

Now Saul was face to face with David's sublime trust in God, his superlative courage and conviction, and his total confidence that God would go with him down into the valley. Now Saul had to accept David as savior or else sow the seeds of his own doom. At this critical moment of decision, Saul's reaction to David was a matter of salvation or defeat. What did Saul do? He scoffed at David.

"You!" we can hear Saul exclaim. "You my savior? Nonsense! You are only a boy. Why, I'm three times the man you are. Goliath would make mincemeat of you." Saul had no use for David. In fact Saul would rather have no savior at all than have to acknowledge a debt of salvation to David.

There was no escaping David, however, so Saul would only accept David on Saul's terms. "If this is a matter of salvation," he said in effect, "then I must share in it. I must at least be allowed to contribute to my own salvation. You will have to fight Goliath in my armor."

David, out of courtesy to Saul, put on the armor and then took it all off again. Saul could receive no personal salvation as long as he insisted on making his own contribution to God's plan of salvation. David would not fight Goliath in Saul's armor. It was incongruous. Likewise, if we are to be saved, we must set aside all confidence in our righteousness, our efforts, our ironclad respectability. Our own armor may fit us, but the Lord will have nothing to do with it. We must stop insisting that Christ be our Savior on our terms.

After ridiculing David, Saul rejected David's claim to be the one and only savior. "Thou art but a youth" (1 S`muel 17:33), he sneered, making the common mistake of judging by outward appearance. Israel had chosen Saul to be king in the first place. They had judged him by his outward appearance. Now Saul rejected David as savior on the same carnal grounds. That is why millions reject Christ. Julian the Apostate called Jesus "the pale Galilean." The Nazis called Him "a crucified, dead Jew." Millions think of Him only as "gentle Jesus, meek and mild," and underestimate Him. However, He is God over all, blessed for evermore.

Saul was reluctant to face one obvious fact about David. David was the only savior God had provided for Israel, just as Christ is the only Savior God has provided for us. There was no salvation anywhere else for Saul, and there is "none other name under heaven given among men, whereby we must be saved" (Acts 4:12).

Rejecting Saul's armor and retaining his shepherd character, David turned his back on Saul and set his face toward the valley. He came to grips with Goliath—"him that had the power of death" (Hebrews 2:14)—and destroyed him. Nobody else could have done that. Not Saul, not Jonathan, not Abner nor Joab nor all the host of Israel could have done that. David, and only David, was God's anointed savior that day.

Having conquered Goliath, David returned victorious from the fight. Across the country, from Dan to Beersheba, from Manasseh to the Mediterranean, from north to south, from east to west, from busy city markets to rural hamlets in the hills, the great shout went up: "Saul hath slain his thousands, *and David his ten thousands*" (1 Samuel 18:7, italics added). The Israelites thought of David and declared, in effect, "Hallelujah! What a savior!" But Saul had no intention of bowing his knee to David or of heralding his praise.

III. HOW DEEPLY HE RESENTED DAVID

Jealousy, rage, and resentment—black as the pit of Hell and as cruel as the grave—entered Saul's soul. He hated David from that day on. Moreover he hated all who dared to make it known that they had accepted David as savior and anticipated his return as sovereign.

Saul's hatred came home to roost in his own home. Both Jonathan and Michal gave their hearts to David. Attempting to change Jonathan's mind, Saul tried persuasion first. He cursed Jonathan and his mother. "Use your head, man," we can hear Saul say. "Can't you see that David will ruin your career? I've never heard anything so senseless in my life. Why throw away all your prospects for the sake of David?"

When Saul found that persuasion was getting him nowhere, he tried outright persecution. He flung a javelin at his son (1 Samuel 20:33). Jonathan, however, possessed a temper equal to Saul's, and Saul never tried that tactic again. But Saul was able to put sufficient pressure on his son to force him to settle for a life of compromise (Jonathan never followed the leading of his heart to go with David). Saul thus robbed Jonathan of his crown at the second coming of David—that is, when David typically returned to come into his kingdom.

To sway Michal, Saul resorted to cunning. He said in effect, "If you're determined to give your heart to David, I can't prevent that. Go ahead and marry him. Just remember, you might be David's wife, but you're still my daughter. You'll do what I tell you or it will be the worse for you." And thus it was. Michal lived such a life of compromise that she brought dishonor on David's name.

Saul resented David and everything David stood for. Saul resented David because he was both savior and sovereign and because he was the Lord's anointed. Saul resented David because his godly life showed up Saul's glaring sins. Saul resented David for his knowledge of God and his popular psalms. Saul hated the thought that people all over the land were singing David's songs and singing his praise. Saul resented David because he avoided the snares that were set for his feet. Saul resented David for not using the same carnal weapons that were used against him. Saul resented David's goodness, his grace, his gifts, his greatness, and his coming glory. Saul resented David because he was always beyond reach. Saul resented David because in the end the kingdom, the power, and the glory would all be his. Saul resented David because he had provided salvation in the dark valley of death and there could have been no salvation without him.

In other words, Saul resented David for the same reasons that people today resent and reject Christ.

IV. HOW DELIBERATELY HE REJECTED DAVID

Saul's life degenerated into a mad crusade against David. He summoned all the allies he could find. He gathered around him men who hated David, and made short work of anyone suspected of siding with David.

The terrible incident in 1 Samuel 22 is an example. Saul finally and fully revealed what a murderous heart he had. When David went to Gath, he stopped near Jerusalem at Nob, the place where the tabernacle was pitched, and appealed to Ahimelech the priest for bread. Ahimelech reluctantly gave David the sacred shewbread from the table of the tabernacle and Goliath's sword, which was kept in the tabernacle compound as a national treasure.

One of Saul's cronies, an evil man named Doeg the Edomite, took great delight in informing Saul of Ahimelech's "disloyalty." That was enough for Saul. He ordered the massacre of the entire priestly family residing at Nob. Eighty-five priests were among the victims in that holocaust. The murder of God's anointed priests was on Saul's conscience until the end of his days. The crime with its attendant guilt was a direct result of Saul's rejection of David.

It is hard for us to realize that some people today hate Christ as much as Saul hated David. They hate Christ and they hate His people. There is no end to the harm these hateful people will try to inflict on believers.

V. HOW DREADFULLY HE REPUDIATED DAVID

David spared Saul's life on two separate occasions. David never stopped loving poor, deluded, demented, demon-driven Saul. David would have saved him, even at the very end, if Saul had let him. David never desired the death of Saul. Some of David's own people never could understand why David did not kill Saul when the opportunity arose. But David, like Jesus, loved even his enemies.

On one of the occasions when David could have slain the king, Saul confessed, "I have played the fool" (1 Samuel 26:21). But he continued to play that role. A man like Saul plays the fool once too often. Saul's bitterness toward David was noted in Heaven. In the end God allowed the Philistines to invade the land. Saul knew that the only man in the kingdom who could deal with the Philistines was David, but even in this emergency he would not call on David to be his savior.

Saul called upon God, but God no longer spoke to him. Saul had sinned away the day of grace. Samuel the prophet was dead and with his death the last restraining influence had passed out of Saul's life. The silence of God in all its abysmal horror descended on Saul's soul. Terrible indeed is the condition of the person to whom God no longer speaks, at the door of whose heart God no longer knocks.

In his desperate need, Saul had only two places to go. He could go to David, plead with him for forgiveness, and in deep contrition hand over the affairs of the kingdom. But Saul would rather die than take such a humble place. Instead of going to David, Saul went to a witch. He turned to the occult. He went down to Endor and pleaded with the witch who lived there to summon up Samuel from the dead.

A great deal of hocus-pocus is circulated about spiritism and astrology, but there is also reality in the whole devilish field. There is a reality behind the occult and it is an evil reality. Those who play with ouija boards or attend seances are opening the doors of their personalities to an occult invasion. Behind the occult lurks the evil one and a vast army of deceiving spirits.

The Bible expressly forbids any communication with a witch (today we would call the person a psychic). The spiritual consequences of such communication are so terrible that God ordered the death penalty for those who practice witchcraft. In defiance of the Word of God King Saul consulted the witch.

The usual practice was for the witch to contact her familiar spirit, who would impersonate the spirit the client wished to contact—or her familiar spirit could have one of his demon colleagues do the impersonation. This time, to the horror and fright of the witch, the impossible happened. Samuel himself appeared. And Samuel pronounced the death sentence on Saul.

Finding the door of Heaven barred against him, this desperate man deliberately repudiated David and knocked on the door of Hell. God opened the door for Saul—and let him fall through it. Within a day he was dead and damned.

A person can ridicule, resent, and repudiate the claims of Christ, and God will let him do it. God will sometimes stay His hand twenty, thirty, forty, or fifty years. Then all of a sudden the sentence will fall. The summons into eternity will come. The Christ-rejecter will be dead and in Hell. That is the lesson of Saul.

4
Lot,
the Saddest Reminder

Genesis 13:11; 14; 19:12; Luke 17:32

The only way a man is ever counted righteous by God is by *believing*. The Bible says, "Abraham believed God, and it was counted unto him for righteousness" (Romans 4:3). Somewhere along the line Lot too put his faith and trust in the

Lord and was accounted righteous in Heaven's sight. Indeed God calls him "that righteous man" (2 Peter 2:8). That is, He puts Lot on a par with Abraham, one of the greatest believers of all time. But we would never guess from what is revealed about Lot in Genesis that he was a believer. Were it not for the fact that the Holy Spirit notes that Lot was righteous, we would probably write him off as one who merely professed to believe.

An old English proverb says, "You can't have both the penny and the bun." Lot wanted both. He wanted the best of both worlds. That is the mistake Lot made.

All people have to ask themselves two questions. The first is, Heaven or Hell? Once we settle that question and strike out for Heaven, the second question follows quickly: Heaven or earth? The devil tries to persuade believers that the second question doesn't matter—that as long as their souls are saved, they can try to get everything this world offers. When we look at Lot, however, we see the enormous cost of choosing to live for worldly gain. In this chapter we will trace the downward course of this man who once made a decision for God that ensured his name would be written in life's eternal book, yet failed to make his calling and election sure.

The world is the sworn enemy of God, and God is the sworn enemy of the world. "If any man love the world, the love of the Father is not in him" (1 John 2:15). "The world," of course, is human life and society with God left out. God has never blessed worldliness, and He never will. The life of Lot is an example of worldliness. His story is told in Genesis to warn others not to make the same mistake he made; he is held up as a lighthouse to help others avoid shipwreck.

I. LOT'S CHOICE

Lot had come under the godly influence of his Uncle Abraham. Swept off his feet by Abraham's dynamic faith, his all-out commitment to God, and his determination to walk the straight and narrow way, Lot too had struck out on the pilgrim way. The two men had traveled a long way together. They had journeyed north from Ur and then west across the fertile crescent. They had continued on past the great city of Damascus and gone down into Canaan. God had led each step of the way and had blessed not only Abraham but Lot as well. "And Abram," we read, "was very rich in cattle, in silver, and in gold. . . . And Lot also, which went with Abram, had flocks, and herds, and tents" (Genesis 13:2,5).

So far so good. But then a dispute arose.

A. The Dispute

"And there was a strife between the herdmen of Abram's cattle and the herdmen of Lot's cattle: and the Canaanite and the Perizzite dwelled then in the land" (Genesis 13:7). The devil had won a victory. Here were two believers in the midst of a crooked and perverse generation, and their testimony for God was being destroyed.

Genesis 13 is the first chapter in the Bible where the word *brethren* appears—and there they were quarreling. At least their servants and supporters were. They squabbled over money, over material things, over what Paul contemptuously called "filthy lucre" (1 Timothy 3:3). Satan had these two households occupied with the things of this world. Having taken their eyes off the Lord and eternal things, they disagreed over who had grazing rights to the limited pastureland.

B. The Discussion

So Abraham and Lot had a discussion. God had deeded the whole land to Abraham. It was all his. However, he turned to Lot and said in effect: "Look here, Lot. We are brethren. The things that divide us are nothing compared with the things that unite us. Here we are squabbling over a few thousand acres of land. Let us keep eternity's values in view. Take your choice, my brother. I'll leave the matter in God's hands. It is far better that we should separate than that we should squabble— especially in front of the ungodly."

A spiritual man—a man who has learned to leave circumstances with God—speaks from a perspective like Abraham's.

C. The Decision

Lot made his choice, and we note what he decided and why. He had a terrible lack in his life. He had no spiritual priorities, no spiritual perspective. He was *weak in his devotions*. We read that Abraham had an altar and that he "called on the name of the Lord" (Genesis 13:4). We do not read that of Lot. He somehow managed to jog along from day to day without any personal quiet time with God. No wonder his life was a spiritual shipwreck. None of us can live the Christian life unless we daily cast our anchor, haul in our sails, and get alone with the Lord. We will drift if we do not do that, and the reefs are waiting for us.

Lot was also *worldly in his desires*. Lot chose the well-watered plain of Jordan because it reminded him of Egypt. In Old Testament typology, Egypt is one of the symbols of the world. Lot was Heaven-born and Heaven-bound, but he had the world in his heart. When Abraham first suggested that they separate, Lot should have become alarmed. He should have said: "What? Leave the fellowship of God's people? Neglect the assembly of the saints? Try to 'go it alone' surrounded by Canaanites and Perizzites? God forbid! The price is too high." Instead Lot made a carnal worldly choice. He had a *"religious"* reason for his choice: the coveted spot was "even as the garden of the Lord." His *"real"* reason was that the plain of Jordan was "like the land of Egypt" (Genesis 13:10).

Lot was *wrong in his decisions*. He thought he was a much stronger believer than he really was. He thought he could live independently of Abraham and his household of like-minded men. Lot thought he could start his own group in Sodom. The Holy Spirit adds this significant comment on Lot's choice: "But the men of Sodom were wicked and sinners before the Lord exceedingly" (Genesis 13:13). God had already marked Sodom for judgment. It was the last place on earth that

Lot should have chosen. But he had no spiritual anchor and no spiritual awareness, so he drifted toward Sodom, blissfully ignorant of the caldrons of fire and brimstone already bubbling and boiling on high. Some might object that Lot did not know that Sodom was doomed. But God knew, and had Lot taken time to wait on God, God would have directed his steps elsewhere.

II. LOT'S CHAINS

Lot moved his family into Sodom. His children grew up with Sodomites instead of with saints. His wife went shopping in Sodom when she should have stayed with Sarah.

Any person who moves out of the will of God will face the consequences sooner or later. Lot was no exception. War broke out and Sodom was defeated. Lot, his wife, and his little ones were caught up in the maelstrom and swept away with the tide. The victorious kings of the East fastened chains on the hands of Lot and his family and marched them away with the ungodly to be sold in the slave markets of Mesopotamia. Lot had chosen the world so God let him have the world—and its chains.

What did Lot think about as he trudged along with a yoke of iron around his neck and a whip cracking over his head? What did he think when he saw one of his little ones stumble and then scream with pain as the slave driver thrashed him and kicked him back into line? What did Lot think when he saw a soldier leering at his wife or overheard one of them telling his friends how much he thought she was worth? What did he think as he marched north and saw the smoke of Abraham's campfires on the hill?

Lot's chains were the direct result of Lot's choice. Let us not deceive ourselves. If we deliberately allow the world to come between us and the Lord and His people, we will pay for it. Our circumstances will close in on us in the end. There will be little hope for us either, unless some Christian brother cares for us the way Abraham cared for Lot. Lot had treated Abraham badly, but that "friend of God" held no grudges. When he heard the news of Lot's chains, Abraham mobilized his forces and called on his brethren for help. Then away he went, at great personal cost and risk, to rescue his nephew. Abraham rescued not only Lot, but also all those who were with him. Genesis 14 records the resounding victory.

Abraham, the man God used to rescue Lot, knew the meaning of true separation. Separation is not isolation, but insulation. The truly separated believer is like a live electrical wire—insulated against that which would cause a short circuit, and in touch with the need at one end and the power at the other. God can use such a man in an hour of crisis.

Lot was rescued. His chains were removed. He could have started all over again. He could have come back into the fellowship of God's people. He could have brought up his family in a spiritual atmosphere instead of in a Sodomite environment. He could have said to his uncle: "Dear Abraham, I was wrong. I am sorry for my selfishness. Will you receive me back into fellowship?" But that was not what Lot did.

III. LOT'S CHANCE

Abraham sat at the Lord's table with Melchizedek. With the bread and wine before him, Abraham poured out his heartfelt thanks in a tangible offering of his tithes. And where was Lot? Absent from the service and in a conference of quite a different kind.

Abraham and Melchizedek were fellowshiping over the emblems of the Lord's body and blood. That was the scene in the camp of Abraham—the separated, victorious believer.

Meanwhile Lot was with the rejoicing, liberated captives. He was talking and laughing with the Sodomites, who were congratulating him for having connections with so mighty a military leader as Abraham.

The king of Sodom was probably talking with the king of

Gomorrah and laughing over some vile joke when Lot came into view. We can almost see the king of Sodom stroke his beard reflectively and say to the king of Gomorrah: "I say, Birsha, we should keep in with that fellow Lot. If his uncle is such a warrior, we need to keep on his good side. I have already tried the old boy out—you know, offered him a king's ransom—but the old fool has religious mania. He refuses any kind of connection with us at all. But there is no denying he knows how to fight. If we can't tie Abraham to our apron strings, we had better tie his nephew Lot to us."

So the king of Sodom summoned Lot. Lot came and bowed respectfully. "Lot," we can hear the king say, "I have taken a great liking to you, my son. You are just the kind of man Sodom needs. We need you in the government. Would you be interested in a well-paying, influential position at court? What do you say to being made a minister of state in Sodom?"

Lot thought that this offer was his big chance. The poor foolish man had not learned a thing. Abraham's efforts to rescue him from his backsliding had all been in vain.

We can trace the progression of worldliness in Lot's life. First he *looked* toward Sodom; then he *pitched his tent* toward Sodom; then he *dwelled* in Sodom. The next time we meet him he is *sitting in the gate* of Sodom, the place of government in cities of old.

IV. LOT'S CHILDREN

The Holy Spirit gives us one more look at Lot on the night of Sodom's judgment. The hot fires of God's wrath against the sexual sins of Sodom had been banked up for years, but grace had held back His hand. That night, however, judgment was to fall.

Two angels of God inspected the city and found the reports of Sodom's unnatural sins to be true beyond all doubt. Those vices did not slink down the back alleys, furtive and ashamed. They stalked brazenly on the major thoroughfares.

The gay community demanded its rights. Society acknowledged the perverted preferences of the gays to be normal and permissible. Their alternative lifestyle was upheld by the laws of the land. The streets of Sodom were utterly vile. Visitors were not safe in Sodom, not even in the home of a minister of state. Judgment must fall, so Lot was sent running through the city to warn his children.

Lot had never asked if Sodom was a good place to raise children. He just asked if the plain of Jordan was a good place to raise cattle. Lot had never worried much about the spiritual welfare of his children. He had thought his example would be sufficient. After all, he had never indulged in those gross sins for which Sodom was famous. He had doubtless told his children about Abraham and God, but he had never wept and prayed for their salvation. He had never cared enough for his children to separate himself from Sodom.

Lot had sent his children to Sodom's schools and he had allowed them to play with Sodom's sons. He had watched his children imbibe Sodom's values and accept Sodom's vices. He had allowed his wife to become more and more involved in the social life of Sodom. Then he had wondered why his family was slipping away from him.

At least two of his daughters had married into Sodomite families. He had lost them! They cared nothing at all for spiritual things. Payday had arrived. He had sowed worldliness, and he had reaped worldliness. He had "vexed his righteous soul from day to day," the New Testament says (2 Peter 2:8), but little good that could do as long as he continued to live in Sodom. Why couldn't he see that? Why didn't he get right with God? Why don't we?

Sometimes we see our children absorbing the world's values. They argue over every little thing. They don't want anything to do with the Lord's people; they prefer their godless friends. And we wonder why. But if we have modeled a lifestyle of worldliness, no wonder our children are like that. Does the hymn writer describe our lifestyle?

Room for pleasure, room for business—
But, for Christ the Crucified,
Not a place where He can enter
In the heart for which He died?

Like so many people today, Lot had a saved soul and a lost life. He made the world his choice and then wondered why his children did not have the slightest interest in spiritual things. Lot pursued worldly goals and had to reap worldly results.

The Bible gives us two dreadful closing glimpses of Lot's children. They had fully absorbed the viewpoint and vices of Sodom.

A. They Had the Viewpoint of Sodom

Look first at his married daughters and their husbands. When Lot hammered on their doors that night of judgment, they rolled over, then turned out of bed to see what on earth was the matter. "Hurry!" we can almost hear Lot say. "Judgment day has come! God is going to destroy Sodom. Two angels have visited me. They have seen for themselves the sins of Sodom and they are going to pour out God's wrath on this place. Hurry! Don't even get dressed. Just seize a cloak and come. They will save us if we hurry."

It was God's solemn, sober truth. "But he seemed as one that mocked unto his sons in law" (Genesis 19:14). His daughters had the viewpoint of Sodom too. They did not believe a word Lot was saying. What else could he have expected? His testimony was not backed up by the kind of life that would have made his words credible. Many a parent has awakened too late to that sad fact.

B. They Had the Vices of Sodom

Now look at the two daughters who still lived at home. The angels dragged them out of the city and the two girls fled for the hills. Their mother was dead—turned into a pillar of salt because she looked back lovingly and longingly at Sodom. The two unwed daughters were now alone in the hills with their father. What they did to him is recorded in Genesis 19. They committed incest. The angels had been able to get the girls out of Sodom, but the angels had not been able to get Sodom out of the girls.

So much for Lot's children. But what about our own? What kind of example are we setting day by day? What are our priorities? What principles guide us in the decisions we make? Our children know.

There is still time to change our ways, but the longer we delay, the more difficult and costly the change will be. We must repent. We must get back into full, participating fellowship with the Lord's people. We must put God first in everything. We must fast and pray and take time to be holy. We must safeguard our daily quiet time as the most important, precious, and vital activity in our lives. We must allow God to transform our lives. We must besiege His throne and hammer at Heaven's door like that importunate woman in the Gospels. We must say to God, as Jacob did, "I will not let thee go, except thou bless me" (Genesis 32:26). We must be importunate with God to save and sanctify our children while we put their feet on the road that leads to eternal life.

Then God will go to work for us. He is waiting to step into our hopeless situations and work spiritual miracles *for* us. But first He has to work spiritual miracles *in* us.

I have often thought what a pity it was that Lot did not take his two unmarried daughters to Hebron, so that at least these two might come under the influence of godly Abraham. Who knows what might have happened then?

5
Stephen,
the First Martyr

Acts 6:1–7:60

I. THE FAITHFUL MINISTER

II. THE FEARLESS MESSENGER

III. THE FIRST MARTYR

T he deacons of the early church were excellent men. Two of them, Stephen and Philip, leaped almost immediately to high prominence, outshining even the apostles.

Stephen became the first great *martyr* of the church. He was the vanguard of the army of faithful Christians who through the centuries would die boldly for the cause of Christ. Nero would sew Christians up in blood-soaked sacks and throw them to wild beasts. He would dip believers in tar and use them as living torches for his revels. Torquemada would torture Christians to death during the Inquisition. They would be burned at the stake and massacred by the thousands. Leading the way was Stephen, one of the deacons.

Stephen's friend Philip became the first *missionary* of the church. He took seriously the words of the Lord Jesus: "Ye shall be witnesses unto me . . . in Samaria" (Acts 1:8). None of the apostles wanted to go to Samaria, although James and John had once been willing enough to call down fire on Samaria (Luke 9:54). So the deacon Philip went to Samaria first. Soon revival broke out there. The ranks of the Jewish church were breached and it was forced to take its first mighty step toward becoming an international community of called-out ones. Leading the way "into all the world" was Philip, one of the deacons.

The early church would not appoint anyone to be a deacon unless he was filled with the Spirit. Stephen was just such a man.

I. THE FAITHFUL MINISTER

The early church was expanding rapidly. Thousands were being saved and added to its ranks, and the apostles were very busy. Extraordinary things were happening. There was a great outpouring of love in the church and the Christians were generously giving money to fund their social welfare program. Then the devil saw an opportunity. (Christians probably squabble over money more than anything else.) Some of the widows began to complain that they were not getting their fair share. A stream of people with petty complaints soon distracted the apostles. We can imagine the grievances. "Mrs. Smith was given four dollars more than I was and I have two more children than she has." "Mrs. Jones got beef and I only got chicken." "Mrs. Murphy was given a wool blanket and I only received a cotton one."

Peter, who was a practical businessman, decided that enough was enough. It was time to delegate the secular and social side of the ministry to other men. But not just anybody! Perhaps anyone could wait on tables in a secular soup kitchen, but only those with the highest qualifications should wait on tables in the church. The apostles did not say, "Find someone who has proved himself successful in handling money." They did not say, "Find someone who has a degree in business management." The qualifications for a deacon were much more stringent than that. The apostles said, "Look ye out among you seven men of honest report, full of the Holy Ghost and wisdom, whom we may appoint over this business" (Acts 6:3). Manward the deacons had to be "men of honest report." Godward they had to be "full of the Holy Ghost." Selfward they had to be "full of . . . wisdom."

In other words, deacons had to be men of *sterling character*. Their integrity had to be beyond question. They had to be people who could be trusted, people who had unstained reputations. They not only had to *be* honest; everybody had to *know* they were honest.

Deacons also had to be men of *spiritual capacity*. In the early church nothing less than a complete filling of the Holy Spirit would suffice—even to do the most humble, menial task.

Finally deacons had to be men of *simple competence*. They had to be full of wisdom. They had to be able to make sensible decisions. (Unfortunately, spirituality and common sense are often strangers to one another.)

Stephen met the qualifications. He was honest, capable, and Spirit-filled—that is, the loveliness of the Lord Jesus characterized everything he did. A person who is filled with the Spirit is intoxicated with the Holy Spirit. He is turned into a different kind of person. He becomes Christlike in his walk and in his talk. He experiences the present, continuous process referred to in Ephesians 5:18: literally, "Be ye being filled."

The Holy Spirit says this about a deacon: "They that have used the office of a deacon well purchase to themselves a good degree, and great boldness in the faith which is in Christ Jesus" (1 Timothy 3:13). In other words, the office of a deacon is one of God's schools for the development of spirituality, character, and talent.

Stephen certainly developed boldness in the faith. He made full proof of his ministry. He was "full of faith and power, [and] did great wonders and miracles among the people" (Acts 6:8). What those miracles were is of little or no importance today. What is important is that Stephen manifested the power of God in his life. He made an impact for God on his generation. He waited on tables, as Dr. Luke put it (Acts 6:2). He ministered in ever-widening circles to the physical and spiritual needs of his flock.

Stephen was not famous just for his mighty works. He soon developed into an effective preacher of the gospel. We read: "Then there arose certain of the . . . Libertines, and Cyrenians, and Alexandrians, and of them of Cilicia and of Asia, disputing with Stephen. And they were not able to resist the wisdom and the spirit by which he spake" (Acts 6:9-10). These hot debates probably took place in the Jerusalem synagogue frequented by Hellenist Jews.

The mention of Cilicia points us to the Roman province of Asia Minor and to its capital city of Tarsus. The strong inference is that the brilliant young Jew, Saul of Tarsus, was a member of the synagogue where the debates took place. Saul was a trained rabbi, a disciple of the famous Gamaliel, and a formidable opponent in debate. He was a dedicated Jew, a convinced Talmudist, and a bigoted Pharisee. He was convinced that Jesus of Nazareth was an apostate and that Christianity was a blasphemous and dangerous cult. Saul had a mind for the universe—narrowed by rabbinic Judaism. He had a mind capable of writing such world-shaking Epistles as Romans, Ephesians, and Thessalonians, but his horizons were limited by the traditions and teachings of men like Hillel and Gamaliel.

We can well imagine that Saul and Stephen frequently locked horns over the issue of Jesus of Nazareth. Stephen would calmly point to the Old Testament Scriptures and say: "There were not to be two *Christs*—one to suffer and one to reign. There were to be two *comings*.

"Look at the evidence of the life that Jesus lived, Saul. Jesus was not a blasphemer. He was the Son of God. He walked on the waves and stilled the storm. He turned water into wine and fed hungry multitudes. He healed the sick and cleansed lepers. He cast out evil spirits and raised the dead. It is impossible to deny the life that He lived. And as for His death—that was redemptive. He died, the just for us the unjust, to bring us to God.

"He fulfilled the law and the words of the prophets. He fulfilled such Scriptures as Isaiah 53, Psalm 22, and Psalm 69. The Scriptures say that His hands and feet were to be pierced. The prophet said He was to be numbered with the transgressors.

"Then to crown it all He rose from the dead. Come, come, Saul! The Sanhedrin says that the disciples stole the body, but you are an intelligent man. You know that can't be true. Why didn't the Sanhedrin arrest Peter and John and the rest and put them on trial? Why didn't Caiaphas make them show where the body was hidden? You know as well as I do, Saul, that they did not dare to do any such thing. There was no body to produce. I can introduce you to more than five hundred people who saw Jesus alive after His resurrection. You can cross-examine them if you like. All Jerusalem knows He rose from the dead. This thing was not done in a corner . . . "

Stephen taught the Scriptures with authority. And so the debate went on until Saul and his friends gnashed their teeth in rage.

II. THE FEARLESS MESSENGER

"If you can't persuade them, persecute them!" Before long the Jewish leaders arrested Stephen, put him on trial, and indicted him on two counts. They accused him of attacking the *Scriptures* and the *sanctuary*. His spoken defense is a masterpiece, one of the truly great sermons in the book of Acts. Stephen's defense ranks alongside Peter's Pentecostal sermon, Paul's sermon in Pisidian Antioch, and Paul's message on Mars Hill.

Throughout the ages the church has produced magnificent preachers and powerful sermons. We think of Jonathan

Edwards and his "Sinners in the Hands of an Angry God" and of Henry Drummond and his "The Greatest Thing in the World." We think of Spurgeon and D. L. Moody, men who could move the masses with their words. Stephen stands in the forefront of them all.

Stephen's defense revolved around three major points. He talked to his enemies about the saviors, the Scriptures, and the sanctuaries God had given them.

God had given them *saviors* like Joseph and Moses, but Israel had rejected them. False witnesses were accusing Stephen of speaking against Moses when Israel's whole national history had been characterized by setting Moses aside. Stephen's accusers were far more guilty than he was.

God had given Israel the *Scriptures,* but they had broken the law. The nation had plunged into the grossest idolatry despite what the Scriptures said about such folly. Now the Jewish leaders were trying to restructure the law by imposing all their vain traditions on it. Stephen's accusers were the ones who were guilty of speaking against the Scriptures.

God had given Israel *sanctuaries:* first a tabernacle and then a temple. The temple was David's idea, not God's, although God accepted David's generous thought. Solomon built the temple, but had enough sense to see that his sanctuary—lavish and magnificent though it was—could not house a God who inhabited all the vast reaches of time and space. In Stephen's day his enemies called their temple a holy place, but all they had done was defile it.

The tabernacle was different. It spoke of the transient and temporary, for God never stands still. God cannot be locked up in a temple, though it be made of gold, silver, precious stones, costly wood, and rich fabrics, and though it be served with expensive offerings and rare perfumes.

"The very idea! To think that the great, eternal, uncreated, self-existent God of the universe, the Creator of stars and worlds unknown, could be shut up in a tiny temple on an obscure hill by a stiff-necked and rebellious crowd of religious fanatics . . . " Stripped down to its bare essentials, that was what Stephen told his accusers, the religious elite of the nation. It made them mad!

But Stephen was not through speaking. Amid a growing uproar of fury and dissent, he hammered home his conclusion. They had accused him of *reviling the holy place*. He accused them of *resisting the Holy Ghost*. They had accused him of *slighting Moses, the man of God*. He accused them of *slaying Jesus, the Son of God*. They had accused him of *blaspheming the law*. He accused them of *breaking the law*. Stephen took the charges leveled against him, picked them up, and flung them back in the faces of his accusers. We read, "When they heard these things, they were cut to the heart, and they gnashed on him with their teeth" (Acts 7:54). (Doubtless Luke heard of what happened at this trial from Paul, who was among that mob of angry men.) They were turned into a pack of wolves. Everywhere Stephen looked he saw faces distorted with fury and rage.

III. THE FIRST MARTYR

Having hammered home God's truth, noble Stephen looked away from that ring of furious faces. He looked up. Luke wrote, "He, being full of the Holy Ghost, looked up stedfastly into heaven, and saw the glory of God [that is, the Shekinah glory cloud, long missing from the earthly temple], and Jesus standing on the right hand of God" (Acts 7:55). And Stephen instantly bore witness to what he saw.

Just two short years before, Jesus had returned to Heaven, having been absent from His homeland for more than thirty-three years. He had come from glory to visit a distant planet in the remote galaxy that men would one day call the Milky Way. He had returned home in a battle-scarred human body, but He had been given a triumphal entry into Heaven. He had assumed once more the glory He had with the Father before the worlds began. We can almost picture His welcome. The gates of glory had swung wide. The trumpets had blared. The angel choirs, massed along the streets of gold leading to the great white throne, had sung the Hallelujah Chorus until it echoed off the everlasting hills. Angels and archangels, thrones and dominions, cherubim and seraphim, had joined the grand procession. Cheering, chanting, and applauding, the mighty throng had paraded up to Zion's hill. All Heaven had rung with the praise of the shining ones: "Holy! Holy! Holy is the Lord!" The twenty-four elders had cast their crowns at His feet, and He had sat down at the right hand of the Majesty on high.

That is where Jesus was when Stephen saw Him. No less than sixteen times in the Bible Jesus is said to be at God's right hand. No less than thirteen times Jesus is said to be seated at the right hand of God. The word *seated* shows that the work of salvation has been completed to the eternal satisfaction of God. The word *seated* shows that though He is man, Jesus is also God. He is God the Son—coequal, coeternal, and coexistent with the Father—God over all, blessed for evermore. Jesus is seated, "henceforth expecting till his enemies be made his footstool" (Hebrews 10:13).

The day Stephen was tried admiring angels still crowded around Jesus. They gazed on the face of incarnate deity. They looked in awe and wonder at the marks of Calvary. Their eyes were riveted on Him, but He was not looking at them. He was looking back to earth where He saw Stephen standing alone surrounded by a howling mob of scribes and Sadducees, rulers and rabbis, priests and Pharisees. Their faces were distorted with rage, their lips drawn back from gnashing teeth. Hatred was in their eyes and death was in their hands. There Stephen stood—one lone man, careless of his life, a latecomer to the ministry—bravely telling the mob the truth about Jesus. This is the scene Jesus saw and it was all too familiar.

The slow fuse Stephen had lighted with his very first word had reached the powder keg. It exploded with fury and violence. The mob seized him and dragged him from the chamber into the blazing sunshine. They marched him through the city streets, dragged him to the foot of a skull-shaped hill, and prepared for the assault.

Saul of Tarsus cheered the mob on. "Here, you fellows, let me hold your coats," he said. The stones began to fly. And with every stone the mob threw at Stephen they were guaranteeing for themselves a full measure of God's righteous wrath. Was it stones they were looking for? He would give them stones. Within a few decades or so He would tear down their precious temple stone by stone. He would summon the Romans to bring their catapults and engines of war and throw stones at the Jews. First they had rejected the Savior and nailed Him to a cross of wood. Now they had rejected the Holy Spirit and were murdering a blood-bought, Spirit-baptized, Spirit-indwelt, Spirit-sealed, Spirit-filled, and Spirit-anointed child of God.

Luke wrote: "They stoned Stephen, calling upon God, and saying, Lord Jesus, receive my spirit. And he kneeled down, and cried with a loud voice, Lord, lay not this sin to their charge. And when he had said this, he fell asleep" (Acts 7:59-60).

Saul was also destined to wear a martyr's crown, although nothing could have been further from his thoughts the day he witnessed Stephen's death. That day iron entered into Saul's soul. Whether it was Stephen's face, or his message, or his calm assurance, or his forgiveness, or his testimony that he had seen the standing Christ, something affected Saul that day. Saul would never forget Stephen. That angel face (Acts 6:15) would haunt him until the face of Stephen was replaced in his soul by the face of Jesus, the Son of God.

When the stoning of Stephen was all over, devout men picked up the battered body of the first Christian martyr. They washed it, wrapped it, and gave it a decent burial. Then they met to decide what to do. It was evident that savage persecution would now be let loose on the church. They had seen the face of Stephen, but they had also seen the face of Saul. They had seen the blood-lust, the hatred, the zeal, the fanaticism, and the determination of that young man.

Doubtless those devout men wept for Stephen too. He had shown such promise. *Why,* they must have wondered, *did God allow this to happen?* Ah, but they could not see Stephen. While they mourned, he was receiving "the stephanus"—the martyr's crown. If they could have seen Stephen at that moment, they would not have wept. They would have laughed for joy. They would have seen angels crowding around him to welcome him home. The mourners would have seen him conducted amid triumphant anthems to where Christ was sitting at God's right hand. They would have seen him bow at Jesus' feet. They would have seen him—the spirit of a just man made perfect—enter into the joy of his reward. They would have heard all Heaven echo with the Lord's "Well Done!" They would have heard Christ say: "Welcome home, Stephen. Now let me tell you about that young man Saul . . . "

6
Anna,
the Godliest Widow

Luke 2:36-38

I. HER VICTORY

She could have been

A. Bitter at the Funeral

B. Bitter over Her Family

C. Bitter over Her Frailty

D. Bitter over Her Finances

II. HER VOCATION

III. HER VISION

Anna was a very old woman. She had been a widow for eighty-four years and had been married for seven years before that. That accounts for ninety-one years. Even if she had married when she was a young teenager, she would still be over a hundred years old. Anna was a woman who had grown old loving God with all her heart and all her mind and all her soul and all her strength.

Anna was from the tribe of Asher. Asher, the least important of all the tribes, had sprung from the son of Jacob and Leah's maid Zilpah. Leah was the unwanted wife and Zilpah was the unwanted slave of the unwanted wife. Asher was the last and least of the four slave-born sons of Jacob.

Yet Asher never allowed that status to bother him. His name means "happy." He made up for the deficiency of his birth by the joy and gladness of his disposition. Just because a person comes from humble circumstances doesn't mean he cannot be happy. Anna was born into the "happy tribe" and she seems to have imbibed the two characteristics of that tribe: she was humble and she was happy.

Anna added another characteristic: she was not only humble and happy—she was holy. She had grown old in godliness.

This Anna is the godly old woman whose name is forever associated with the birth of the Lord Jesus Christ. She is the woman whom God allowed to see His Son when He was a tiny infant, a baby six or seven weeks old. She saw a little one who was dependent for every human need upon the ministry of a mother; yet Anna realized He was the One on whom the worlds depended. He was the creator and sustainer of the universe— the One who, even when cradled in this mother's arms, upheld all things by the word of His power.

The Lord Jesus had been circumcised when he was eight days old, probably on the last and greatest day of the feast of tabernacles. After the appropriate lapse of time, Mary had now come to the temple with her holy child to offer the sacrifice demanded by the law to cover her uncleanness. A mother had to bring such a sacrifice forty days after the birth of a son, or eighty days after the birth of a daughter (Leviticus 12:2-5).

On this particular occasion God allowed two people to hold His Son in their arms. One was a woman; one was a man. Both were old. The two who were given a special glimpse of Him at this time were Anna and Simeon. They make an interesting pair, but we are only going to look at what the Holy

Spirit records about Anna. We are going to consider the victory, the vocation, and the vision of this remarkable woman.

I. HER VICTORY

When studying people in the Bible of whom very little is told, we must read between the lines. We must flesh out the stories and put ourselves in the people's shoes. When we read between the lines of Luke 2:36-38, we can at once see that Anna was a woman who had achieved victory over bitterness. She could have been very bitter over her lot in life.

A. Bitter at the Funeral

She was young, she was married, and she was happy. She was probably in her late teens or early twenties when the tragedy happened: her husband died and she was left a widow.

Anna could have been very bitter at her husband's funeral. We all know people who have turned bitter after a bereavement. They blame God for their sorrow; they speak rashly and accuse Him of cruelty. Satan wins a victory by distorting their picture of God. But death is not God's fault; death is our fault. The wages of sin is death. We have no one but ourselves to thank for the fact that death stalks the earth invading every home, breaking up every marriage, and turning this world into one vast graveyard. The blame for this blight can all be laid at the door of sin.

Anna might easily have blamed God. She could have decided to turn against Him; millions do. But had she become bitter, in time she would have turned into a sour old woman nobody liked.

With her husband dead, Anna probably had to work to make ends meet. At harvest time she would glean in the fields, doing hard labor for the equivalent of a minimal wage just to survive the winter. She would come home at night and see her husband's work shoes in the corner of the room and his old robe hanging in the closet. The house would be empty and silent but full of haunting memories. Her life was so very, very dark.

But then Anna would take down the family Bible, find a well-worn passage in the prophecy of Isaiah, and read there of "the *treasures* of darkness" (Isaiah 45:3, italics added). Anna learned to trust God in the dark. She would say, "Dear Lord, I don't know why You took my beloved from me, but I trust You anyway. You have promised to be the friend of the widow. Dear Lord, I need You to be my friend."

So Anna entered into victory. She could have been bitter at the funeral. Instead she entered into the treasures of darkness. She decided she would make God's house her home.

The temple courts in Anna's day were both commodious and elaborate. The outer court, as rebuilt and extended by Herod, did not form a part of the sacred area. Gentiles were allowed to walk there so it was called the court of the Gentiles. The ruling religious authorities had concessions set up in this court. Their agents were always busy there changing money for buying and selling animals for sacrifices. Anna would make her way across this court until she came to some steps which led to a barrier.

This barrier was known as the middle wall of partition. On the wall notices in Greek and Latin were posted to warn Gentiles not to penetrate beyond that point. The penalty for not heeding this warning was death. Ritually unclean Jews were also forbidden to go beyond the wall. Nine massive gates led through this barrier. One of the gates, known as the beautiful gate, was sometimes called the Corinthian gate because it was overlaid with costly Corinthian bronze.

Anna would make her way through one of the gates and enter the court of the women. In this court the temple treasury was located. Jewish men could go farther—into the court of Israel. Descendants of Aaron could go farther still—into the court of the priests. Anna could go as far as the court of the women.

In this court she found a quiet corner that became her real

home. She "departed not from the temple," says the Holy Spirit (Luke 2:37). She made God her husband, she made His house her home, and she entered into the treasures of darkness. She said with Job, "Though he slay me, yet will I trust in him" (Job 13:15).

So instead of becoming bitter at the funeral, Anna dedicated her widowhood to God. She determined to be the happiest, holiest widow in Jerusalem.

B. Bitter over Her Family

Anna could have reacted against God even before she became a widow. She could have resented the fact that her parents made her go to the temple so often when she was a little girl. And then when tragedy struck she might have said, "If that's all the thanks I get for going to the temple all the time, that's it. I'll never darken the doors of the temple again." It is astonishing how many people offer excuses like that. Actually the most precious privilege ever granted to a human being is that of being born into a Christian home—a home where parents love the Lord, keep fellowship with God's people, require their children to go to Sunday school and church, and protect their children as far as possible from the ways of the world.

Think of it—one could have been born into a Hindu home. Until recently some little Hindu girls were subjected to the horrors of child marriage.[1] Others were destined to serve as temple prostitutes. Hindus have some 300 million gods, they worship idols, and they venerate rats and vermin. Some time ago *National Geographic* carried an illustrated article showing food actually being set out for the benefit of rats that are regarded as sacred—in a land that traditionally has had trouble feeding its millions of people.[2]

Or one could have been born into a Muslim home. Muslims are taught to worship Allah and to revere the teachings of a fierce and lustful prophet. Their creed revolves around the formula, "There is no god but Allah and Muhammad is his prophet."

Or one might have been born into a communist home. Communists indoctrinate their children in the lie that there is no God. Millions of communists die in their sins without God, without Christ, without hope—never having heard of John 3:16.

Those who are born into Christian homes are greatly privileged. Yet some resent their Christian upbringing and cannot wait to get away from it. Like the prodigal son they throw off the restraints and requirements of a godly home. They have been brought up surrounded by sublime truth. They have been taught that Jesus is the eternal uncreated Son of the living God, that He deliberately incarnated Himself in human form at Bethlehem, that He "went about doing good," that He lives in the power of an endless life, and that He is mighty to save. Yet they want to throw their heritage away.

When a person decides to turn his back on all that is Christian, God sometimes lets him. It will be more tolerable for some shivering naked cannibal standing at the great white throne on the day of judgment than for such a rebel.

Anna's father must have been a very godly man. His name was Phanuel, which means "the face of God." Anna grew up in a home where her father was a living image of God to her childish soul. She saw the face of God in the face of her father. She knew what God was like because she knew what her father was like.

My own father had his faults and failings like anyone else, but he showed me the face of God. I have never known another man who could pray like my father prayed. When my father stood up to lead God's people in prayer, he lifted them into the very throne room of the universe.

Why do so many Christian parents see their children go astray? Sometimes it is because the children look at their parents and do not see the face of God. Christian parents must do more than talk about what is right. Their supreme responsibility is to live Christ so that their children will think of the face of God whenever they think of their parents.

C. Bitter over Her Frailty

Even though Anna was not bitter over her family, she could have been bitter over her declining health. A person does not arrive at the age of approximately 110 without accumulating the inevitable physical consequences of old age. Perhaps she had arthritis or rheumatism. She might have had a weak heart or bad circulation. She could easily have pleaded her old age as an excuse for no longer going to the temple. But Anna's chief delight was to be where God's people came together.

Her friends might have said, "Granny, you'd better give it up. You could fall down and break your hip on those stairs." "Granny, you can't go to the house of God today. It's raining." "Granny, now that you're so old, why not ease up a little? Why not settle for the sabbath? Just go to the temple on the sabbath."

But Anna would have said, "I'm looking for the coming of the Lord, and when He comes I know where I want Him to find me. I can think of a thousand places where I don't want Him to find me. I know where I would like Him to find me; and I know where I'm most likely to find Him—in the temple. You'll never keep me away from God's house."

When Jesus was twelve years old and Mary and Joseph lost Him, they went back to Jerusalem and spent three days searching the city. Astonishingly, they never thought of looking in the temple. Yet Jesus had haunted that temple. Anna was like Jesus: she loved the place where God's people met. So did Peter and John. Acts 4:23 says that after they were threatened by the Sanhedrin, "being let go, [Peter and John] went to their own company." There is more truth than poetry in the old saying that birds of a feather flock together.

D. Bitter over Her Finances

Anna could have used her financial status as well as her frailty as an excuse for not going to the temple. There were vested interests in that temple. There were those who under the guise of religion fleeced the widows and the helpless. Jesus spoke of those charlatans who "devour widows' houses, and for a pretence make long prayers" (Mark 12:40).

Under Jewish law a widow could not dispose of her property except through the rabbis, some of whom were cheats. Quite possibly Anna herself had been cheated. But the fact that some people use religion as a cloak to cover up their wickedness made no difference to Anna. She was not going to let their hypocrisy rob her of her own joy in the Lord.

The Holy Spirit says of Anna that she "departed not from the temple" (Luke 2:37). The word *not* is strong, expressing full and direct negation: absolutely not. There were no ifs, ands, or buts: Anna lived solely for the place where God had put His name. Her whole life revolved around the temple.

A verse in Anna's Bible told her that the Lord would come suddenly into His temple (Malachi 3:1). She did not know where else He would come, but she knew He would come there. So the temple was where Anna wanted to be.

Anna triumphed over all the big and little excuses people make for staying away from the gathering place of the people of God. She was not infatuated by the temple itself, but she wanted to be where God Himself had promised to be. Her presence in the temple was evidence of her victory over bitterness.

II. HER VOCATION

Luke 2:37 tells us that this remarkable woman "served God with fastings and prayers night and day." The word translated "served" signifies "worshiped." Anna devoted her whole life to praying for the Lord's coming. She could see wrongs all about her, even in the temple, and she longed for the Lord to come and right those wrongs.

When we read of Anna's vocation we can picture an old woman, bent and feeble, *doing what the high priest should have been doing*. (The high priest, as everyone knew, was more interested in the politics of his office than anything else.) We can also picture an old woman *doing what the shining seraphim and cherubim are doing.* We see Anna, as the hymn says, "gazing on the Lord in glory." We see her day and night ceasing not to cry, "Holy, holy, holy, is the Lord. . . . Thou art worthy, O Lord, to receive glory and honour and power: for thou hast created all things, and for thy pleasure they are and were created" (Isaiah 6:3; Revelation 4:11).

Anna brought her body under control and she set her spirit free. Her life's work was to praise the Lord and to pray— for her family and friends, for the leaders of her nation, for the spiritual life of her people, for those who ruled the land, for God's kingdom to come, and for His will to be done on earth as it is in Heaven.

The name *Anna* (Hannah) means "God is gracious." People might have said to her, "God is gracious? He took away your husband in your youth when you had been married barely seven years. God is gracious?" But Anna would have said, "Oh yes! That was His gracious way of wedding me to Himself. Do you think I have been a widow these past eighty-four years? Oh no! I have been married to Another, even to Him who is to be raised from the dead."

Anna's vocation was to pray. God has few saints like her on earth. He has plenty of people who are willing to preach. He has only a few who are willing to pray, and even fewer who feel called to make prayer and fasting the great and controlling ministry of their lives.

III. HER VISION

One day Anna's prayers were answered!

The day began like any other day. Anna probably woke up that morning at the usual time. With her poor old bones and joints all stiff, she took a little while to get going. She dressed, went outside, picked up her pitcher, and hobbled down to the well. There she exchanged a few pleasantries with other women from the neighborhood. Then she went back home to make herself a little porridge for breakfast.

Taking her well-worn staff, off she went to the temple. She knew her way blindfolded; she knew every house and shop, every man and woman, every stick and stone.

She puffed and panted a little as she came to the temple mount. Rising from the deep valleys, the mount was like an island surrounded by a sea of walls, palaces, streets, and houses. Rising terrace after terrace, the mount was crowned by a mass of snowy marble and glittering gold. Anna paused to admire the splendor of the view. She had seen it thousands of times but it never failed to take her breath away. She had seen that gigantic sacred enclosure thronged with as many as two hundred thousand people on high days and holy days.

Once within the temple gates Anna saw colonnades and porches everywhere—the most famous was the ancient eastern colonnade known as Solomon's porch. She saw the pinnacle of the temple towering 450 feet above the Kidron valley.

Once past the colonnades she entered the court of the Gentiles. As she walked through she looked with disapproval at the way it had been turned into a market. Coming to the middle wall of partition she labored up the fourteen steps to enter, through one of the splendid gates, the court of the women. There Anna found her habitual corner and began her daily round of prayer.

But this day was different from any other day, for on this day Jesus came!

Anna noticed a man and a woman coming. They were obviously poor and had with them a baby wrapped in a blanket. Then Anna saw an old man approach them. She knew that old man. He was Simeon. She couldn't help overhearing what Simeon said as he intercepted the couple and took the baby in his arms: "Lord, now lettest thou thy servant depart in peace, according to thy word: For mine eyes have seen thy salvation" (Luke 2:29-30).

Anna's heart leaped. *It was the Lord! Hallelujah! He'd come! Of course! Of course! He was to come as a baby. A virgin was to conceive and bear a Son.* And Anna burst into thanksgiving and praise.

She now had a new vocation. She spoke of Him to all who looked for redemption in Jerusalem (Luke 2:38). She knew every believer in town. "He's here!" she would say to each and every one of them. "I've seen Him. His name is *Jesus.* Keep your eyes open. He'll be back in your lifetime. Be sure you are ready."

So instead of becoming bitter, Anna became a blessing. Anna's joy over the coming of Jesus is ample testimony to God's faithfulness in rewarding a life like hers.

———————

1. What those horrors were has been amply documented in a harrowing book entitled *Mother India* by Katherine Mayo (New York: Harcourt, Brace, 1927).
2. *National Geographic,* July 1977, 71.

7
Ananias and Sapphira, the Biggest Liars

Acts 5:1-11

I. A LESSON IN DISCIPLESHIP: Great Power
   A. The Men
   B. The Message
II. A LESSON IN FELLOWSHIP: Great Grace
III. A LESSON IN MEMBERSHIP: Great Fear

A*nanias* and *Sapphira*—the two names sound like music in our ears. The name *Ananias* means "Jehovah has graciously given." It reminds us of words from an old hymn:

> Savior, Thy dying love
> Thou gavest me,
> Nor should I aught withhold,
> Dear Lord, from Thee.
>
> . . . .

All that I am and have,
Thy gifts so free,
In joy, in grief, thro' life,
Dear Lord, for Thee!
                                    (Sylvanus D. Phelps)

Sapphira, an Aramaic word, simply means "beautiful." One name captures the thought of *bounty;* the other captures the thought of *beauty.* If the pair had lived up to their names, they would have been permanent ornaments of the church—enduring examples of the bounty and beauty of the Lord Jesus. Instead they were a pair of Achans in the camp (Joshua 7). Like their Old Testament counterpart, they perished under the judgment hand of God.

The Holy Spirit associates the story of Ananias and Sapphira with three expressions: "great power," "great grace," and "great fear." In other words, this story provides lessons in discipleship, fellowship, and membership.

I. A LESSON IN DISCIPLESHIP: Great Power

The story of Ananias and Sapphira was told in the context of a description of the early church. Let us consider the men who established the church and the power of their message.

A. The Men

"With great power gave the apostles witness" (Acts 4:33). The apostles themselves were ordinary men. In fact the Sanhedrin contemptuously called them "unlearned and ignorant" (4:13). *What under the sun,* thought the Jewish religious leaders, *is there to fear from a dozen fishermen, tax collectors, and peasants? Why, there isn't a single educated man among them. They are not rich. They are not sophisticated. They are not from the upper crust of society. They are common Galileans.* But the apostles had been with Jesus! That was the secret of their power. What distinguished the apostles from other men was the amount of time they had spent in the personal company of the Lord Jesus.

It is almost redundant to say that we do not have apostles in the church today. The gift of the apostle was special and specialized. The nursery no longer exists where apostles can be born and raised. John lived longer than any of the other apostles and when he died, the office of the apostle died.

The word *apostle,* however, simply means "sent one." There are many "sent ones" today. Indeed, all Christians are "sent ones." The *work* of the apostle remains though the *gift* of the apostle has ceased.

The early apostles had spent time with the Son of God and had been baptized, indwelt, sealed, filled, and anointed by the Spirit of God. In the sense that anyone can become acquainted with the Son of God and make himself available to the Spirit of God, anyone can be an apostle. That is the kind of man God uses to build His church. In the early days the Jerusalem church was uniquely blessed in that it had about a dozen such men in its ranks.

B. The Message

The early church had only one message: Christ—alive from the dead, ascended on high, seated at God's right hand, and coming again. "With great power gave the apostles witness of the resurrection of the Lord Jesus" (Acts 4:33).

The resurrection of Christ is the one great irrefutable argument for Christianity. During the French revolution a Frenchman named Lepeaux was disappointed in the poor success he was having in launching a new religion, which to his mind was far superior to Christianity. He appealed to Charles Maurice de Tallyrand, a statesman-bishop who became a leader of the godless French revolution. Lepeaux asked Tallyrand, "What should I do to get my plans off the ground?" "My dear M. Lepeaux," the statesman said, "it is a very difficult thing to start a new religion. But there is one thing you might at least try. I suggest you get yourself crucified and then rise again on the third day."

The resurrection was the dynamic of the apostles' message, and of course it is gloriously true. "God hath raised him from the dead," wrote Paul to the Romans (Romans 10:9).

Eusebius, an early church father and historian, told us that when the news began to circulate in Jerusalem that Jesus Christ was alive from the dead, Pontius Pilate, the Roman governor, considered the story to be of sufficient importance that he officially referred the matter to Tiberius. Under Roman law the Roman senate had the authority to rule on all claims to deity. Eusebius wrote: "An ancient law prevailed that no one should be made a God by the Romans except by a vote and decree of the Senate. The Senate rejected the Nazarene's claim to deity" (*Ecclesiastical History,* Book 2, chapter 2). Apparently the Lord Jesus did not think it worthwhile to get the Romans' approval before claiming to be God and proving it by rising from the dead!

The well-publicized case of Lord Lyttleton and Gilbert West illustrates the power of the apostles' message. These two men, unbelieving and skeptical, decided that the best way to overthrow Christianity was to undermine belief in its two cardinal historical facts: the resurrection of Christ and the conversion of the apostle Paul. Lyttleton undertook to discredit the account of the conversion of Paul and West undertook to disprove the resurrection of Christ. When meeting to discuss their progress, they made a great discovery: they had both been so convinced by the evidence that they had written their books to prove the opposite of what they had set out to prove. Some years ago I checked West's book out of the Moody Bible Institute library and read its clear message of a Christ who died, was buried, and rose again.

For a number of years Allan Redpath was the pastor of Moody Memorial Church in Chicago. At one Moody Bible Institute Founders Week Conference I heard him use the following illustration in a sermon.

It seems that Redpath was an Englishman and though he had lived in the United States for a long time, he retained his love for English sports. He was especially interested in the annual cricket test match (the highest level of competition) between England and Australia. But he could find few people in the United States who even knew what cricket was and still fewer who cared anything about the test match.

The match began each day at 11:00 a.m., stopped at 1:00 p.m. for lunch, resumed at 1:45 p.m., stopped at 3:30 p.m. for tea (cricket is a gentlemanly sport), resumed at 4:00 p.m., and stopped at 6:30 p.m. Each year the match went on like that for five days.

One year when Redpath was living in Chicago, he wanted to know how the annual match was going. He bought every Chicago newspaper he could lay his hands on but he couldn't find a word about the match. The American journalists were only interested in the Cubs and the Sox. So a friend from England kindly airmailed him a copy of a London paper. The headline on the front page was "England Facing Defeat." This news was more depressing than no news at all. Worse still, nobody seemed to care. But two days later Redpath received another British newspaper. This time the headline read, "England In Sight Of Victory." In two days the whole situation had changed.

Likewise it was a sad day at Calvary when Joseph took Jesus down from the cross, wrapped His body in graveclothes, and put Him in a tomb. The world went on its way. Few people cared. But the disciples were utterly demoralized and defeated. Thomas became an avowed skeptic, Peter ate his heart out with remorse, and John did his best to comfort the Lord's mother Mary. Then came the resurrection morning! In three days the whole situation had changed.

That was the point of Redpath's illustration and that was the message of the early church: the whole situation had changed. And the news spread. As Paul said to King Agrippa, "This thing was not done in a corner" (Acts 26:26). Peter, James,

John, Matthew, Thomas, and all the rest of the disciples were eyewitnesses of the risen Christ. Their powerful message would turn the world upside down.

II. A LESSON IN FELLOWSHIP: Great Grace

Adding to his description of the early church, Luke said, "Great grace was upon them all" (Acts 4:33). That outstanding characteristic and quality of life which marked the Christ now marked the Christians. The overflow of love among Christians was such that a brother who had money in the bank would share his money with a brother in great need. Before long the prevailing custom was share and share alike. This generous lifestyle was an experiment in pure socialism—that is, socialism based on the utmost ideal and motivated by what the Holy Spirit calls "great grace." The experiment did not last and it did not work, but it was an interesting attempt to have all things in common.

Acts 4:36-37 gives us the example of Barnabas. He was a Levite who owned property on the island of Cyprus. Carried away with the spirit of the early church, this "son of consolation" sold his property and put the proceeds at the apostles' feet. The Holy Spirit neither approves nor disapproves the deed. He simply cites it as an example of the overflowing love and fellowship of the early church.

This kind of socialism is neither commanded nor commended in the Epistles. The noble experiment was simply recorded as a phase through which the early church passed. Before long, abuses arose and Jerusalem was known far and wide for its poor saints. There was never enough to go around.

Brief though it was, the early experiment in sharing is a lesson in fellowship. Although the Holy Spirit does not require a Christian with means to beggar himself in order to help the poor, He certainly does expect the Christian to be concerned about the physical and material needs of the less fortunate.

"The poor always ye have with you," Jesus said (John 12:8). We can find plenty of outlets for our generosity if we have the compassion of Christ in our hearts.

Caring for the sick, the poor, the orphaned, the aged, and the illiterate has always been and still is one of the great concerns of the church. The early church was very much alive to the needs of the unfortunate and the poor. Always a leader in social reform, the church built the first hospitals, asylums, orphan homes, and rescue missions. But the modern church has surrendered half its mission to the government. Such surrender leads to socialism without a soul and a welfare state without a conscience.

The gospel of Christ always quickens the conscience of the individual so that he becomes aware of the social ills of mankind. For example, Lord Shaftesbury, a Christian, became aware of the plight of little children working like slaves to feed the jaw of the "Moloch" of Britain's industrial machine and started a campaign against this injustice. William Wilberforce, a Christian, aroused a lethargic British parliament to abolish slavery throughout the empire. George Muller, a Christian, reached out to the destitute orphans in England's streets. Amy Wilson Carmichael, a missionary to India, gave impetus to helping wretched widows and rescuing little children destined for prostitution in Hindu temples. And the early Christians were aware of each other's needs and "distribution was made unto every man according as he had need" (Acts 4:35).

After describing the generosity that characterized the early church, Luke told the story of Ananias and Sapphira.

III. A LESSON IN MEMBERSHIP: Great Fear

The facts behind the story are that two great protagonists came to the floor of the church. Satan came to battle the Spirit of God. God demonstrated His power and great fear came upon the church.

What Ananias and Sapphira did is linked by a conjunction

to what Barnabas had done. They had been impressed by his gift. They had particularly liked the applause that, all unsought and unwanted, he had received. His gift seems to have been exceptionally generous since the Holy Spirit draws such special attention to it. Anyway, Ananias and Sapphira had a family conference and decided to emulate the generosity of Barnabas. Acts 5:1 says they "sold a possession."

But Acts 5:2 says they "kept back part of the price." Within a stone's throw of Pentecost Ananias and Sapphira entered into an agreement to deceive. (Deception is Satan's favorite device.) Their fall into sin was not sudden. Ananias and Sapphira were not overwhelmed by temptation. Their deception was planned and deliberate.

When Ananias and Sapphira sold the property, the proceeds were more than they expected. "We don't have to give it all," they agreed. Later when Peter demanded an explanation from Sapphira he said, "How is it that ye have agreed together to tempt the Spirit of the Lord?" (Acts 5:9) Peter used the word *sumphoneo* from which our word "symphony" is derived. Evidently Ananias and Sapphira shared a harmony of purpose. (The word *sumphoneo* is used in Acts 15:15 to describe the harmony of the Old and New Testament Scriptures: "To this agree the words of the prophets.")

Little did Ananias and Sapphira realize that there was an unseen listener to their whispered pact.

"How much did you get, Ananias?" we can hear Sapphira say.

"Twice what I asked for," we can hear Ananias reply. "The man wanted the land badly. He wants to build a bank on the corner. It's right near the temple."

"Do you think we have to give it all?"

"How about if we give all we originally intended and keep back the extra?"

"That's a good idea, Ananias. Do we need to tell anybody what the real market price was? It was a cash deal, wasn't it?"

"Yes, my friend wanted to deal in cash."

"Well, that's all right then. We'll tell everyone that we got such-and-such a price."

The unseen listener knew the market price. The Holy Spirit was there when the deal was struck. He knew to whom the property was sold and for how much. And He did not keep the information to Himself. He went and told Peter.

If the Savior detested one sin more than any other when He trod these scenes of time, that sin was hypocrisy. Honest doubts never angered Him, but He scathingly denounced hypocrisy. He who was and is the truth never made peace with a lie. Nor has His Holy Spirit.

Pretending to a holiness and a generosity they lacked, Ananias and Sapphira lied to the Holy Ghost and "kept back" *(nosphizomai)* part of the price (Acts 5:2-3). Note that Greek expression. When the translators of the Septuagint came to the story of Achan they used an almost identical word. They recorded that "the children of Israel committed a trespass in the accursed thing: for Achan . . . took *[enosphisanto]* of the accursed thing" (Joshua 7:1). This Greek expression means "took for himself." Achan hindered the blessing of God and so did Ananias and Sapphira. Their sin was covetousness, the love of money. They held on to what had been promised to God.

The Spirit of God acted at once. He did something Jesus never did—He smote. Once, twice, and two of God's people lay dead on the floor. That morning they had been wrapped in smug complacency. Before the day was done they were lying in their coffins.

How swiftly and terribly Ananias and Sapphira were exposed. Their story is a preview of the judgment seat of Christ. Never once did Peter question their salvation. The church has no business judging people who are "without"—only those who are "within" (1 Corinthians 5:12).

Now let's backtrack to an earlier point in the story. Ananias laid his offering at the apostles' feet just as Barnabas had done. "Well bless you, my brother," we can hear Peter say. "This is a generous sum. I take it this is the full price you received for the property?" Ananias could have told the truth. He could have said, "No, as a matter of fact I did get more for the land but I decided to keep some of the proceeds for our own needs." That would have been perfectly acceptable (Acts 5:4). The Lord is not against private ownership of property.

The Lord said, "Sell all that thou hast, and distribute unto the poor" (Luke 18:22), but this is the counsel of perfection. It is not an obligation. It is not a necessary part of being a believer. It is not an evidence of grace. The idea of "lordship salvation" is not found in the New Testament. We must not confuse conversion with consecration. Selling all that we have and giving it to the poor is an evidence of growth, not grace. In the case of the rich young ruler, the Lord saw that his love of money was a stumbling block to his salvation.

Ananias was a free agent as far as his property was concerned. He could keep it, sell it, give all of it away, or give part of it away. There was no physical necessity, church necessity, or spiritual necessity for him to sell the property and give any of the proceeds away. The only compulsion was love—the compulsion to be like Jesus, to express the compassion of Christ for the poor, to lay up treasure in Heaven.

Ananias could have told the truth, but he told his lie and judgment fell. "Thou hast not lied unto men," Peter said, "but unto God" (Acts 5:4). The man dropped dead on the spot and within an hour he was in his tomb.

Three hours later his wife came in. Where had she been the past three hours? Maybe she'd gone to the bank to deposit the nice little nest egg they had left over. Perhaps she had been in the market deciding how to spend the extra money. Possibly she had been at home waiting for Ananias to return and had decided to go to the church to see if he were there.

Anyway, Sapphira came in all smiles. By now their generous gift would be the talk of the church. She nodded to this one and that one. Too eager to receive the praise of men, she did not notice the strained silence. Casually Peter asked her the fateful question. The interrogation probably went like this:

"By the way, Sapphira, how much did you get for that piece of property? Ananias was here a little while ago. He did mention a price. Do I have the figure right? Was it such and such?"

Apparently Sapphira took no alarm at Peter's question. She was so preoccupied with material things that she failed to detect the tenseness of the atmosphere and the pointedness of the question. Or did she suspect something at the last moment, but tried to protect her husband?

Alarmed or not, Sapphira answered Peter's question with a barefaced lie and her doom was swift. Peter's terrible words fell on her ears: "How is it that ye have agreed together to tempt the Spirit of the Lord? behold, the feet of them which have buried thy husband are at the door, and shall carry thee out" (Acts 5:9). She had no time for reflection, no time for repentance. Caught red-handed lying to the Spirit of God, she dropped dead at Peter's feet.

"Great fear came upon all the church" (Acts 5:11). Suddenly people woke up to the fact that the church was a place of terrifying holiness. Fear fell on the unsaved and on those who came to church for the loaves and fishes (the fringe benefits of Christianity). Nobody dared join the church (5:13).

Nowadays almost anyone can join most churches—the only requirement for membership is a letter of transfer, a glib profession of faith, or an agreement to get baptized. Why does not God's judgment fall today? People get away with lying to the Holy Spirit. They promise to tithe, teach a Sunday school class, study their Bibles, go to the mission field, or visit the sick. Then they break their promises and nothing happens.

In contrast to many churches today, the early church was energized by great power, great grace, and great fear. If the church of today had the *dynamic* of the church of that day, it would have the *discipline* of that day. And if the church of today had the *discipline* of that day, it would have the *dynamic* of that day.

8
Herod Agrippa I, the Meanest Murderer

Acts 12:1-25

I. THE HOLLOW CROWN
II. THE HIDEOUS CRIME
  A. The Death of James
  B. The Detention of Peter
III. THE HAUGHTY CLAIM

Herod Agrippa I wielded a murderous hand at the helm. He was a scheming, grasping, treacherous individual. The Herods were a bad lot. They were true children of Esau, Edomites with hands dyed red with the blood of innocent men, women, boys, and girls. Disregarding the laws of God or man, the Herods were a law unto themselves. A man would be better off trusting a rattlesnake than trusting a Herod. The family was not without wit, charm, and genius. Herod the so-called Great was a magnificent builder, bold ruler, and crafty negotiator. But woe would betide the man who crossed a

245

Herod, or who had something a Herod wanted, or who stood in a Herod's way.

Herod Agrippa I, whom we meet in the early chapters of Acts, is not the Herod we meet in the Gospels. The man who murdered John and mocked at Jesus was Herod Antipas, an uncle of Herod Agrippa I.

I. THE HOLLOW CROWN

The Herods thought they were big men, but they were only as big as God in Heaven and caesar on earth allowed them to be. Nevertheless they made plenty of noise and threw their weight around in their own small puddles. If you'd heard them talk and seen them strut, you'd have thought they ruled the world, not just bits and pieces of a little land held in Rome's iron hand. A Herod's crown was hollow.

The grandfather of Herod Agrippa I was Herod the Great, the big-time builder. One of his projects was the temple in Jerusalem. It took about eighty-four years to build the temple, and about six years after it was completed it was destroyed by the Romans in accordance with the words of Christ. The Roman general Titus had ordered it to be preserved. Jesus had declared it would be razed. Jesus proved to be right.

Another landmark of Herod the Great's building genius was the Roman city of Caesarea on the coastline of his realm. Caesarea was an architectural marvel because its builders had to overcome enormous obstacles when constructing the harbor.

Herod the Great, however, is best known to us as the one who murdered the babes of Bethlehem in an effort to destroy the newborn Christ of God.

The grandmother of Herod Agrippa I was the beautiful Mariamne. Herod the Great was madly in love with this princess, yet that did not stop him from murdering her and her two brothers. After that he became insane. His nights were haunted by the beautiful woman he had married and murdered and his days were spent trying to find another woman like her.

On one occasion he saw a woman of the streets who reminded him of his dead princess. Despite all warnings, he wanted her. He got what he wanted and contracted a foul disease that rotted his body through and through.

The father of Herod Agrippa I was Aristobulus, who was also murdered by his father Herod the Great. Agrippa's parents were first cousins. Agrippa himself was married to his first cousin, the daughter of an aunt who was married to an uncle. No wonder there was a trace of madness in the Herods.

When Herod the Great murdered Aristobulus in a fit of jealous rage, Agrippa was sent off to Rome by his mother so that he would be out of the reach of his evil grandfather. No wonder Caesar Augustus said it was better to be Herod the Great's hog than his son.

Agrippa's uncle Philip married the bloodthirsty Herodias. Then Agrippa's uncle Antipas ran away with Herodias. Agrippa's cousin Salome (daughter of Herodias) performed a provocative dance before her stepfather Antipas and so inflamed the lustful king that he promised her half his kingdom. She settled instead, under the urging of her she-wolf mother, to demand the head of John the Baptist on a platter.

Agrippa's brother Herod of Chalcis married his niece Berenice. Later on Berenice showed up as the consort of her brother Agrippa II under circumstances that caused the tongues of the scandalmongers to wag.

Such was the Herod family. They had little or no moral scruples. The only law they consulted was the law of their own lustful desires.

While the young Herod Agrippa I was in Rome he made an important friend. That friend was Gaius, the grandnephew of Tiberius Caesar. Gaius is better known today as Caligula. When Tiberius died, Caligula became the emperor. Caligula remembered his friend Agrippa and sent him back to Palestine as king. Later on the emperor Claudius enlarged the domains of Herod Agrippa I so that he actually ruled a kingdom almost as large as that of his grandfather Herod the Great.

However, the crown was hollow. The king who wore it could never forget that he was, after all, a puppet of the caesar. When Agrippa was on his way back to Palestine, he stopped in Alexandria, Egypt. There the Greeks openly mocked and derided him. Nor was he greatly liked by his subjects. He was too much the child of Roman vice, too much given to Greek frivolity, too glib with his lip service to Judaism, too much a savage Herod, and too much an Idumean.

So Herod Agrippa I wore a crown, but it commanded little or no respect from the Jews. True, he could claim descent from Mariamne, daughter of an ancient line of Jewish priest-kings. But the wild blood of Esau ran too strongly in the veins of the Herods for any of them to be able to command much respect in the Jewish promised land. Agrippa, however, sought to make friends among the Jews when he could. He was an old hand at buttering the toast of those who wielded real power. He played up to Caiaphas, Annas, and the college of Jewish cardinals who sat in the Sanhedrin and pulled important strings.

II. THE HIDEOUS CRIME

Agrippa was politician enough to know that if he wanted to gain favor with Caiaphas and his crowd, he must side with them against the church. Most of the Sanhedrin viewed the church with hatred. They hated Christ. They hated the ignorant and unlearned men who were fast rendering Judaism obsolete. Caiaphas and his friends resented the success of the handful of Galilean fishermen who were winning thousands of converts to Christ. The Jewish leaders resented the boldness of the Christians and their complete indifference to the commands and threats issued by the Sanhedrin.

It did not take Agrippa long to put two and two together. A good way to ingratiate himself with the Jewish authorities would be to do their dirty work for them. Having no scruples, he acted to please the Sanhedrin.

A. The Death of James

"Now about that time [about the time that Paul and Barnabas showed up with a substantial cash donation from the dynamic Gentile church in Antioch for the support of poor Christians in Jerusalem] Herod the king stretched forth his hands to vex certain of the church. And he killed James the brother of John with the sword" (Acts 12:1-2). The Greek word translated "vex," *kakoō,* means "to do evil to someone, especially to harm physically or maltreat someone." In the case of James the maltreatment took the form of coldblooded murder—premeditated and malicious. Herod acted without any cause or provocation, but he thought he could get away with the crime because he sat in a seat of dictatorial power.

James had been a Galilean fisherman. He and his brother John were first cousins of Jesus. James' mother was one of the Lord's most devoted followers and accompanied Him even to the cross. At the call of Jesus, James and John left their fishing business and became the Lord's most intimate disciples. James was one of the three disciples chosen by Jesus to witness the raising of Jairus's daughter, to be present on the mount of transfiguration, and to watch and pray with Him in the garden of Gethsemane.

We can well imagine that in the infant church James was much in demand as a speaker. New converts would be eager to hear him tell over and over again of the many marvelous and mighty works of Jesus. He would recount for them firsthand the sermon on the mount, the Olivet discourse, and the many parables. He would tell how Jesus cleansed lepers, gave sight to the blind, fed multitudes, and raised the dead.

James would tell them with an embarrassed laugh how he and John had persuaded their mother to ask Jesus to give them high posts of honor in His kingdom (Matthew 20:21-28). "How little we understood about the kingdom in those days," he would say. He would look around the group and add: "Jesus answered, 'Ye know not what ye ask. Are ye able to drink of the cup that I shall drink of, and to be baptized with the baptism that I am baptized with?' We boasted that we could. Well, He gave us a chance to taste of that cup when He took us to Gethsemane, and we fell asleep. We had the chance to follow Him to Golgotha, and we ran away."

So James went quietly about his business, telling the story of Jesus to this person and that group until he filled Jerusalem with the knowledge of Christ. James' testimony was so effective that when Herod decided to vex the church, he thought it would be a good idea to get rid of James first. Thus James became the first martyr among the apostles. Herod simply ordered his henchmen to execute James and then the king sat back to reap the approval and applause of the Jewish religious elite.

B. The Detention of Peter

"Because he saw it [James' death] pleased the Jews, he proceeded further to take Peter also" (Acts 12:3). Peter was taken on the anniversary of Christ's murder. It was the feast of unleavened bread, which is closely associated with Passover. Herod was delighted with the new friendliness of the Jewish high priest and his toadies. Arresting Peter was a cheap and easy way to keep the troublesome Sanhedrin happy and content.

Herod doubtless imprisoned Peter in the strongly garrisoned fortress of Antonia, which frowned down on the temple court. Peter was locked up as tightly as any prisoner today on death row. Between him and freedom stood two iron chains, sixteen soldiers, various keepers, and an iron gate. Four relays of soldiers guarded him around the clock. There were four guards in each relay. Two of the guards stood at the door. The other two guards stood one on either side of him; doubtless, in keeping with Roman custom, Peter was actually chained to these two. Moreover, the death sentence had been signed and would be carried out the next day.

So what did Peter do? Did he pray, pleading with God to

set him free? (God had given him the keys of the kingdom, but a lot of good they were doing him now.) Did he pace the floor of his cell, grit his teeth, and bravely resolve to die like a man? Did he ask God to give him dying grace? No. He simply committed his soul to God, said goodnight to his jailers, and went to sleep! He was not just a conqueror; he was more than a conqueror.

Peter had already learned how to be crucified with Christ. The life that he now lived he lived by the faith of the Son of God (Galatians 2:20). To Peter death was simply a matter of being absent from the body and present with the Lord (2 Corinthians 5:8).

We can imagine what the angel who visited Peter in his cell said when he reported back to the courts of bliss. "What was Peter doing when I arrived? Bless you, he was sound asleep! I had to give him quite a blow to wake him up. You'd have thought he was safe and sound in his own bed."

Meanwhile the church was praying. The church knew how to pray in those days. Luke wrote, "But prayer was made without ceasing of the church unto God for him" (Acts 12:5). Peter was asleep but his brothers in Christ were wide awake. Across Jerusalem and up and down Judea all-night prayer meetings were in progress. The court of Heaven was being bombarded and blitzed by an enormous barrage of intercessory prayer.

The church could not imagine itself without big, blustering, bossy, beloved Peter. He had such a happy knack of putting his foot in his mouth and making people love him for it. God had used Peter to perform miracles. Peter was the one who preached on the day of Pentecost, the birthday of the church. Peter was the one who was speaking when the Holy Ghost was given to the Samaritans. Peter had flung wide the door of the church to the Gentiles. Peter was always way out in front of everyone else or lagging his feet far behind. Peter could tell inimitable stories about Jesus. Peter was famous for his bluff honesty; he would shout a person down one moment and weep with sorrow and regret the next. Peter had bravely faced the Sanhedrin. Peter was one of the chosen three, along with James and John, who knew Jesus best. The church could not imagine itself without Peter, so the church prayed.

On the surface it seemed as if all the odds were with Herod Agrippa I. He had the fortress and the soldiers, the power and the authority. He had the confidence of the caesar and the great seal to legitimize his actions. Behind Herod stood imperial Rome and its armies of iron. Alongside Herod stood the powerful Sanhedrin, which spoke for hundreds of thousands of Jews at home and abroad.

On the other hand there was a praying church—ordinary men, women, boys, and girls who loved Jesus. An unsaved betting man would have put his money on Herod, especially after the martyrdom of James. The God of the Christians had not lifted a finger to help him.

Then the miracle happened. Down from the heights of Heaven came Peter's angel. How we would like to know more about these angels! We each have one. Peter and Paul saw theirs. Little children have angels. Individual churches have angels.

Jacob's ladder swarms with angels. In Genesis 28 we see them ascending and descending that shining stairway. They trudge upwards weighed down with the sad stories of man's injustices, atrocities, and downright wickedness. They come back down refreshed and revived, their eyes alight with new resolve; they are returning to earth with new orders from the throne of God.

Peter's angel came to the jail. What cared the angel for iron gates and iron men? A snap of his fingers and all the guards were sound asleep. An imperious beckoning of his hand and Peter followed. (Peter, dazed and still half asleep, thought he was having a particularly interesting and vivid dream.) The door swung open of its own accord. The iron gate felt a sudden impulse to fling itself open. The gate let the great apostle of the Lamb pass and then shut itself again with a triumphant clang.

The night air smelled sweet and fresh after the fetid atmosphere of the prison. Peter turned around to thank his benefactor but he was gone! Peter was free—but by no means safe. God never does for us what we can do for ourselves, so Peter set off for the house of Mary, the mother of John Mark. Mary's house was one of the primary meeting places of the Jerusalem church.

We have all chuckled over what happened next. Rhoda, who couldn't believe that Peter was really at the door, left him standing there while she ran in to tell the news to the people who had gathered to pray. It was incredible. God had answered prayer! "It's his angel!" said the people (Acts 12:15). But Peter's persistent banging on the door at last produced the desired result. We can imagine the hubbub in that house.

Peter prudently decided to go into hiding before the morning came and off he went into the night. As for Herod, he simply added to his other crimes by ordering the execution of Peter's unoffending guards.

III. THE HAUGHTY CLAIM

Herod went back to Caesarea after all this "and there abode," the Holy Spirit says (Acts 12:19). The Greek word translated "abode," *diatribō,* literally means "to rub away, to spend time." Herod went on rubbing away the little bit of time he had left.

Then a crisis arose in the coastal cities of Tyre and Sidon, old Phoenician trading centers. Herod exerted pressure, things came to a head, and the cities gave in. When the cities sent a delegation to Caesarea to make their peace with the royal tyrant, Herod decided to make an occasion out of it. He would accept the surrender with suitable festivities and all due pomp and circumstance.

On the second day of the festivities Herod decided to make an especially grand entrance. He put on a gorgeous robe woven throughout with strands of silver. He entered the theater where everyone was assembled at the break of day so that the first rays of the rising sun would shine on him. His robe blazed and flashed as though with fire and the people cried out, "This is a god!"

Then the watching angel smote him. As Herod drank in the adulation of his subjects, God summoned worms to gnaw at his intestines. Five days later he died in agony. The invisible watcher made his report; the invisible worm did his work. Herod was only fifty-four. He had been king for less than seven years.

The judgment of God is not always that obvious but it is always certain. We may not see the immediate sequence of cause and effect, but we can be sure that it is there.

Herod Agrippa I was dead and damned "but the word of God grew and multiplied" (Acts 12:24). The Word of God lived on. It lives on still, and will live on and on even when time will be no more. God buries the opposition, and His work and His Word go on.

9
Philip,
the Busiest Deacon

Acts 6:2-5; 8:5-40

I. THE CLAN
II. THE MAN
III. THE PLAN

There was a problem in the Jerusalem church—too many apostles in too small a space. They were all there. Their horizons began and ended in Jerusalem, their native Galilee, and surrounding Judea. The Lord's last words had been plain enough: "Ye shall be witnesses unto me both in Jerusalem, and in all Judaea, and in Samaria, and unto the uttermost part of the earth" (Acts 1:8). But no one took these words seriously, except Philip—and he wasn't even an apostle.

I. THE CLAN

In those days Christianity was clannish. One had to be a Jew to get into the church. One had to subscribe to a temple-oriented, ritual-related, legalistically-leavened form of Christianity. Peter endorsed that idea, as did James. Even though James was a latecomer, the fact that he had been the Lord's brother gave him special leverage within the Jerusalem church. James was a born legalist, a dedicated ascetic, and a convinced *Jewish* Christian. The other Christians were all intimidated by James.

The church was a Jewish church. The central and pivotal point of gathering was the temple. Christians tried to keep the peace with the Sanhedrin, the synagogue, and the sanctuary. The martyrdom of Stephen had rocked the boat; Christians had to be careful. They tried not to do anything that would cause offense.

The church, let it be said, was a big clan because a great many Jews had become Christians. That is, they had become Jewish Christians—law-keeping, circumcision-advocating, Sabbath-observing Christians. In their minds Christianity was just another form of Judaism, albeit an elevated and enlightened form. A great many priests had become Christians and the Pharisees were inclined to lean toward a Christianity that upheld the Mosaic law.

Peter, James, John, Thomas, Matthew, Philip, Nathanael, and the rest of the apostles were at the heart of the clan. We can be sure they were all very busy because there were thousands of people in the Jerusalem church alone.

Doubtless the apostles were popular speakers. They would be in demand for all kinds of meetings: gatherings in the temple courts, meetings for teaching doctrine, meetings for fellowship, meetings for breaking of bread, prayer meetings, home meetings, and baptisms. Many people would want to hear the authentic story of Jesus firsthand from those who had spent three and one-half years in His company.

The apostles were the proper custodians of the gospel. They could describe the Lord's many miracles and recount His wonderful teachings word for word. They knew His parables, His famous sermon on the mount, His Olivet discourse, and His teaching in the upper room by heart. None of Christ's words had as yet been written down, so the memories of the apostles were vital.

So the apostles were kept busy enough speaking. And it was still the age of miracles. Was anyone sick? Let him call for an apostle. Gifts of healing were still part of the accrediting phenomena of an apostle. Peter had even raised the dead.

The apostles would receive messages from all over the country. "Can Peter come to Capernaum and preach in the synagogue for the next three sabbaths?" "Can John come to Joppa? A brother here is desperately ill." "Can Thomas come to Tiberius and tell how the Lord convinced him that the resurrection was real?" Invitations kept pouring in. How could the apostles respond to these calls when they could hardly keep up with the work in Jerusalem?

The social side of the gospel continued to be somewhat of a headache also. The poor seemed to be getting poorer. There was no longer any question of unfairness in the distribution of funds, but there never seemed to be enough money to go around.

The church was all very correct, very conservative, very clannish, very careful, and reasonably comfortable. But God never intended for the apostles to be comfortable. He intended for them to get going to the ends of the earth. A ship tied up in harbor is usually very safe. But ships are built for the high seas—for breasting angry waves and defying storms.

The clan had comfortably forgotten the words of the Master (Acts 1:8). The apostles had evangelized Jerusalem and Judea and were content. Actually Jerusalem and Judea had more or less evangelized themselves. With the tremendous impetus of Pentecost the gospel had quickly spread over the homeland. But what about Samaria?

We can imagine the apostles themselves discussing that question. Jude the obscure might have said, "What about Samaria? Aren't we supposed to evangelize Samaria? That would be a good job for you, Peter. You always seem to like the lead and the limelight. Why don't you take the lead and go to Samaria?"

Peter would say, "Well I like that! Don't you people forget

that I'm the apostle to the circumcision. John, you wanted to call down fire on Samaria some years ago. Now's your chance. Go and call down some Pentecostal fire on Samaria. You're just the man for the job."

John would reply, "I don't feel any leading in that direction at all. Thomas, you're a converted skeptic. That would be a good place for you to go. We all know how skeptical the Samaritans would be if one of us Jews showed up and offered to be friendly. As a cured skeptic you'd be just the man to break down their barriers."

Thomas would say, "Thanks for nothing. Matthew's the man for that job, it seems to me. After all he was a tax collector at one time. He had no scruples in those days, so scruples shouldn't bother him now. We Jews have scruples about the Samaritans. Evangelizing *them* would be a good job for Matthew."

We can hear Matthew reply, "Let's put our hands on Simon the Zealot. What a marvelous job for him!"

Finally the Holy Spirit left them to their complacent inaction and turned to one of the new deacons instead. He said in effect, "Come on, Philip. You come with me. You and I will go on down to Samaria. We'll show them how it's done."

So Philip went to Samaria and revival broke out. Lives were transformed. Miracles happened. People were saved. The whole place turned upside down. "And the people *with one accord,*" Luke said, "gave heed" (Acts 8:6, italics added). Luke said the same thing of the disciples when just before Pentecost they were in the upper room eagerly awaiting the coming of the Holy Spirit: "They were all with one accord" (Acts 2:1).

There was great joy in Samaria (Acts 8:8) and there was great joy when the Welsh revival broke out. G. Campbell Morgan recorded his impression of the Welsh revival: "No song books, but ah, me! I nearly wept tonight over the singing of our last hymn. No choir did I say? It was all choir. And hymns! I stood and listened with wonder and amazement as the congregation sang hymn after hymn without hymn books. No advertising. The thing advertises itself. All over the country people were converted just by reading the newspaper accounts."

Revival came to Samaria and sure enough the devil had his counterfeit all ready and waiting, a scoundrel by the name of Simon Magus. All sorts of extraordinary and extrabiblical stories are told about Simon Magus.[1] It was said that he could make statues walk. He could roll himself in fire without being burned. He could turn stones into loaves, open bolted doors, melt iron, and produce phantoms at banquets. He could cause vessels in his house to move about and wait on him at the dinner table. Probably mesmerism was involved. Still, the stories circulated and continued after his apostasy.

Simon Magus was fascinated by the power of the Holy Ghost displayed by Philip. In fact Simon made a profession of faith in Christ and was baptized. It must have been the talk of the town. "Have you heard about Simon the sorcerer?"

"No, what has he done now?"

"He has become a Christian. He has been baptized. Can you believe it? They say he sits right up front at all the preacher's meetings."

Meanwhile the news of the revival in Samaria filtered back to Jerusalem and made its belated impact on the clan. The apostles decided they must get involved and sent both Peter and John.

Inevitably Simon met Simon. Simon Magus watched with astonishment as the Samaritan believers received the Holy Ghost when Simon Peter laid his hands on them. The laying on of hands was a method that was essential in the case of the Samaritans. The centuries-long animosity between the Jews and Samaritans made it absolutely necessary that the leaders of the Jerusalem church extend some special gesture of goodwill to the Samaritans so that they would not feel themselves to be second-class citizens in the kingdom of God.

Simon Magus was fascinated by the signs that accompanied the giving of the Holy Spirit. It was not long before he betrayed himself. "Sell me the secret," he said in effect. "I'd like to be able to give the Holy Ghost by the laying on of hands."

Peter turned on him in a flash. "Thy money perish with thee. . . . Thou hast neither part nor lot in this matter: for thy heart is not right in the sight of God. . . . thou art in the gall of bitterness, and in the bond of iniquity" (Acts 8:20-23). But Peter did not go beyond reading the innermost secrets of this unregenerate soul. Death had followed the sin of Ananias and Sapphira because they were truly saved and came under apostolic jurisdiction. But Simon Magus was not genuinely saved and Peter left his punishment to God.

Simon Peter exposed the man as an impostor and turned away and left him. Frightened, Simon Magus asked Peter to pray for him. But that was not what the wretched man needed; he needed to pray for himself. If tradition is to be believed, he went back to his sorcery and founded one of the gnostic cults. He is said to have turned up in Rome where he performed his magic tricks even in the court of the caesar.

The events in Samaria made a deep impression on the clan. Peter and John "preached the gospel in many villages of the Samaritans" (Acts 8:25).

As for Philip, God called him away to another task.

II. THE MAN

God is just as interested in individuals as He is in nations. He cared about an Ethiopian eunuch as much as He cared about Samaria.

Any one of the apostles might have had the opportunity of meeting the man from Ethiopia, leading him to Christ, and being instrumental in planting the church in the heart of Africa. But no! The Holy Spirit knew that Peter's and John's hearts were in Jerusalem even while they were touring Samaria. So the Holy Spirit whispered again to Philip the deacon: "Come on, Philip. You and I have an appointment with the secretary of the treasury of the kingdom of Ethiopia."

Responsive as always to the Holy Spirit (one of the qualifications required of a deacon in the Jerusalem church) Philip went off to the desert. He left behind him a flourishing revival. Philip had no question, no quarrel, and no quibble about leaving the limelight to Peter. Philip responded quickly and quietly to the Spirit of God.

So Philip went toward Gaza, to the high road to Egypt. There he waited until on the distant horizon he saw a cloud of dust that soon resolved itself into a group of chariots. They carried the chancellor of the Ethiopian exchequer and his escort.

Like the Samaritans this man stood in a kind of "half relationship" to the nation of Israel. The Samaritans were pagan cousins; the Ethiopian seems to have been a proselyte cousin. He had gone to Jerusalem to worship but apparently he was bitterly disappointed. Possibly he was as disappointed as Martin Luther, who upon arriving at Rome, the city of his dreams, found it full of religious arrogance, pomp, power, and pride and turned from it with disgust and dismay.

We can picture this Ethiopian as he wandered around the city about which he had read and heard so much. Jerusalem was associated with Melchizedek, David, Solomon, and the queen of Sheba! Jerusalem was the city of poets and prophets, the home of the temple, and the heart of a spiritual empire.

No doubt the Ethiopian attended the Jerusalem synagogues and listened to the rules, regulations, and accumulated religious rubbish that the rabbis propounded in the name of God. He probably went to the temple, only to find himself shut out of most of it. The court of the Gentiles would be about as far as he could go and that was more like a mercantile exchange than a sanctuary. He probably wondered, *Why don't the temple authorities clean up this temple traffic?* We can imagine his shock when he discovered that the authorities owned the concessions.

Wandering around the markets of Jerusalem he probably found a shop where portions of the Scriptures were for sale--hand-copied, authorized, and very expensive. Perhaps while browsing through a beautiful copy of the prophecy of Isaiah the word *Ethiopia* caught his eye and he decided to buy it. He could not have made a better choice if he'd asked the chief rabbi himself for advice.

Maybe the Ethiopian heard rumors about the church and went to Annas or Caiaphas with his inquiries. (A man in high social and political position would go to the top.) We can well imagine what kind of answers the high priest and his crowd would have given. And we can wonder why Andrew or Thomas did not lead the Ethiopian to Christ. Perhaps the church avoided him because he was black and a Gentile.

We can speculate that he was sad at heart, empty of soul, and disillusioned as he wandered about the holy city. We know for certain that he went to Jerusalem to worship and that he came away as hungry of heart as when he arrived.

Still seeking, still longing, the Ethiopian headed for home. His entourage arrived first at Gaza and then headed toward Egypt. Ahead of him lay a journey of hundreds and hundreds of miles back to his native land.

When Philip caught up to him, he was reading the prophecy of Isaiah. Although the Ethiopian could not understand what he was reading, he had persevered through fifty-two chapters and was in the middle of the fifty-third. Suddenly he heard a voice that seemed to come from Heaven itself. The speaker must have suspected his bewilderment: "Excuse me, sir. Do you understand what you're reading?" The Ethiopian looked up and saw running alongside his chariot a messenger of God—very earthy and dusty and out-of-breath.

The Spirit had been waiting until this critical moment. Then He had whispered to Philip, "Run, Philip. That's the man, the one in the first chariot, the one reading that book. Run!" Thus the text, the teacher, and the traveler converged on Isaiah 53:7. The Ethiopian was reading these words: "He was led as a sheep to the slaughter; and like a lamb dumb before his shearer, so opened he not his mouth . . . his life is taken from the earth" (as quoted in Acts 8:32-33).

"Of whom speakest the prophet this?" asked the Ethiopian. "Of himself, or of some other man?" (Acts 8:34) Could anyone have asked a more appropriate question? What an opening for a soul-winner. And Philip "began at the same scripture, and preached unto him Jesus" (8:35). Of course he did! Fortunately for the Ethiopian, Philip had not studied at a liberal theological seminary. If he had he would have begun, "Well you see, sir, I subscribe to the deutero-Isaiah hypothesis. Before I can answer your question we must first settle which Isaiah we are talking about."

Thankfully Philip did not expose the inquirer to that kind of high-sounding nonsense. Philip was simply a humble, Bible-believing evangelist. From that magnificent text he led the Ethiopian straight into the arms of Jesus. The preaching of Philip is a classic in personal evangelism.

Philip also instructed the new convert in the first steps of the Christian walk. Philip told the Ethiopian he needed to be baptized now that he had accepted Christ. The Holy Spirit, still in charge, arranged for another of those divine "coincidences" that so often occur in soulwinning: an oasis was nearby. The Ethiopian wasted no time. "See, here is water," he said. "What doth hinder me to be baptized?"

In front of his wondering entourage this high-placed government official stopped his chariot and followed Philip into the water. Having acknowledged the Ethiopian's confession of faith, Philip immersed his illustrious convert.

What happened next is one of those mysteries we will explore with greater understanding when we receive our resurrection bodies and stand with the Ethiopian in Heaven. Then we will hear his testimony from his own lips. For now we can just imagine what he will say.

"I came up out of the water, I rubbed the water from my eyes, and I turned to say something to the man who had appeared out of nowhere, but he wasn't there. He had vanished back into nowhere. I asked my servants, 'Where's that Jewish preacher I picked up a little while back south of Gaza?'

'He seems to have vanished, my lord,' one of them replied. 'Well, he can't have gone far,' I said. 'The country is as flat as a pond. Stand on the high point of the chariot and find out if you can see him.'"

But Philip had vanished. The Holy Spirit gives us the only explanation we will have this side of glory: "The Spirit of the Lord caught away Philip, that the eunuch saw him no more." The Ethiopian, however, had no doubt that God had sent him a special messenger. "He went on his way rejoicing" (Acts 8:39). Meanwhile Philip had been miraculously and instantly transported twenty miles up the coast to the old Philistine city of Ashdod (Azotus).

III. THE PLAN

The divine plan of course was to evangelize the whole Gentile world. The Lord's mandate was to "be witnesses unto me . . . unto the uttermost part of the earth" (Acts 1:8). Nothing could be done about the mandate, however, until the apostles took the divine plan seriously.

The Lord was about to jolt Peter out of his complacency and send him, whether he liked it or not, to the home of a Gentile. Even then the Jerusalem apostles would still be content to drag their feet, but once the door was officially open to Gentiles, the Lord would call and anoint a new apostle—Paul.

In the meantime Philip made tentative attempts at Gentile evangelism himself. He headed up the old Philistine-Phoenician coastline and visited city after city. Ashdod, Lydda, and Joppa were all on his route. On and on he journeyed northward until at last he came to Caesarea.

Caesarea was a bustling modern city with an atmosphere like Rome's. Caesarea was as unlike the sleepy old Palestinian towns as one could imagine. It was the seat of the Roman government in Palestine. An engineering marvel, Caesarea was a bustling seaport. It was the home of the occupying garrison and had such Roman necessities as baths and stadium. The Jews shunned the place like the plague.

Here Philip took up his residence. Long after Peter had come to Caesarea to win Cornelius and his family to Christ, Philip stayed on in this strategic, outward-looking Roman city. Here he brought up his family for God and sought to be a witness for Christ in a thoroughly Gentile atmosphere. He and his family (including four prophetess daughters) were still in Caesarea twenty years later when the great apostle Paul was imprisoned in this city. Paul was attended by his Gentile companion Luke who recorded Philip's story in the book of Acts.

Philip was one man who readily entered into the divine plan to evangelize the whole world. The last glimpse the Holy Spirit gives us of Philip is in Caesarea. The next time we see him we will be in Heaven.

---

1. G. H. Pember, *Earth's Earliest Ages* (Glasgow: Pickering & Inglis, n.d.) 295-299.

10
Cornelius, the Noblest Roman

Acts 10:1–11:18

```
I. THE ROMAN
II. THE REFUSAL
III. THE REVIVAL
IV. THE REACTION
```

The conversion of Cornelius is a landmark in world history. At that point in time, divine decree and apostolic action flung open the doors of the church to the great Gentile world that stood beyond the pale of Jewish ritual religion. Until that momentous day the Jews had a virtual monopoly on the things of God. Gentiles had to become Jews in order to participate in the revealed worship of God.

What made matters worse was that the Jews detested the Gentiles and said abominable things about them.[1] The Jews said Gentile idolaters should be cut down with the sword. The Jews said that just as the best kind of serpent was a crushed serpent, so the best kind of Gentile was a dead Gentile. They asserted that of all nations, God loved only Israel. According to the rabbis it was not lawful for a Jew to help a Gentile woman in childbirth because he would be helping to bring another Gentile into the world. If a Jew were to marry a Gentile, from that time forward that Jew was to be considered as dead. Just entering a Gentile house would render a Jew unclean.

A Gentile visiting the Jewish temple in Jerusalem could only go as far as the court of the Gentiles, which was the first and lowest of the various courts. Even there the rabbis showed contempt. They turned that court into a marketplace for buying cattle and changing money.

Beyond the court of the Gentiles was the court of the women, then the court of Israel, and then the court of the priests. Finally, on the highest plane, was the temple. If a Gentile approached the court of the women, he was stopped by a barrier that stood four or five feet high. This barrier was called "the middle wall of partition." Prominent notices displayed on the wall stated in both Greek and Latin that no Gentile was permitted to pass the wall and that the penalty for trespassing was death. Paul himself was nearly torn apart by the Jews because of a false rumor that he had taken a Gentile beyond the barrier.

Naturally the Gentiles responded in kind. They hated and persecuted the Jews. But as far as God was concerned, all difference between Jew and Gentile was abolished and the enmity between Jew and Gentile was removed when Cornelius was converted.

Paul wrote to the Ephesians that in Christ the old enmity is abolished (Ephesians 2:15). Jew and Gentile are made one. There is not a Jewish church and a Gentile church; there is just one church in which all differences of race and caste are forgotten. Before Christ, barriers went up. In Christ, barriers came down, just as the walls of Jericho tumbled before the trumpets of Joshua.

Little did Peter understand the significance of what he did that day when he put his pride and prejudice in his pocket, walked from Joppa to Caesarea, and entered the home of a Gentile soldier to lead him to Christ. Already the Samaritans had been invited into the church. Already an Ethiopian Jewish proselyte had been invited in. Now a full-blooded Gentile and his family were invited in. Soon churches would spring up in Galatia, Corinth, Ephesus, and Rome. The Jewish church headquartered in Jerusalem had tens of thousands of members, but soon Antioch would replace Jerusalem as the center of Christianity, Greek would replace Hebrew as the language of divine revelation, and Gentile Christians would enormously outnumber Jewish Christians.

I. THE ROMAN

In Shakespeare's *Julius Caesar* Antony said of the fallen Brutus: "This was the noblest Roman of them all." Not so! The noblest Roman of them all was a mere centurion named Cornelius. He was stationed on the coast of Palestine at Caesarea, an important seaport built by Herod the Great.

Herod had a long career in creating monuments of magnificent proportions. His trophies included the temple in Jerusalem, the winter palace in Jericho, and the practically impregnable Dead Sea fortress of Masada. His crowning achievement was Caesarea, named in honor of Caesar Augustus.

Herod hoped Caesarea would become a great metropolis rivaling Alexandria in Egypt. Caesarea stood on a direct trade route running east and west from Babylon to Rome. Byzantium was only a twenty-day sail away and Rome itself just two months by sea. Caesarea's layout was the grid plan favored by the Romans. The city contained a forum, baths, offices, temples, houses, villas, and marble statues. A great lighthouse guided ships from afar and an aqueduct brought water from mount Carmel, nine miles away.

Roman engineers had overcome enormous technical difficulties because the site had no natural advantages. It had no coastal bays, headland, or islands to which the harbor could be anchored. The strong current, heavy silting, and rough seas had all posed structural problems. Herod had even used hydraulic concrete, which hardens under water! The magnificent city with its two harbors was a monumental achievement.

Caesarea, with all its paganism and luxury, was the natural capital of Rome in conquered Palestine. Forty-seven miles from Jerusalem, Caesarea was the place where the governor lived. The Jews hated the place. The Romans loved it. It was here that the centurion Cornelius lived.

Cornelius was a noncommissioned officer in the tenth legion of the Roman army. He commanded a special regiment known as the Italian band, a cohort of one thousand men whose duty was to help keep the peace in the province of Palestine. The Italian band was made up of troops drawn exclusively from Italy, and since no provincial troops or mercenaries were in the ranks, this cohort was considered especially reliable. Cornelius, the leader of this privileged regiment, was one of those centurions who were the backbone of the Roman army. They were chosen for their ability to lead men, for their courage, and for their willingness to stand and fight to the last man.

Cornelius was an extraordinary person. He was a devout God-fearing Gentile, though not a Jewish proselyte. Being a proselyte involved circumcision and becoming more or less a Jew. A proselyte was offered admittance to the rites and ordinances of the Jewish religion, but most Gentiles felt that the benefits were not worth the cost. Cornelius was one of those men who were disillusioned by the pagan religions of their day and were greatly attracted to the ethical, moral, and spiritual beliefs of the Jews. But they drew the line at becoming virtually Jews themselves.

The Jews called such people "proselytes of the gate" and sometimes "God-fearers." As far as the Jews were concerned, "God-fearers" were still Gentiles, still outside the covenant, and still aliens to the commonwealth of Israel.

Yet the Holy Spirit speaks highly of Cornelius: "A devout

man, and one that feared God with all his house, which gave much alms to the people, and prayed to God alway" (Acts 10:2). Cornelius had achieved as much as a man of his character, background, training, and ability could achieve, and his name was known in Heaven.

But the Jewish Christians did not seem to care about Cornelius and his fellow Gentiles. In the eight years since Pentecost nobody had come from Jerusalem to tell him, or any member of the Roman garrison, that Jesus had died for sinners on that skull-shaped hill in Jerusalem, that He had been buried, that He had risen from the dead, and that He had ascended to the right hand of the Majesty on high. Nobody had told him that the Holy Spirit had come and the church was being formed. Nobody had told him that the living God of the universe "so loved the world, that he gave his only begotten Son, that whosoever believeth in him should not perish, but have everlasting life" (John 3:16). Peter, James, and John had never bothered with Caesarea. To enter such a place, they reasoned, would be to contaminate themselves. "The uttermost part of the earth" was at their doorstep, yet they had little concern.

So God sent an angel to Cornelius, but He did not commission that angel to preach the gospel to him. (Preaching is our job, not the job of the angels. Had that angel been commissioned to preach the gospel, he would have taken Rome by storm. Soon Britain, Gaul, Parthia, Media, and the ends of the earth would have been reached for Christ. The job would have been completed ten times over in eight years.) God allowed that angel to say but one thing: in essence, "Send for one Simon staying with one Simon" (Acts 10:5-6). And that is exactly what Cornelius did.

II. THE REFUSAL

Simon Peter was staying in the house of Simon the tanner. That fact is significant. The Jews held the trade of the tanner in horror and disgust because it involved handling the skins of dead animals. To touch a dead body under the Levitical ritual code rendered a man ceremonially unclean. By rabbinic law a tanner's house had to be located at least fifty cubits outside a city to decrease the danger of accidental contamination of a devout Jew. If a Jewish girl married a man and found out later that her husband was a tanner, her marriage could be automatically declared null and void. So Simon Peter's prejudices were wearing thin if he could stay with Simon the tanner.

One afternoon Peter announced that he was hungry. His host suggested he retire to the flat roof of the house with its grand view of the Mediterranean and rest while food was being prepared. Peter fell asleep and had the famous vision of the sheet. Down it came from Heaven. The sheet was full of all sorts of creatures pronounced unclean by the Mosaic law: crabs, oysters, shrimp, rabbits, pigs, and all the rest. He heard a voice saying, "Rise, Peter; kill, and eat" (Acts 10:13). Righteously indignant, Peter said, "Not so, Lord; for I have never eaten any thing that is common or unclean" (10:14). G. Campbell Morgan points out that "Not so, Lord" is not a strong enough translation. "Lord, by no means" would be a more accurate rendering. Back came the divine decree: "What God hath cleansed, that call not thou common" (10:15).

The vision occurred three times. Then as Peter rubbed his eyes and tried to decide what the vision meant, the Holy Spirit said to him, "Behold, three men seek thee. Arise therefore, and get thee down, and go with them, doubting nothing: for I have sent them" (Acts 10:19-20). And sure enough there was a knock at the door. His host called up the stairs, "Peter, are you awake? There are three men to see you—Gentiles from Caesarea. One of the soldiers sent them." "Ask them in, Simon," Peter said. "I'm coming right down."

The men had a message and an invitation: "Cornelius the centurion, a just man, and one that feareth God, and of good report among all the nation of the Jews, was warned from God by an holy angel to send for thee into his house, and to hear words of thee" (Acts 10:22).

So that was the meaning of the vision, Peter may have thought. *I must not call Gentiles like Cornelius common or unclean for God has cleansed them. I must go.* It didn't take long for Peter to decide. For the first time in his life he would go to a Gentile city and accept the hospitality of a Gentile home.

It was too late to walk the thirty miles to Caesarea that day so Peter threw caution to the winds. "This," we can hear him say, "is my host, Simon the tanner. I am Simon Peter, an apostle of the Lord Jesus Christ, the Messiah of Israel and the Savior of the world. You fellows had best stay for supper and spend the night here. We'll leave first thing tomorrow morning."

We can imagine too what a lively discussion Peter and his guests had that night. Peter would have asked, "Have you met a man named Philip? He's a friend and colleague of mine. I understand he's living somewhere in Caesarea."

"No sir, we have never heard of the gentleman. Is he a purveyor to the garrison?"

"No, as a matter of fact he's a preacher."

"I wonder why the centurion sent us all the way to Joppa if there's a preacher in town."

"My visit to Cornelius is a much bigger matter than talking to a preacher. This involves a radical departure from anything we have ever done before. This involves opening the door of the church to Gentiles. Until now it has been made up of just Jews. This step calls for the involvement of a prophet and an apostle. Let me tell you about the dream I had this afternoon just about the time you were approaching Joppa . . . "

Perhaps Peter asked questions about Cornelius. Perhaps the men asked questions about Christ. The night must have been far too short for answering all the questions.

Wasting no time, off they went the next day—Peter, the three men, and some Jewish Christians invited by Peter to come along and be impartial witnesses to the historic event that would soon take place in a Gentile city. Significantly, Caesarea faced the Mediterranean sea and looked toward an enormous Gentile world.

III. THE REVIVAL

The centurion treated Peter as though he were more than a man. That is not surprising when we think about it. How many people have ever been given your name and address by an angel? In all the years I have been preaching nobody has ever asked me to come to a meeting because an angel gave him my name and address.

When Peter arrived the house was packed. The word had spread to friends and relatives that Cornelius had seen an angel. *Cornelius?* they may have thought. *The centurion? Surely not. He's not the type. Mrs. Cornelius maybe, but not him. You don't get to be a centurion in the Italian cohort if you're the type that sees angels.*

Peter had an eager and receptive audience. He began by explaining why he, a Jew, was willing to accept an invitation to the home of a Gentile. Then he went straight into the story of Jesus.

Peter's sermon in the house of Cornelius is usually considered to be the draft for Mark's Gospel. The book of Mark was the first of the four Gospels to be written. It was written especially for Romans and reflects the preaching of Peter. Mark's Gospel divides into two parts, as focused by the key verse: "For even the Son of man came not to be ministered unto, but to minister, and to give his life a ransom for many" (Mark 10:45). First we see the Lord Jesus giving His life in *service* and then we see Him giving His life in *sacrifice*.

The message of Mark is just what Peter preached to Cornelius. First Peter spoke of Jesus giving His life in service. "God anointed Jesus of Nazareth with the Holy Ghost and with power: who went about doing good, and healing all that were oppressed of the devil; for God was with him" (Acts 10:38). Then Peter spoke of Jesus giving His life in sacrifice. "Whom they [the Jews and the Gentiles alike] slew and hanged on a tree: Him God raised up the third day, and shewed him openly" (10:39-40).

And then it happened. Revival broke out in that home. The Holy Spirit came down just like at Pentecost. The same signs appeared. God did not send these signs to convince the Gentiles. They needed no convincing. They were ready to believe whatever Peter told them. God sent the signs to convince Peter and the Jewish brothers who accompanied him.

Probably nothing less than this dramatic pouring out of the Holy Spirit on the Gentiles would have convinced the Jerusalem church that it was no longer an exclusive Jewish club. The "middle wall of partition" was broken down. Judaism, even in its Christian form, was obsolete. Gentiles did not have to become Jews in order to become Christians.

But it took the conversion of the apostle Paul, the outbreak of revival in Antioch, the first church conference in Jerusalem, the united testimony of Peter and Barnabas and Paul and James, the writing of the letter to the Galatians, and the writing of the letter to the Ephesians to make the truth begin to sink in. The Jerusalem church was broken up, its people were scattered and deported, the temple was destroyed, and the nation of Israel was dissolved before the truth finally sank in. Judaism was not essential to Christianity; in fact Judaism was a ball and chain around Christianity's leg.

Even to this day some people have the idea that Messianic Jews should have their own separate church in which the various dead forms of Judaism can be observed as part of Christianity. That kind of thinking shows how difficult it is to slay error.

Peter and his friends stayed on at Caesarea for a few days. No doubt he did some sightseeing, but that was not the reason he stayed. He stayed to teach the new Gentile Christians the rudiments of New Testament faith and then he hurried back home.

IV. THE REACTION

While Peter was preaching and teaching and building up the infant Gentile congregation in pagan Caesarea, news filtered back to Jerusalem. (It is amazing how things get around.) One would think that the Jerusalem church would have been delighted to hear what had happened in the home of Cornelius. Not so. The elders in Jerusalem were horrified. They could hardly believe their ears. Peter had disgraced himself, betrayed the church, and practically denied the faith. He had not only gone to the pagan city of Caesarea; he had actually entered a Gentile's house. Worse still, he had taken others with him. Worse yet, he had remained there. Rumor and gossip embellished the story so that by the time Peter came back the Jewish church was ready to excommunicate him.

It says something about the spiritual state of the Jerusalem church that so soon after Pentecost and the great commission the chief apostle could be put on trial for doing exactly what an apostle was supposed to do—what the whole church was supposed to do. He was supposed to preach the gospel to all men everywhere without regard to color, class, or creed. Just because Peter had failed to dot his *i's* and cross his *t's* the way they expected, the Jerusalem believers were outraged. Here was legalism at its worst.

Peter must have been thankful for his independent witnesses as he told the Jerusalem church the story from beginning to end. "The Holy Ghost fell on them, as on us," he said. "What was I, that I could withstand God?" (Acts 11:15,17)

The unbelieving Jewish Christians would never have believed in a thousand years that God could love Gentiles the way He loved Jews if the sign gifts had not followed the baptism of the Holy Spirit in Caesarea. Tongues were a sign to the Jews and in the end they were convinced. Grudgingly they conceded that Peter's preaching to Cornelius was of God, but they didn't like it and they did nothing to follow it up. They sent no missionaries to Caesarea. They did not invite Cornelius to come to Jerusalem and meet the church. But God already had His man in Caesarea. Philip was there to do, as before, what they failed to do.

As for us, we can say, "Peter, we are glad you went to Caesarea. We are glad you met Cornelius. We are glad that a second Pentecost put Cornelius and us on the same spiritual footing before God as you. The Lord knew what He was doing when He enrolled you in the apostolic band."

---

1. Alfred Edersheim, *The Life and Times of Jesus the Messiah* (Grand Rapids: Eerdmans, 1959) I:90-92.

11
Saul of Tarsus, the Greatest Convert

I. THE MIRACLE OF SAUL'S CONVERSION
   A. The Vigor of His Personality
   B. The Violence of His Persuasion
   C. The Vindictiveness of His Passion
II. THE MANNER OF SAUL'S CONVERSION
   A. A Tremendous Revelation
   B. A Total Revolution
   C. A Typical Resolution
III. THE MEANING OF SAUL'S CONVERSION
   A. Complete the Inspiring of the Word
   B. Commence the Evangelizing of the World

W hen young Saul of Tarsus had his first taste of blood at the stoning of Stephen, it turned him into a tiger. "Here, you fellows," we can imagine he said to the men who were marching Stephen to the place of execution.

"Put your coats down here. I'll keep an eye on them." Off those coats came, and down they went in a heap at the feet of that imperious young man. "Now then, you fellows, let's see what you can do. Fifty shekels to the man who bounces the first stone off that apostate's head. . . . Well hit, sir. . . . Come on! Hit him again. He's still alive. Listen to the canting hypocrite praying for us. Come on! A hundred shekels to the man who finishes him off."

We can be sure that Stephen will receive a martyr's crown at the judgment seat of Christ. He will be the first in a long and noble lineup of people who washed their robes in the blood of the Lamb and were willing to sacrifice their lives for the cause of Christ. There can be little doubt that Stephen will also receive a soul-winner's crown for the subsequent conversion of Saul, because Saul came away from Stephen's blood-splashed golgotha with three memories embedded deeply in his soul.

First, Saul came away from the stoning of Stephen with some *unforgettable facts*. There is at least a hint in the New Testament that Saul of Tarsus had debated the great truths of the gospel with this keen, Spirit-filled deacon of the Jerusalem church. Let's assume Saul had and imagine what the debate was like.

Saul brought to the encounter a formidable mind, schooled by the brightest teachers of his day. He was a trained rabbi, far ahead of all others in his class. He was the future Gamaliel, perhaps the future high priest of Israel. Saul had the drive, determination, discipline, and dedication required.

He was quite sure that in a debate he could make mincemeat out of Stephen, but Stephen made mincemeat out of Saul. Saul should not have been surprised because he was debating a man full of the Holy Ghost. Saul was up against the Mind that designed the universe, the Mind that inspired Moses, David, Daniel, and Isaiah. Saul was up against the One who wrote all thirty-nine books of the Old Testament and who was busy writing all twenty-seven books of the New Testament. Saul was up against the Holy Spirit.

Stephen looked into Saul's flushed face, straight into his fiery eyes, and said: "But Saul, it behooved Christ to suffer. David said, 'They pierced my hands and my feet.' Of whom did the prophet speak, Saul? Of himself or of some other man? Did not Isaiah say, 'Who hath believed our report? He was led as a lamb to the slaughter'?"

Saul hated what he heard, but he could not gainsay what the Scriptures said. After the debate the stubborn facts of Scripture lay like dormant seeds in his soul. These facts waited like lurking lions in the underbrush of his mind for the moment when they could leap out and tear him to pieces deep inside. He could stone Stephen, but he could not silence Stephen. Even when dead, Stephen still spoke.

Second, Saul came away from the stoning of Stephen with the vision of an *unforgettable faith*. Never could Saul forget Stephen's testimony before the Sanhedrin. Friendless and forsaken, alone in the arena, surrounded by hostile and bitter men, Stephen had been bold under God. The words of his testimony had made the courtroom ring. Stephen's faith embraced the whole Old Testament revelation and he had poured it out like molten lava, heated seven times in the furnace of Calvary. Saul beat his ears with his hands but that noble testimony still rang in his soul. He considered himself to be a man of faith, but his faith was like a cup of tea compared to the vast ocean-fullness of Stephen's faith.

Third, Saul came away from the stoning of Stephen with the memory of an *unforgettable face*. Saul had never seen anyone die looking like an angel. Saul had known that men would die for their faith. He had known that men would die out of fanaticism in spite of the fear that their eyes betrayed. But he had not known anyone could die the way Stephen did. The religious elite of Israel had gnashed on Stephen with their teeth like so many wild animals. Yet the more they had allowed hate and wrath to distort their faces, the more the face of Stephen had shone. It had glowed with the light of another world.

That angel face haunted Saul. It looked at him through the

darkness of his bedroom. It hovered over every landscape. In *Oliver Twist* Charles Dickens told how the face of Nancy haunted Bill Sikes, her murderer, and drove him to a frenzy. Similarly the face of Stephen haunted Saul until it drove him to Jesus. When at last on the Damascus road he saw the face of Jesus, it reminded him of the face of Stephen. Stephen had become so like his Lord that the likeness showed in his very face.

I. THE MIRACLE OF SAUL'S CONVERSION

The conversion of Saul of Tarsus was a miracle of grace that may still be the talk of every quarter and canton of the celestial city.

Imagine for a moment that we are in Jerusalem before Saul's conversion. Here comes a member of the Sanhedrin. Ask him if he thinks Saul will ever become a Christian.

"Saul? Saul of Tarsus become a Christian?" he exclaims. "Why he'd rather eat pork or worship Jupiter!"

Here comes a new widow with her fatherless children. Ask her. The activities of Saul, grand inquisitor of the Sanhedrin, led to her husband's death.

"Saul? Saul of Tarsus become a Christian?" she responds. "It would take a special dispensation of God's grace to make a Christian out of that man, but I pray for him."

But Saul of Tarsus *did* become a Christian in spite of all the obstacles of birth, breeding, background, belief, and behavior. He became a Christian in spite of the vigor of his personality, the violence of his persuasion, and the vindictiveness of his passion.

A. The Vigor of His Personality

Some people are pliable and easily molded, but not Saul. His personality was hewn out of rock—he was all granite and iron. He would not even bow to the established party line, though it was enunciated by his teacher and mentor Gamaliel.

"Leave them alone lest you end up fighting against God" was Gamaliel's advice. *Nonsense!* thought Saul. *Coexist with Christianity? With all due respect, Gamaliel is getting old and soft.*

Saul was hard as a diamond, inflexible and adamant. He summoned all the power of his forceful personality for the fight ahead. He summoned all the flaming fervor of his natural eloquence, all the thundering energy of his being, all the drive of his unbridled will. He became a pulsating engine of destruction. No Alexander, Caesar, or Napoleon ever outshone Saul of Tarsus in dynamism and determination. All his mind, soul, heart, and strength were set ablaze by his hatred for Jesus and the detested cult of the Nazarene.

B. The Violence of His Persuasion

Saul had his own convictions about the Christ of God and what kind of a Messiah He would be. The meek and lowly Jesus of Nazareth was certainly no Messiah according to Saul's book. Jesus was nothing but a weak and watery impostor.

Saul envisioned a militant Messiah—a true son of David, a man of war. The Messiah would smite the power of Rome and make Jerusalem the capital of a new world empire founded on the Mosaic law in accordance with the sayings of the prophets.

Saul was looking for a martial Messiah, not a meek Messiah. The very expression *meek Messiah* was a contradiction in terms. Saul wanted a Messiah who would let Himself be crowned, not a Messiah who would let Himself be crucified. Saul wanted a Messiah who came to reign, not a Messiah who came to redeem.

The thought of Calvary was revolting. That scene should not be the grand finale of the Messiah's sojourn on this planet. The idea that great David's greater Son should come but end up being crucified by the Romans was preposterous!

Saul knew his Bible. He knew by heart the Scripture "Cursed is every one that hangeth on a tree" (Galatians 3:13; Deuteronomy 21:23). That God's Son should hang on a tree was utterly ridiculous. Worse, it was blasphemy. Away with

anyone who preached such outrageous heresy! With Saul of
Tarsus it was no matter for mere discussion and debate.

C. The Vindictiveness of His Passion

Saul nursed in his soul such a fierce hatred of Christianity
that he offered himself to the Sanhedrin as their grand
inquisitor, their Torquemada, their licensed instrument to
stamp out this heretical cult. The wealthy aristocratic men who
ran the Sanhedrin were only too glad to have their dislike of
Jesus of Nazareth confirmed by the fiery eloquence of young
Saul and to have someone do their dirty work for them. They
gave him a mandate and a free hand.

In later years Saul himself said wonderingly that he had
been "exceedingly mad" against the Christians (Acts 26:11).
Acts 8:3 says that he "made havock of the church" and Greek
scholars tell us that no stronger metaphor could have been
used. It was used in classical Greek to describe the ravages of
a wild boar uprooting a vineyard. This metaphor occurs
nowhere else in the New Testament.

Saul had one controlling passion. It drove sleep from his
eyes and mastered all other passions and lusts. He wanted to
beat, brand, bully, and bludgeon every man, woman, boy, and
girl who named the name of Christ. He was in just such a mood
when he was racing toward Damascus the day he was saved.

Saul's attendants on the road to Damascus must have
cursed him underneath their breath. At high noon when the
merciless Syrian sun beat down from a brazen sky, any sensible
man would stop by the side of the road, find shade and shelter
beneath some palm trees, and have some lunch and a
refreshing siesta. But Saul was driven on by his hate. He was
like a man possessed. He was in a fever of rage and was afraid
that someone would get to Damascus before him and spread
the word that he was coming. He couldn't bear the thought that
some of his enemies might escape.

So the salvation of Saul of Tarsus was a miracle. He was
saved when humanly speaking everything was against his

being converted. He was saved in spite of the vigor of his personality, in spite of the violence of his persuasion, and in spite of the vindictiveness of his passion. He was saved even though he could not be reached with reasoning—one cannot reason with a man who knows he's right, who is as stubborn as a mule, and who is driven by a burning hate. Saul's conversion was nothing less than a miracle.

Actually, every conversion is a miracle. That someone born in sin, shaped in iniquity, blind to the truth of God, deaf to the gospel, dead to the Son of God, and determined to go his own way should come face to face with the risen Christ and enthrone Him as Savior and Lord is a miracle indeed. It is a miracle that happens hundreds of times every day.

II. THE MANNER OF SAUL'S CONVERSION

Some souls seem to be born gradually into the kingdom of God. Others seem to be hurled in headfirst. For some the light dawns so slowly they can never say for sure exactly when they were saved. For others the light dawns like a lightning flash and the truth penetrates like a thunderclap. When Saul was saved, there was a burning voice and a blinding vision and all of a sudden he was prostrate in the dust confessing his newfound faith.

A. A Tremendous Revelation

In all his later writings Saul hardly ever referred to the human life of Jesus of Nazareth. Saul first saw Him, first knew Him, and first enthroned Him as "the Lord from heaven" (1 Corinthians 15:47). Ever afterwards that was how he thought of Jesus.

"Who art thou, Lord?" Saul cried. "I am Jesus whom thou persecutest," the Lord replied (Acts 9:5). At once Saul's world collapsed like a house of cards. His religion was useless.

Saul was a circumcised Jew, a Benjamite, a Hebrew of the Hebrews, a Pharisee, a firebrand of the Jewish faith, a moral

man, and a law-abiding citizen. He observed the rites of
religion and performed the deeds of the law, but his every
thought had been sinful. All his religion had done for him was
make him an active enemy of Christ. It had simply confirmed
him in his sins and persuaded him he did not need a Savior. As
a religious man he felt no need to confess his sin and accept
Christ as Savior.

What a tremendous revelation it was to Saul that he was
lost and undone and on his way to a Christless eternity. He
realized he was the enemy of the gospel and the committed foe
of the living, risen, ascended Son of the living God. Without
such conviction of sin no religious man can ever hope to be
saved.

B. A Total Revolution

One moment Saul of Tarsus was the chief of sinners; the
next moment he was a devout believer with his feet set on the
road to becoming the chief of saints. One moment he thought
Jesus of Nazareth to be an impostor; the next moment he
owned Him as Lord and God. One moment he was a terrorist
committed to the ruthless extermination of the church; the next
moment he was a new creature in Christ Jesus. In Acts 9:1 he
was breathing out threats; in Acts 9:11 the Lord said, "Behold,
he prayeth."

There was a total revolution within Saul. He was changed
in a moment, in the twinkling of an eye. He did not go through
a long drawn-out process of psychological reconditioning. He
experienced *conversion:* a life-transforming change that affects
the mind, heart, will, conscience, body, soul, and spirit.

C. A Typical Resolution

"Lord," Saul said, "What wilt thou have me to do?" (Acts
9:6) Before his conversion Saul had served the Sanhedrin; now
he wanted to serve the Savior. He knew that "faith without
works is dead" (James 2:26). Saul resolved from that day
forward he would allow no rivals, no refusals, no retreat. Jesus

would be Lord of every thought and action. (Sooner or later every genuine born-again believer must acknowledge in some measure the sovereignty of the Spirit of God in his life.)

So Saul of Tarsus was already well on the way to becoming the great apostle Paul. Within a decade the world was going to hear from this man. He was an apostle "born out of due time" (1 Corinthians 15:8) but he would come "not a whit behind the very chiefest apostles" (2 Corinthians 11:5).

III. THE MEANING OF SAUL'S CONVERSION

What does a newly saved person do? To a large extent it depends on the person. We probably would have said: "The best thing for you to do, Saul, is to go to Jerusalem and attend the services of the church and learn all you can about the Christian life. There are some good Bible teachers there like Peter and John. You can learn a lot from them."

Well that is just what Saul did *not* do. He decided to get away from people altogether. He needed time to think, read his Bible, and pray. So off he went toward the silences of Sinai— to Horeb, the mount where God had met with Moses. Saul dropped out of sight for a number of years until even his name was thankfully forgotten by the persecuted saints of God.

Saul, however, was not forgotten by God. He was in God's school. His teacher was the Holy Spirit and his textbook was the Bible. God was preparing him for the greatest of all ministries, second only to that of his beloved Lord from Heaven.

Saul, God said, "is a chosen vessel unto me" (Acts 9:15). God had built into him a combination of qualifications He had not built into any of the other believers in the ever-growing Christian community. Saul was a Jew, a Roman, and a Greek. He was a Jew by birth, training, religion, and education. He was a Greek by scholarship, learning, and language. He was a Roman by citizenship—free-born. Saul of Tarsus was cosmopolitan, a man made for the world. With the conversion of such a uniquely qualified man, the time had come for God to complete the inspiring of the Word and commence the evangelizing of the world.

A. Complete the Inspiring of the Word

There were new truths to be conveyed to men. Saul was the man for the job. He was an intellectual giant with a mind commensurate to the task. A major part of the Bible had not yet been written and Saul was chosen to write it. God needed a man with his genius, boldness, and authority.

When Saul of Tarsus departed for Arabia, the Christian vocabulary did not yet exist. Words like *Adam, Moses, law, sin, death, grace, works, atonement, redemption, adoption, justification, faith,* and *righteousness* existed in the general vocabulary of the Hebrew people. But such words had not yet attained their full stature in Christ. Words inspired by the Holy Spirit came to the mind of Saul when he was in Arabia. He later wrote, "I conferred not with flesh and blood" (Galatians 1:16). Saul took Genesis, Leviticus, Psalms, and Isaiah in his backpack when he went into the wilderness. He returned with Romans, Ephesians, and Thessalonians in his heart.

B. Commence the Evangelizing of the World

There were new tribes to be converted to God. Saul of Tarsus was the man for that task too.

When Saul was saved, the church was exclusively Jewish. When he died, churches dedicated to the worship of Jesus existed in every major city of the Roman empire. Gentiles had poured into the church in a living tide. Saul had taken the pagan world by storm.

When Saul was saved, Jerusalem was the geographic center of the Christian world. Peter, James, and John were the pillars of the church. When Saul died, Rome was the center of the Christian world and Jerusalem had become a mere suburb. An unimportant center on the backwaters of history, Jerusalem would soon be wiped off the map for centuries.

What was the meaning of Saul's conversion? His experience on the Damascus road was a major turning point in the history of mankind. Every conversion is intended to be just such a turning point. The conversion of men like Martin Luther, William Carey, David Livingstone, D. L. Moody, and the like have all been high-water marks in the history of this planet. God intends that your conversion and mine should be the same. May each of us make sure it is.

12
Paul,
the Ablest Missionary

Acts 28:30-31

I. HOW PAUL REVIEWED THE PAST
   A. His Unregenerate Past
   B. His Unrecorded Past
   C. His Unrivaled Past
II. HOW PAUL REDEEMED THE PRESENT
III. HOW PAUL REGARDED THE FUTURE

The book of Acts ends with Paul in prison in Rome. His terms of imprisonment appear to be light, as would befit the detention of a Roman citizen. He was chained to a soldier and probably he could not come and go as he pleased, but he was free to receive any visitors he wished.

We can visualize the great apostle running his house like the courtroom of a king. Correspondence flowed in from all over the empire. A constant stream of visitors came and went. His attendants, including his beloved physician, executed his

decisions. There was no pomp or ceremony; Paul had no use
for that kind of thing. But even the most disinterested jailer
must have been impressed by the power, influence, and
diligence of this extraordinary Jew who possessed Roman
citizenship, spoke flawless Greek, and wrote words that
commanded greater respect than those of the emperor.

Paul was permitted to live in his own rented house. We
are going to spend some time with him there. We are going to
picture how he reviewed the past, redeemed the present, and
regarded the future. We will see a man who had few regrets
(and all those under the blood), who was wholly committed to
a single cause, and who was quite unafraid of the days ahead.

I. HOW PAUL REVIEWED THE PAST

Everyone has a past. It must be a good feeling to be
comfortable with one's past. We can do nothing about the past
except applaud it or apologize for it. What has been done has
been done and can never be undone. Only God can do
anything about the sinful past. He promises to blot it out. He
promises even more. He says He can restore the years that the
locusts have eaten (Joel 2:25).

As we picture Paul reviewing his life we think of his
unregenerate past, his unrecorded past, and his unrivaled past.

A. His Unregenerate Past

Paul was raised by devout Jewish parents in the port city
of Tarsus on the coast of Asia Minor. His father was a Roman
citizen. How he acquired this priceless honor we are not told.
Most likely a Roman general or administrator in southeastern
Asia Minor granted citizenship to him for rendering some
valuable service. The service may have been rendered to
Pompey or Mark Antony. As Roman citizens Paul's family must
have associated with the cream of society in Tarsus and Cilicia,
even though their strict observance of Jewish law made it
impossible for them to exploit their advantages fully.

Paul described himself as a Hebrew of the Hebrews—a Hebrew sprung from Hebrews (Philippians 3:5). He was proud of his heritage as a Jew and of his status as a Roman. He grew up in a bustling seaport thronged with sailors and merchants from all over the known world. A cosmopolitan Hellenist and Greek-speaking Jew, he was also a trained rabbi for he sat at the feet of Gamaliel. That in itself set Paul apart from the rank and file, even among the Jews.

Gamaliel, the grandson of the illustrious rabbi Hillel, was a Pharisee. His learning was so great that he was one of only seven doctors of Jewish law who were given the title *rabban*. Upon his death this proverb was circulated among the Jews: "Since Rabban Gamaliel died the glory of the law has ceased." They were wrong of course. They would have been more correct to say, "Since the Lord Jesus died the glory of the law has ceased."

At the feet of this distinguished teacher young Paul imbibed his views of Judaism. Already the first shoots of the Talmud were flourishing, and a Jewish student being taught by a learned rabbi would learn more about the Midrash and the Mishna than about the Bible.

Paul of course memorized all 613 commandments of the Mosaic law. But he was even more conversant with the work of Hillel, who brought to full flower the system of exegesis that applied Greek reasoning to the Hebrew Scriptures. He knew by heart all the intricate rules, regulations, teachings, and traditions that the Jews had hedged around the law. For instance, young Paul had at his fingertips all the dos and don'ts with which the Jews tried to protect the sabbath. (Christ swept all these rules away as so much high-sounding nonsense.)

Yet this star pupil—brilliant, sincere, protected, privileged, and promoted—later wrote the word *ignorant* over that early period of his life. Ignorance was his only excuse for his rabid persecution of the church. "I did it ignorantly," he said (1 Timothy 1:13).

Paul was totally ignorant of the law of God all the time he

studied it in those days. He played with it as a child plays with an ornament. No one—father, mother, schoolmaster, or fellow student—ever took the Sword out of its sheath to show him its glittering edge, its divine workmanship, and its ability to pierce the conscience, stab the soul, and bring fearful conviction of sin. Gamaliel taught those eager young men who thronged his academy what Rabbi So-and-So said and what Rabbi Such-and-Such said. Gamaliel so distorted, dissected, and dissipated the Word of God that by the time Paul graduated, the Sanhedrin had marked him as the young man most likely to succeed. The church had marked him as the young man most likely to persecute Christians.

A persecutor is what Paul became. He made havoc of the church. He cheered those who stoned Stephen and held their coats. He obtained warrants from Caiaphas and Annas and persecuted the church at home and abroad with a single-mindedness and savagery that struck terror into the hearts of Christians everywhere.

Paul's later words reveal a deep pang of remorse: "I persecuted this way unto the death, binding and delivering into prisons both men and women. . . . I imprisoned and beat in every synagogue them that believed. . . . when they were put to death, I gave my voice against them. . . . [I] compelled them to blaspheme. . . . beyond measure I persecuted the church of God, and wasted it" (Acts 22:4,19; 26:10-11; Galatians 1:13).

How Paul thanked God after his conversion for the precious blood of Christ. All his sins against the Christians were under the blood. God forgave his sins and forgot them, but Paul could not forgive himself nor could he forget. The faces of men, women, boys, and girls rose up to haunt him. At night he would see faces, hear voices, and wake up bathed in cold sweat—even after he had been saved for years and those sins had been cast behind God's back, buried in the depth of the sea, and blotted out as by a cloud.

No wonder Paul had such a burden for the poor saints of Jerusalem. No wonder he took collections for them everywhere he went. No wonder he begged and pleaded with his Gentile converts in city after city to contribute funds for the needy Christians in Jerusalem. Many of them he had widowed, orphaned, and beggared. Their faces were ever before him even though God had eternally banished his sins from His mind and memory.

B. His Unrecorded Past

With constant delight the great apostle remembered that never-to-be-forgotten experience on the Damascus road, the startling heavenly vision of the risen ascended Christ. How that experience colored all his thinking ever afterwards! Paul had never known Jesus during the days of His flesh; he knew Him only as "the Lord from heaven" (1 Corinthians 15:47). That blinding vision was the beginning of his understanding of the great commission. "Once I was blind, but now I can see," he must often have said.

The Holy Spirit draws the veil of silence over the next few years in Paul's life. But the new convert was not wasting his time. In Arabia under the guidance of the Holy Spirit Paul formulated the theology of the New Testament. Those years in Arabia were essential for him to sort out fact from rabbinical fable. He had so much to unlearn. Much of the teaching he had received from Gamaliel was worthless to him in his new life in Christ.

During this silent period Paul seems to have been disinherited by his family (Philippians 3:8 says that he "suffered the loss of all things") and he had already received the "mighty ordination of the nail-pierced hands" for his work among the Gentiles (Acts 9:15), so there was nothing to stop him from getting busy for God. Paul was not the kind of man to sit around waiting for a call from the Jerusalem church—they were glad he was somewhere else. Paul, saved or unsaved, was trouble as far as the Christians in Jerusalem were concerned.

As Paul reviewed his past he remembered his first visit to Jerusalem after his conversion. He remembered the incredible loneliness he felt. The whole church eyed him with the greatest suspicion. They thought he was simply pretending to be saved to worm his way into the congregations in Jerusalem as a Sanhedrin spy and informer. Then Barnabas, a true son of consolation, befriended him and introduced him to the apostles.

Paul looked back with pleasure on the time he spent in Jerusalem with Peter. "Here's the upper room, brother Paul," he could hear Peter saying. "Here's where Jesus entered into Jerusalem to the hallelujahs and hosannas of the crowd. Here's where He overturned the tables of the money-changers. Here's where we all went to sleep while He wept and prayed over yonder. Here's where I denied Him, to my shame."

God warned Paul that Jerusalem was a dangerous place for him, yet he felt drawn to it. Ultimately events there led to his imprisonment. He spent years of his life in prison at Caesarea and Rome, thanks to the thoughtlessness of the Jerusalem church.

C. His Unrivaled Past

Paul remembered when the real call came. First the Antioch church needed a teacher, and his friend Barnabas came to recruit him for that ministry. Then the Antioch church needed a missionary, and Paul and Barnabas with young Mark in tow set out to evangelize the regions beyond.

Paul thought of his years as a missionary. There was his first missionary journey to Cyprus and the thrilling confrontation with Elymus the sorcerer and the conversion of Sergius Paulus, the island's Roman governor.

Then the great Taurus range beckoned to him to return to Cilicia where he had already labored for years on his own. Taking a firm hold on the leadership of the missionary team, he announced his decision: "We'll head north, pass through the Cilician gates, and then travel on into Galatia. Danger? What's the matter with you, John Mark? If we're in the will of God, so what if there's danger? There's danger everywhere. You're quitting? Well, my young friend, all I can say is that you have a great deal to learn about discipleship."

Paul conducted evangelistic campaigns in Pisidian Antioch, Iconium, Lystra, and Derbe. A pattern soon developed. Paul's policy was to go to the Jews of the local synagogue first. Inevitably the synagogue divided right down the middle. The unbelieving Jews were bitterly hostile. Rage, jealousy, blasphemy, and persecution always followed.

Paul remembered being hailed as a god at Lystra one moment and being stoned as a troublemaker the next. *It was just as well that John Mark went home,* Paul thought. How he valued dear patient Barnabas, always willing to play second fiddle. He never complained and was willing to suffer with Paul for the cause of Christ.

Paul remembered the joy of planting churches everywhere. Hundreds of people became Christians, were baptized, and learned the rudiments of the gospel and sound exegesis of the Old Testament. Going back to ordain elders was a wonderful memory also.

Then came the Jerusalem conference and his confrontation with the Jewish church over the freedom of Gentile Christians from the law of Moses, from circumcision, from sabbath-keeping, and from Israel's dietary laws. Even in prison as Paul sat reminiscing, he could not hold back a grateful *Amen!* for God's sovereign overruling of that conference. It was still hard to believe that Peter and the ascetic, legalistic, narrow-minded James took his side. He would have liked to free Jews as well as Gentiles from the bondage of the law, but God would take care of that in His own time. Paul was sure the destruction of the temple, foretold by Jesus, would help.

Paul thought also of his next two missionary journeys. The disagreement with Barnabas over John Mark was sad, but God stepped in and provided Silas, Timothy, Titus, and a host of other young men to take Barnabas's place. Paul went back to Galatia and on to Troas.

Then God overruled again. Paul met the man from Macedonia, first in vision and then in the flesh as dear Dr. Luke walked into his life to confirm Paul's call to evangelize Europe.

Memories arose: Philippi and the jail; Thessalonica and revival; Berea and a people zealous to test all teaching by the Book; Athens and the once-in-a-lifetime opportunity to speak for God on Mars hill. *How strange that the Greeks could be so brilliant in philosophy, politics, art, and science and be so blind in religion,* Paul mused.

When Paul traveled on to Corinth and Ephesus, hundreds of thousands of people found Christ. Paul planted church after church in city after city in country after country. Almost single-handedly, in cooperation with the Spirit of God, he evangelized all the Eastern European Mediterranean. What a life he had lived since Jesus came into his heart. The soldier chained to his wrist suddenly awoke as Paul shouted, "Hallelujah!"

II. HOW PAUL REDEEMED THE PRESENT

We picture Paul looking at his prayer book. It listed so many places and so many people. Barnabas, Mark, Timothy, Titus, Priscilla, Aquila, Aristarchus, Apollos, Rufus, Alexander, Demas, Crispus—name after name was listed. Paul thought of the hundreds of men he had discipled. Now in the ministry, they were blazing gospel trails to vast regions beyond. Paul's prayer list was enough to keep him busy from morning to night.

He was praying for others too: Lydia; the Philippian jailer and his wife and children; the poor little slave girl; Alexander the coppersmith; Festus; Felix; King Agrippa; that poor lost man known to the world as Nero Claudius Caesar Augustus Germanicus; the soldiers; and the members of the praetorian guard, many of whom he had already won to Christ.

Reminded of the soldier chained to him, Paul said, "Tell me, my friend, you're new to the guard, aren't you? Where are you from? Are you married? Two little boys, eh! What are their names? Tell me, Marcus, has anyone ever told you about Jesus? Let me tell you how I met Him."

We picture Paul witnessing, praying, and redeeming many long hours by writing letters. While sitting in his rented house he carried on a voluminous correspondence. Some of his letters have been preserved. No greater letters have ever been written than Paul's prison letters to the Ephesians, the Philippians, the Colossians, and Philemon. Paul wrote these letters under the direct control of the Holy Spirit. They are God-breathed, inerrant, divinely inspired, and part of the living fabric of the Word of God. They will outlast all the suns and stars in space. These jewels of inspiration will dwell in our minds for the endless ages of eternity.

Much happened to Paul between the time he wrote his Epistle to the Romans from Corinth and the time he wrote his Epistle to the Ephesians from Rome. He called at Philippi and Ephesus on his way to Jerusalem. He warned the Ephesian elders that heresy was on the prowl and that they were responsible for the flock. He brought to Jerusalem a magnificent financial gift from the Gentile churches of the West. He was conned into going into the temple court to prove his Jewishness. He was beaten up by the mob and rescued by the Roman garrison. He addressed the multitude and then the Sanhedrin. Because a conspiracy to murder him was afoot he was hurried off to the Roman city of Caesarea. There he lingered in jail for two long years. He appeared before Felix, Festus, and King Agrippa. In exasperation Paul appealed to caesar and now the apostle was in Rome, where he languished in prison.

The wheels of justice creaked on just as slowly in Rome as they did everywhere else. However, Paul faced an added element of danger. He now realized that it was well within the bounds of possibility that he would be executed. When he had appealed to caesar in A.D. 59 there were no indications that Nero would degenerate into a monster. But by A.D. 62 the official attitude toward Christians had changed. Nero's wise tutor Seneca was retired. The Jewess Poppaea wound the imperial tyrant around her little finger. The corrupt Tigellinus had Nero's ear. In just two years Nero would set fire to Rome and blame the Christians for the holocaust.

Through all that happened between the writing of the Epistle to the Romans and the writing of the Epistle to the Ephesians, Paul grew to the full measure of his stature in Christ. His letters from prison had a new emphasis on the lordship of Christ and on the mystery of the church and its relationship to Christ.

So we picture Paul redeeming the present by writing, by witnessing, and by interceding. The past was past. The future was future. He had today. He saw to it that each passing moment was freighted with precious cargo to be weighed in for reward at the judgment seat of Christ.

III. HOW PAUL REGARDED THE FUTURE

Paul never worried about the future. Whenever he tried to lift the veil and peer into the future, all he could see was Christ. The Lord Jesus dominated his horizon.

If caesar should set him free, then for him to live was Christ. He would evangelize Spain. Beyond Spain were Northern Europe, the Germanic tribes across the Danube, and the Angles on the tiny island of Britannia. If Nero set him free, Paul would fling himself into global evangelism with a passion and a purpose that would make the past seem like wasted time.

If Nero were to command his execution, then hallelujah! To die would be gain. He would be absent from the body and present with the Lord.

Paul already had one glimpse of glory. He was caught up into the third heaven and saw things untranslatable. He could never decide afterwards if he had been in the body or out of the body during that experience. All he knew was that the experience was real, tangible, and audible—what lay beyond the grave was as solid as what lay on this side. What he saw and sensed over there filled him with "a desire to depart, and to be with Christ; which is far better" (Philippians 1:23).

The word Paul used for *desire* in writing to the Philippians is the usual word for *lust* in the New Testament. Indeed the original word is translated "lust" some thirty times. Paul was lusting to go to Heaven. He tasted the powers of the world to come and became an addict of glory. Let Nero execute him. All Nero could do was promote him to glory. Paul's future would be Jesus! Paul's future would be forever. His future would be "joy unspeakable and full of glory" (1 Peter 1:8). Neither caesar nor the Sanhedrin nor Satan could rob Paul of his future. His future would be glorious.

In the end Paul witnessed before Nero, and Nero had him executed. But when Paul arrived in glory, Jesus had him crowned.

VOLUME 3

CONTENTS

1
Philip
the Plodder

John 1:43-45; 6:5-7; 12:20-22; 14:8-9

I. WHAT PHILIP FOUND
II. WHAT PHILIP FIGURED
III. WHERE PHILIP FALTERED
IV. WHAT PHILIP FELT

hilip had a Greek name. The most famous Philip in Greek history was Philip of Macedon, the father of Alexander the Great. After Alexander's conquests the Greek influence was pronounced throughout the Middle East. Perhaps that is why Philip, the Lord's disciple, had a Greek name. The fact that Philip had a Greek name may have been one of the reasons Jesus chose him.

This disciple may have been named after another Philip, closer in time and territory: Philip the Tetrarch, one of the sons of Herod the Great. Philip the Tetrarch's brother Herod Philip married their niece Herodias, who afterward eloped with her husband's half brother, Herod Antipas. Herod Philip and Herodias had a daughter, Salome, who was a major player in the drama of John the Baptist's murder. Philip the Tetrarch married Salome. The Herods were a bad lot. Philip the Tetrarch was the best of them. Like his father, Philip the Tetrarch was a builder. One monument he left behind him was Caesarea Philippi at the foot of mount Hermon. He was well-liked by his subjects. Doubtless it was not at all unusual for people in those days, as in our own day, to name their sons after well-known figures such as the tetrarch.

The fact that Philip, the Lord's disciple, had this Gentile name suggests that his parents were not narrow-minded Hebrews, but more liberal-minded Hellenists. But even Hellenists would have made sure that their son had a thoroughly Jewish education.

Philip came from the city of Bethsaida, which is called by the Gospel writer "the city of Andrew and Peter" (John 1:44). Perhaps John was suggesting that these two leading men in the apostolic company were friends of Philip. (At the time Jesus was choosing His disciples, Andrew and Peter were living in Capernaum [Mark 1:21,29], but Bethsaida and Capernaum were quite close, possibly twin cities.) Not long after Andrew and Peter gave themselves to Christ, Philip did the same. Andrew had been a disciple of John the Baptist before he became a disciple of Jesus. We can imagine how Andrew would have talked enthusiastically about the Baptist and the imminent coming of Christ. No doubt Philip had been included in some of those impassioned conversations.

Philip apparently did not make much of an impact on the other disciples. If John had not rescued him from complete anonymity, all we would know about Philip would be his name and the fact that he ranks as number five in the general listing of the Lord's disciples. John told us what Philip found, what he figured, where he faltered, and what he felt.

I. WHAT PHILIP FOUND

There can be no doubt that Philip was interested in what Moses had to say about the coming of Christ. Philip knew that the Messiah was to be a kinsman-redeemer, just like Moses. "A

Prophet...like unto me" was Moses' way of describing the Messiah (Deuteronomy 18:15)! Christ would come armed with might and miracle. He would redeem Israel.

Philip, we can be sure, was at home with the glowing prophecies that spoke of the coming Son of David who would put down all His foes and reign in wisdom, love, and power. One day the desert would blossom as the rose, the lion would lie down with the lamb, a child would be able to play with a scorpion, and a man would be a mere youth at a hundred. Jerusalem would become the capital of a new world empire and the Gentiles would lay their tribute at this mighty Messiah's feet.

But Philip also knew about strange, somber, and startling prophecies that spoke of a suffering Messiah. Philip would read Isaiah 53, Psalm 22, and Psalm 69 again and again and puzzle over seeming contradictions. The Messiah was to be born in Bethlehem, yet He was to be called out of Egypt. He was to be militant, yet He was to be meek. He was to be the happy man of Psalm 1, yet He was to be the man of sorrows of Isaiah 53. Philip pondered often over the prophetic Scriptures. He may have been slow on the uptake, but he was a patient plodder. He was not the kind of man to be in a hurry to make up his mind, but he was the kind of man who arrived at a conclusion in the end. No doubt he thought, *When we finally find the Messiah, we'll see that He has fulfilled prophecy just as it's written*.

Actually Philip didn't find the Messiah, for we read that the day after Andrew brought his brother Simon to Jesus, Jesus found Philip. Philip thus became the archetype of all those people who have a personal encounter with Christ without the aid of any intermediary. They find Him by reading the Scriptures. Or they find Him simply by being found by the Lord Himself. The seeking Savior finds the seeking sinner. Jesus found Philip (John 1:43), yet Philip told Nathanael, "*We have found him,* of whom Moses in the law, and the prophets, did write, Jesus of Nazareth" (1:45, italics added). So Jesus found

Philip, and he found Jesus! The seeking sinner meets the seeking Savior.

Over and over again in the Bible we see God seeking men and men seeking God. The first question asked in the Old Testament is "Where art thou?" (Genesis 3:9) and the first question asked in the New Testament is "Where is he?" (Matthew 2:2)—a seeking Savior and a seeking sinner. There can only be one outcome: each finds the other.

"We have found him," said Philip to Nathanael! We all like to find things. We are especially pleased if what we find turns out to be valuable. We are even more pleased if we can tell other seekers that we have found what they have been looking for.

The perennial appeal of Robert Louis Stevenson's *Treasure Island* lies in the fact that the book is all about searching for buried treasure. We are intrigued with the story from the day young Jim Hawkins finds the map in the old sea captain's trunk and only narrowly escapes being killed by pirates. We follow with interest the fitting-out of the *Hispaniola* and Squire Trelawney's careless way of engaging a crew. We hold our breath when he recruits Long John Silver, the one-legged cook. We hide with Jim Hawkins in the barrel and learn of the plot by the remnant of Flint's old crew—now enlisted seamen aboard the *Hispaniola*--to seize the ship, murder the squire and the captain (and their loyal subordinates), find the treasure, and set sail for the Spanish Main.

Our interest mounts when Jim Hawkins becomes Long John Silver's prisoner and is dragged along on the pirates' final treasure hunt. "Look out for squalls," advises the squire's friend Dr. Livesey, who had given the map to the rascally cook. Our interest is sustained to the climax: the map leads the pirates to the place where the treasure was buried, but the treasure is gone! The pirates discover that their crimes have all been for nothing. Poor old Ben Gunn, marooned on the lonely island, had found the treasure and removed it long ago.

The pirates found a hole. Philip found Him! "We have

found him," said Philip and he invited his friend to come and find Him too. Those who find Him find a treasure beyond the price of buried gold and precious stones.

Philip was still trying to sort out the clues in his treasure hunt when the Lord Jesus turned the tables on him and found him instead. Philip was still poring over the old prophecies in the Word. He was still pondering about the new preacher in the wilderness. He was still searching his Bible when he found that he had been found!

II. WHAT PHILIP FIGURED

John next mentioned Philip in connection with an incident that took place near Bethsaida-Julias (not the same Bethsaida where Philip was raised) on the east bank of the Jordan river where it runs into the sea of Galilee. Jesus and His disciples had retreated to this area, which was a few hours' sail from Capernaum and an even shorter distance by land around the head of the lake.

The Passover feast was approaching and many caravans were forming as pilgrims prepared to set out on the journey to Jerusalem. Jesus could see the crowds gathering—thousands of men and an uncounted number of women and children—and His heart was moved with compassion. John the Baptist had only recently been murdered and buried, and here were all these "sheep" without a shepherd. So Jesus taught them, hour after hour throughout the day. Toward evening the disciples suggested it was time to send the crowds away. Having gathered in a desert place, the people would need to scatter to find food and lodging. "Send the multitude away," the disciples urged (Luke 9:12). "Send them away."

Philip was of the same mind as the other disciples when the Lord challenged him. "Whence shall we buy bread, that these may eat?" He asked (John 6:5). Philip was astounded. He had already been doing his homework and had arrived at an estimate of the size of the crowd—about five thousand men plus the women and the children. He had already figured how many loaves would be needed just to give each person a few mouthfuls. "Two hundred pennyworth of bread is not sufficient," he said (6:7). Perhaps that amount was the sum total of what was in the bag, or perhaps the amount was Philip's estimate of how much money would be needed. In any case two hundred pennyworth represented a considerable sum since a penny was a working man's daily wage.

The Lord had only asked Philip the question to test him and Philip failed the test. He was too much occupied with mathematics and money to be occupied with the Master. "Two hundred pennyworth of bread is not sufficient"! Those words were Philip's final offering at the altar of truth and trust. "No way!" he was saying, "not with our resources. We don't have enough money so there's no way we can feed the people."

It was a pity that Philip had not read his Bible with more attention. Had he done so he would have balked at using the number *two hundred,* for it was a number of ominous significance. The number *two hundred* is used, for instance, in connection with Achan. After the overthrow of Jericho, Achan was tempted. He knew that all the spoil of Jericho was God's first fruit and was not to be touched. Yet he stole some gold and a garment—and *two hundred* shekels of silver (Joshua 7:21). Those two hundred shekels of silver were *insufficient* to redeem his life from destruction when the day of judgment came.

The number is also used in connection with Absalom, the young rebel who sought to overthrow his father David and seize the kingdom for himself. Absalom was popular with the people, he had charm and charisma and a persuasive tongue, and he found a ready ally in the golden-tongued Ahithophel, the cleverest man in the kingdom. Moreover Absalom was handsome and his good looks were framed by a remarkable head of hair, his crown of glory. In counting up his assets Absalom did not overlook his hair—he weighed it at every year's end. "He weighed the hair of his head at *two hundred* shekels after the king's weight" (2 Samuel 14:26, italics added).

Yet that hair caused his death! When in the battle with David the tide turned against Absalom and he fled, his hair was caught in the branches of an oak—and he hung there until Joab's darts put an end to him.

The number *two hundred* is used in connection with Micah's graven image (Judges 17). First this unscrupulous man stole eleven hundred shekels of silver from his mother. Then, frightened by her curses, he gave them back to her. Then his mother took *two hundred* of those shekels and had them melted down and made into a couple of images. Next he persuaded a landless Levite to be the priest of his idol temple for an annual ten shekels, a suit, and his meals. Later the tribe of Dan persuaded the young Levite to abandon his patron, take Micah's idols, and become priest to the whole tribe. (The young Levite's name was Jonathan. He was the son of Gershom, the son of Moses. So incensed were the later Hebrew scribes with this defection of a grandson of Moses that they changed the name of the grandfather from Moses to Manasseh— to spare Moses' name and memory.) Those two hundred shekels of silver and the silver idols made from them brought disaster on the tribe of Dan. Its name is blotted out from the blessing recorded in Revelation 7.

When Ezra brought his contingent of Jews back to the promised land, he had with him *two hundred* singing men and singing women (Ezra 2:65). When they arrived back in the land and inaugurated the true worship of God, Ezra realized that his two-hundred-voice choir was *not sufficient:* the people needed to hear him read the book of the law. He "opened the book" and taught the people out of the Word of God (Nehemiah 8:1-8). Evan Roberts, the Welsh revivalist, might have learned a lesson from Ezra. The Welsh revival—impressive and far-reaching as it was—produced no long-lasting results because it was carried on the wings of song instead of being grounded on the preaching of the Word.

So Philip ought to have sensed at once that there was something wrong with his thinking when he arrived at the ominous number *two hundred*. Unconsciously he even labeled the number himself as "not sufficient." "Two hundred pennyworth of bread is *not sufficient*," he figured. His figuring was wrong. He figured without Christ.

III. WHERE PHILIP FALTERED

John 12:20-22 provides another glimpse of Philip. It was three days before the Passover. The Lord had just cursed the fig tree, thus pronouncing doom upon the nation of Israel for its apostasy and unbelief, and we can only imagine how full of sorrow His heart was. With His death just a few days ahead, Jesus was in the temple teaching.

Then it was that certain Greeks approached Philip and asked to be introduced to Jesus. These men were not Hellenists (Greek-speaking Jews). They were Greeks who had come up to Jerusalem for the Passover feast. In other words they were proselytes of the Jewish religion. These Gentiles had groped their way to the portals of Judaism and, having heard and seen something of Jesus, realized that their Judaism was a poor substitute for Him. We can imagine that they were awed by the temple and by the tremendous crowds thronging Jesus. But hearing one of the men who was evidently one of the Lord's personal disciples being addressed by his companions as Philip, they ventured to approach him. Here was a disciple of Jesus who had a Greek name! Maybe he would introduce them to Jesus.

But poor old Philip muffed it again. All sorts of doubts and difficulties came up in his mind: *Proselytes they may be, but they are Gentiles. When Jesus sent the twelve of us on a Messianic mission to the tribes, He expressly told us, "Go not into the way of the Gentiles, and into any city of the Samaritans enter ye not: But go rather to the lost sheep of the house of Israel"* (Matthew 10:5-6). *When the Syrophenician woman besought the Lord to heal her child, He said, "It is not meet to take the children's bread, and to cast it unto the dogs"* (Mark 7:27).

Pondering these words of Jesus, Philip was not at all sure the Lord would want to be introduced to any Greeks, however devout they were. Philip had failed to grasp the total change in dispensations that had been ushered in by the Jewish rejection of their Christ and the subsequent cursing of the fig tree. So instead of joyfully bringing a couple of would-be converts to Christ, he gave them the cold shoulder and told them he would have to make inquires. Even then he didn't go directly to Jesus with his predicament; he went first to Andrew. It's a wonder the Greeks didn't go away in a rage (as Naaman would have done).

IV. WHAT PHILIP FELT

Finally John showed us Philip in the upper room. The last few hours had come and the Lord and His disciples were together. Jesus had washed their feet and had declared He was about to be betrayed. He had also told Peter that he was about to deny Him three times.

Then the Lord began His last heart-to-heart talk with His disciples. "I'm going home!" He told them in effect. "Let me tell you about My Father's house. It is a house of many mansions...." He saw their sad faces and the dawning of the realization that He really was going away. They would be left as orphans in the world. They could not imagine life without Him. The last three-and-a-half years had been absolutely marvelous! They thought of all the miracles they had seen and the tremendous teaching they had heard. They thought of His wisdom, His love, and His power. They thought of His goodness, His greatness, and His grace. They could not imagine life without Him.

"Let not your heart be troubled," Jesus said. "I'll be coming back. I'm only going to get things ready for you. I'm going to pave the way for you to the Father." Then it was that Philip blurted out what was in his heart: "You keep on talking about the Father. Show us the Father, and it sufficeth us. That will be sufficient." The same old calculating mind came up short once again. Before he had said, "Not sufficient." This time he said, "*That* will be sufficient." It bordered on the insulting: "You're not sufficient. Show us the Father and that will be sufficient."

It speaks volumes for the patience of our Lord Jesus that He simply took Philip's comment in His stride. The Lord's answer was sublime. John 14:9 gives us His exact words: "Have I been so long time with you, and yet hast thou not known me, Philip? he that hath seen me hath seen the Father; and how sayest thou then, Shew us the Father?"

"What you are asking for," He was saying, "is redundant. There is not one particle of difference between the Father and Me. What He is I am; what He says I say; what He does I do. If you have seen Me, you have seen Him. If I were to show you Him, I would simply be showing you Myself. Don't you realize that for the past thirty-three years I have been the visible expression of the invisible God? I am God as He is God— except that I am God manifest in flesh. Ever since I was born I have been giving people a moment-by-moment, three-dimensional, full-color, audio-visual demonstration of God." At least Philip's blundering statement gave Jesus the opportunity to explain these truths to us!

We cannot help wondering what happened to Philip. He was in the upper room on the day of Pentecost, so he too was baptized by the Spirit of God into the body of Christ. He too was endued with power from on high, so we can be sure that Philip let his light shine in some small corner of this world.

Tradition tells us he went to Scythia—part of southern Russia—and settled in Hierapolis in Phrygia. Hierapolis, a resort town attracting people from all over the Roman world, was near the great medical center at Laodicea, so Philip would not have been far from his dear friend John, who settled at Ephesus.

Thus if tradition and conjecture are true, careful and

methodical Philip helped carry the gospel tidings into Europe. He reminds us that the Lord can use ordinary, prosaic, and dull people just as He can use clever and quick-witted people.

2

Nathanael
the Guileless

John 1:45-51; 21:2

```
I. WHAT HE CONTENDED
II. WHAT HE CONFRONTED
   A. He Was Discerned
   B. He Was Displayed
   C. He Was Described
III. WHAT HE CONFESSED
```

John always called him Nathanael. The synoptic writers called him Bartholomew. *Bartholomew* is a patronymic—that is, a surname consisting of one's father's name or an ancestor's name plus a prefix or suffix. The surname Johnson, for example, is a patronymic and thus *William Johnson* means "William, son of John." So *Bartholomew* is a surname meaning "son of Tolmai." The prefixes *Ben* and *Bar* always signal patronymics; examples from the Bible include Bartimaeus, Barabbas, Ben-hadad, and Benjamin. Peter is called Simon Barjona because his father's name was Jonah. We do not know which ancestor is indicated by the name Bar-tolmai although we know there was a Jewish sect known as the Tholmaens, who were dedicated to the study of the Scriptures.

317

The name Nathanael is more familiar to us since we are acquainted with the Old Testament prophet Nathan. *Nathan* means "gift" and *El* is a name for God, so *Nathanael* means "gift of God." The choice of the name Nathanael revealed the pious hope of the boy's parents that he would indeed be the gift of God. From what we know of Nathanael's character even before he met Christ, we can be sure they were not disappointed.

Nathanael was fortunate in his choice of friends. One of his closest friends was Philip. As soon as the Lord Jesus found Philip, he rushed off to find Nathanael. Philip was brimming over with great news: "We have found him, of whom Moses in the law, and the prophets, did write, Jesus of Nazareth" (John 1:45). Probably the two friends had often pored over the Old Testament Scriptures together, searching for the many prophecies concerning the coming of Christ. They had found Moses' prophecy that the Messiah would be a prophet like him and they had read Isaiah 53, Isaiah 63, Psalm 22, Psalm 69, and Daniel 9. Then the preaching of John the Baptist had heightened their expectations.

We can imagine then that Nathanael pricked up his ears and leaped to his feet when Philip came bursting into Nathanael's hiding place under the fig tree with the momentous words, "We have found him, of whom Moses in the law, and the prophets, did write." But when Philip added, "Jesus of Nazareth, the son of Joseph," Nathanael sat back down.

I. WHAT HE CONTENDED

"Can there any good thing come out of Nazareth?" Philip exclaimed (John 1:46). Nathanael knew Nazareth. He was a native of Cana (John 21:2), which was only five miles away, and he didn't think much of Nazareth.

The sophisticated Jews of the capital didn't think much of Galilee. With more than a touch of contempt, they called the province "Galilee of the Gentiles" (see Matthew 4:15). Remote from the theological stronghold of Judea, Galilee stood astride a busy international corridor, crossed by the great military roads from the north and by ancient caravan routes from the east. "Out of Galilee ariseth no prophet," the leaders of the Sanhedrin sneered when Nicodemus ventured to put in a tentative word for Christ (John 7:52).

They were dead wrong of course. Barak the deliverer, Elon the judge, and Anna the prophetess had come from Galilee. Jonah, the only prophet to whom Jesus directly likened Himself, came from Gath-hepher, only a few miles from Nazareth itself. Elijah, Nahum, and Hosea had either come from Galilee or carried on much of their ministry there.

The sophisticated Jerusalem and Judean Jews mocked at the grammatical errors and mispronunciations common among Galileans. All Galileans were regarded as stupid yokels. The fact that the region had a mixed population of Phoenicians, Arabs, and Greeks, as well as Jews, increased the contempt in which Galilee was held by her neighbors to the south.

The Galileans themselves were scornful of Nazareth. This provincial village seems to have had some kind of unsavory reputation, but the Lord Jesus spent thirty years of His life there. He lived in deep obscurity in the most despised province of the country, in the most despised valley of that province, and in the most despised village in that valley. For thirty years he was unknown, unrecognized, and unnoticed. So very ordinary did those years seem to His contemporaries in Nazareth that when at last in their local synagogue He proclaimed Himself to be the Messiah, they tried to assassinate Him for blasphemy.

Thus it was that when Philip added the words, "Jesus of Nazareth, the son of Joseph," he punctured the balloon of rising hope his first words had begun to inflate.

Nathanael might have argued, "Let us concede that a prophet can arise out of Galilee. Jonah came from Gath-hepher, a town of Zebulun. Hosea was of the tribe of Issachar. Nahum came from Elkosh. Elijah was the Tishbite from Tishbeh in the territory of Naphtali. A prophet can arise out of Galilee—but

Nazareth? Philip, show me one passage of Scripture that links
Nazareth with the Messiah!"

Philip was a wise man. He did not attempt to argue the
point with his friend Nathanael. Philip did not try to change
Nathanael's opinion of Nazareth. Philip simply said, "Come
and see" (John 1:46). He would introduce Nathanael to Jesus
and let Jesus do the rest. That is the very essence of soulwinning.

"Come and see" is what Jesus said to two disciples of John
the Baptist. When they heard their master announce that Jesus
was the Lamb of God, they left John the Baptist and followed
Jesus. The Lord saw them following Him and asked, "What
seek ye?" They replied, "Where dwellest thou?" He answered,
"Come and see." The Bible says, "They came and saw where
he dwelt, and abode with him that day" (John 1:35-39). The
reference is to John the Beloved and Andrew. What a time they
must have had! What an endless stream of questions they must
have asked Him. Perhaps, as later with the travelers on the
Emmaus road, He began at Moses and the prophets and
"expounded unto them in all the scriptures the things concerning himself" (Luke 24:27). Whatever happened, John and
Andrew abode with Him and thenceforth they were His!

"Come and see," said Philip. It did not take Nathanael long
to discover that some good thing could indeed come out of
Nazareth! Nothing so good had ever come out of any city in all
the long ages of time. Goodness is a rare attribute that belongs
essentially to God alone. It is one of the choice fruits of the
Spirit. It is a pearl of great price, a gem more valuable than
rubies. Nathanael found himself up against absolute goodness.
He looked into a pair of eyes that, seeing right through him,
stripped away all of life's comfortable little disguises. He heard
a voice that spoke the truth with a gentleness and candor that
left him breathless. The words he heard were undiluted and
memorable. He was in the presence of a personality that was
wholly unafraid and awesome and unfathomable. Nathanael
was confronted by a sincerity that hurt because it made all
pretense, sham, and hypocrisy wither on contact. And love,

unutterable love, shone out of those all-seeing eyes and resounded through that arresting voice. Nathanael came and saw for himself.

II. WHAT HE CONFRONTED

A. He Was Discerned

Jesus said to Nathanael, "Before that Philip called thee, when thou wast under the fig tree, I saw thee" (John 1:48). Perhaps that fig tree was in Nathanael's garden. Perhaps that fig tree was in some remote unfrequented spot, a place where Nathanael liked to get away from it all. Perhaps that fig tree shaded Nathanael from the hot Syrian sun in a place where he could be alone and muse over a verse of Scripture that had caught his attention. Wherever that fig tree was, Jesus had seen him there.

Jesus' statement must have been somewhat disquieting. It was disquieting for Adam and Eve when they first discovered the truth that it is impossible to hide from God. As they cowered among the trees of the garden in their wretched aprons of fig leaves, they heard a voice calling to them, "Where art thou?" (Genesis 3:9) They knew at once it was useless to hide. That voice penetrated every nook and cranny of Eden. The eye of God stripped aside all foliage and made every hiding place bare.

It was a terrifying truth to Adam and Eve that there was no hiding place from God. It was a tender and tremendous truth to poor, unhappy, runaway Hagar. Goaded beyond endurance by Sarah's acid tongue, Hagar had fled from Sarah and Abraham and was heading for Egypt. Hagar was totally disillusioned by the behavior of these believers. By sunrise she would cross the Egyptian frontier and bury herself again in Egypt's lifestyle and religion. But God had other plans. He could not allow her to go back into the world, back into the dark, back to the demon gods of her people, carrying with her a distorted idea of Himself. The Lord revealed Himself to Hagar, spoke to her, and gave her as fresh and as real and as unique a revelation of Himself as He ever gave to Abraham. God unfolded the prophetic page before her. He gave her an exceeding great and precious promise and told her to go back to the one place on all this earth where He had put His name. "Thou God seest me," she exclaimed (Genesis 16:13).

The fact that we cannot hide from God is a terrific or a terrifying truth depending on our relationship with Him. "I saw you," Jesus said, and Nathanael wondered what He had seen. Nathanael's innermost thoughts were to be demonstrated to be an open book to the One before whom he stood.

B. He Was Displayed

It seems that Nathanael had been reading his Bible when Jesus saw him under the fig tree. The Lord now referred to Genesis 28:12, apparently the chapter and the verse Nathanael had been meditating on when His all-seeing eye was cast upon him. "Hereafter," Jesus said, "ye shall see heaven open, and the angels of God ascending and descending upon the Son of man" (John 1:51).

Genesis 28 tells us of a day in the life of Jacob. Jacob's wiles had gotten the better of him. He had double-crossed his twin brother once too often. Esau was now breathing out threatenings and slaughter, and Jacob was forced to leave home. His first encampment proved to be memorable, for that night he dreamed of a ladder, a shining stairway linking earth to Heaven. Moreover he saw the angels of God ascending and descending that ladder.

The activity of the angel hosts in Jacob's vision is significant, for they weren't descending and ascending; they were ascending and descending. They weren't coming down from Heaven to earth and going back from earth to Heaven. They were ascending to Heaven from earth and then returning to earth from Heaven. We cannot miss the meaning—they were already here; they were stationed down here.

This world is a battlefield, a planet that has been invaded from outer space by beings of great power, intelligence, and wickedness. The planet has also been invaded by countless hosts of angelic beings from the high halls of Heaven. The ranks of the holy angels include martial angels, ministering angels, and messenger angels. These beings owe their allegiance to God and they battle principalities and powers, rulers of this world's darkness, and wicked spirits in high places who owe their allegiance to Satan.

The angels of God, it seems, have a shining stairway they use, or used to use, in order to communicate with the great white throne of God. Jacob saw them ascending. Up that endless ladder they went, laden down with sad tales of wickedness and woe. What stories of injustices and tyrannies and oppressions they carried with them, what tales of hate and malice and envy and rage, what stories of war and famine and pestilence and persecution, what tales of treachery and murder and abuse! That ladder must have seemed a veritable Everest of difficulty and pain for the angels who were weighed down with amazement that Adam's race could be so callous and cruel.

Jacob also saw the angels descending. They had made their reports and received new instructions. Down they came, having taken fresh courage from the untroubled calm and confidence that radiates from the throne of God. Iniquity was just as much a mystery to the angels as to men, but the angels sensed from the peace and power emanating from God's throne that all was well. They were reassured that although God's present purposes may be inscrutable, they are perfect and peerless. So descending the stairway with confident steps, the angels came to resume their duties. What a noble and awesome vision for a runaway young man! No wonder it changed Jacob's life.

"Well, Nathanael," Jesus said in effect, "I am that ladder. I am that living link between earth and Heaven. The angels of God ascend and descend upon Me. I am the way, the truth, and the life and no one comes to the Father but by Me."

C. He Was Described

The moment Jesus set eyes on Nathanael, He said, "Behold an Israelite indeed, in whom is no guile!" (John 1:47) The word translated "guile" here is the same word used in the Septuagint version of Genesis 27:35 to convey the idea of guile or subtlety. Genesis 27 tells us of Jacob's guile.

When Jacob stole Esau's blessing and Esau pleaded, "Bless me, even me also, O my father" (Genesis 27:34), "he found no place of repentance, though he sought it carefully with tears" (Hebrews 12:17). He had bartered his birthright years before and had forfeited the blessing along with it—not that either birthright or blessing was ever really his to sell. Nevertheless, overwhelmed suddenly and too late by the immensity of what he had thrown away, Esau burst out in anguish. Isaac, now fully aware of what had really happened, put it bluntly enough to Esau: "Thy brother came with subtilty, and hath taken away thy blessing" (Genesis 27:35).

Jesus used the same word Isaac did when He described Nathanael as an Israelite in whom was no subtlety or guile. John 1:47 has frequently been paraphrased, "Behold an Israelite indeed in whom is no Jacob!"

It took God twenty years to get to the root of the Jacob-nature in the pilgrim patriarch and bring him to the place where He could change his name to Israel. Even then the old Jacob-nature often reasserted itself. Indeed it is not until we come to the closing chapters of Jacob's life that we see him living as Israel.

But standing before Jesus was an Israelite singularly free from the guile, crookedness, and subtlety of Jacob. The Lord appreciated the guilelessness of the man. True to his nature, Nathanael did not depreciate the Lord's comment with false humility, but accepted it at face value. "Whence knowest thou me?" he said (John 1:48). In other words, "How do you know so much about me?"

Nathanael was free from the double-dealing characteristic

of some of Jacob's seed. There was something inherently transparent about Nathanael. He harbored no mixed motives in his heart. He was a man who could be trusted. He scorned the use of what are commonly called the tricks of the trade. People always knew where they stood with Nathanael. The Lord Jesus recognized this rare quality at once and spoke words intended to evoke the response that demonstrated Nathanael's guilelessness.

III. WHAT HE CONFESSED

Nathanael was quick to grasp the truth. "Rabbi," he exclaimed, "thou art the Son of God; thou art the King of Israel" (John 1:49).

"The Son of God"! That identification put Him on the throne of the universe. Nathanael's statement was a startling confession of faith. Peter took years to come to a like confession. Nathanael was far ahead of the majority of the nation of Israel in his comprehension of Christ. Nicodemus, the learned and thoughtful member of the Sanhedrin, did not rise to that realization until after Calvary. When he sought his famous midnight interview with Jesus, he hailed Him as "Rabbi...a teacher come from God" (John 3:2).

When we stand at the foot of the cross, we hear another man confess Jesus to be the Son of God: the Roman centurion in charge of His execution. But that confession was wrung out of him by the sheer weight of the evidence—darkening skies, rending rocks, bursting graves, and terrors in the temple. No such physical phenomena elicited the confession from Nathanael's soul. It was evidence enough for him that Jesus had demonstrated His deity by reading him like a book.

"The King of Israel"! That identification put Him on the throne of David. For a thousand years the Hebrew people had looked for the coming of the Messiah.

The Davidic kingdom had waxed and waned and had finally been swept away by Nebuchadnezzar, and the times of the Gentiles had begun. Cyrus the Persian had eventually restored a remnant of the Jews to the promised land and hope had revived, but Ezra, Zerubbabel, and Nehemiah had presided only over a dependency. Their mandate had been to build a temple, not a palace—to raise up an altar, not a throne. The terrible sufferings of the Hebrew people during the Syro-Egyptian struggles and the coming of the monstrous Antiochus Epiphanes had hardened the clay of persistent Jewish unbelief. The sects of the Pharisees and Sadducees and the institution of the synagogue and the Sanhedrin had hardened the clay still further. Rabbinical handling of the Scriptures had caused belief in the Bible to degenerate into adherence to the sterile traditions of the elders.

Then came the voice of John the Baptist kindling new hope. And when Christ confronted Nathanael, it took him about two minutes to make up his mind: Jesus was the King of Israel. All the Messianic promises could now be fulfilled. The King had come and soon the kingdom would come!

"Thou art the Son of God," Nathanael said. Jesus countered, "Ye shall see heaven open, and the angels of God ascending and descending upon the Son of man." Jesus was indeed that ladder of Jacob's dream. As Son of God He placed His hand upon highest Heaven. As Son of man He planted His feet firmly on the earth. God manifest in flesh, He was truly God in every sense of the word and truly man in every essential of humanity apart from sin.

Nathanael was quick to recognize the Messiah, and that is about all we know of him. Really that is all we need to know. We can be sure that a man who began with such a head start finished way out ahead. At the judgment seat of Christ it will be supremely interesting to see and hear what proof Nathanael made of his ministry in after years.

3
James
the Less

Matthew 10:3

I. HIS DESIGNATION
II. HIS DISTINCTION
III. HIS DESTINATION

He is called James the Less (sometimes James the Younger) and that's about all we know of him—just a name. But that's about all we know of hundreds of people whose names appear here and there in the Bible. At least his name *occurs* in the Bible—and that's more than can be said of the pharaoh of the oppression in the days of Moses. That's more than can be said for Alexander the Great or for the philosophers and scholars of Athens. That's more than can be said for Julius Caesar. There were millions of people on earth when James responded to the call of Christ, and the vast majority lived and died and were forgotten. Yet James had his name written in the Bible five times. That's better than making *Who's Who*.

I. HIS DESIGNATION

He is designated "James the son of Alphaeus" (Matthew 10:3). Matthew is also identified as the son of Alphaeus

(Mark 2:14). If both references are to the same Alphaeus, Matthew and James were brothers and James was a Levite. The tribe of Levi was the priestly tribe. The Levites were the legal experts of the day. Thomas is also thought to have been a brother of this James.[1]

One tradition is that before responding to the call of Christ, James the Less was a Zealot. If that tradition is true, Matthew and James could have had little or nothing in common until they both met Christ. Matthew, a Roman tax collector, was a detested publican, a collaborator with Rome, and a traitor to the Jews, while James, a vehement foe of all things Roman, was determined to strike the blow that would shake off the hated shackles of the occupying power.

The name Alphaeus is the Greek form of the Hebrew name Cleophas. The Cleophas mentioned in the New Testament was the husband of that Mary who went with the mother of Jesus and other women to Calvary on the day of the crucifixion (John 19:25).

The Bible tells us nothing else about James the Less. He asked no questions and did nothing to distinguish himself as an individual. He simply marched in step with the others. He was a listener not a talker, a follower not a leader.

But James stands at the head of a long line of men and women who love the Lord and seek to live for Him quietly and inconspicuously in the daily rounds and common tasks of life. We do not know the names of the majority of those who were thrown to the lions in the days of the persecuting caesars. We do not know the names of those hewers of wood and drawers of water who built St. Paul's Cathedral or Westminster Abbey. We do not know the names of millions who down through the ages have made up the rank and file of the faith. James the Less heads the procession of the foot soldiers of the cross.

There are four lists of the twelve apostles in the New Testament. Three are in the Gospels (Matthew 10:2-4; Mark 3:16-19; Luke 6:14-16) and one is in the book of Acts (1:13,26). In each list the names are divided into three groups of four disciples. The same disciples are always grouped together and in every case each group is headed by the same apostle. The first group includes the more prominent and conspicuous apostles and is always headed by Peter. The second group includes less well-known disciples and is always headed by Philip. The third group includes the least known disciples; they are obscure except for Judas Iscariot, whose name always appears last, covered with infamy. This third group is always headed by James the Less. His place in the lists suggests that he had at least some leadership qualities.

We can also, more or less positively, infer from Scripture that James came from Capernaum. Jesus made Capernaum His headquarters during the early part of His ministry; Peter and Andrew lived there; Matthew had his customs office there; the Lord performed many of His greatest miracles there.

It is not at all unlikely that the Lord kept an eye on Matthew and James the Less for quite a while. He saw something in this obscure James that rang true and when the time came for Him to make up the list of His personal disciples, He decided that James would make an excellent apostle.

We would have chosen someone who cut a more dashing figure. We would have wanted a banker or a millionaire. We would have thought that someone like Nicodemus or Joseph of Arimathaea was better than the retiring James. But when we stand at the judgment seat of Christ, we will applaud with cheers and hosannas the Lord's choice of this man. The Lord chose him as He chose only eleven other men in all the history of this world. And the Lord made no mistakes—not even when He chose Judas Iscariot and certainly not when He chose James the Less.

II. HIS DISTINCTION

James' distinction lies in his almost complete anonymity. He is conspicuous because he was inconspicuous. He is outstanding because he is obscure. Some of the greatest forces in the universe work silently, secretly, and unseen. Silently the snowflakes fall, building barricades and stopping the march of armies. Silently the atoms whirl, their electrons rushing around their nuclei billions of times in a millionth of a second. Silently great forests grow.

In the church James the Less is the precursor of all those who have trusted Christ, who have walked humbly with their God, and who have sought to serve Him in some small corner of the harvest field. They are unknown, unsung heroes of the faith. Consider the impact of such inconspicuous men on John Wesley, Alexander Cruden, William Booth, John Knox, and John Bunyan.

Let us begin with John Wesley. The Irish historian William Lecky, who cannot be suspected of any bias toward Christianity, declared that the Wesleyan revival saved England from the blood bath of the French revolution. He went so far as to say that the religious revolution begun in England by the preaching of the Wesleys was more important than all the splendid victories won on land and sea under the British prime minister William Pitt.

Conditions in England at the time of the Wesleys were terrible almost beyond belief. The stage was decadent, the royal court reeked of licentiousness, and the church and religion were openly scorned. Infidelity and drunkenness were epidemic. In London one house in every six was a gin mill. Bands of thugs sallied forth from the taverns to commit mayhem on ordinary citizens. The priests of the Church of England were fox-hunting parsons and a converted minister was as rare as a comet. Every kind of immorality was championed by the press. It was taken for granted that Christianity was defunct—no longer even a subject for inquiry. Then John and Charles Wesley came on the scene.

But how did John Wesley come to know Christ? He had always been religious. He admitted that as a young lad he stole from his mother's purse—but he always tithed what he stole and gave some of it to the poor! He had crossed the Atlantic to be a missionary only to discover that he himself was not right with God. Returning to England, he groped in a kind of twilight zone for some time. "What have I learned?" he asked himself. "I have learned that I who went to America to convert the Indians was never myself converted."

His journal tells us that he came to Christ in the middle of a persistent and passionate quest for the truth of God. One evening he went reluctantly to a meeting of a Christian society in London where someone was reading Luther's preface to the Epistle to the Romans. About a quarter of the way through the reading, the light suddenly dawned in John Wesley's soul. The man who was destined to bring revival to England passed from death unto life. But who invited John Wesley to the meeting? And who was reading Luther's commentary? One of the church's nobodies.

John Wesley went on to write 118 books and articles. He and his brother Charles published 49 books of hymns and poetry. John traveled some 250,000 miles, mostly on horseback, preached 40,000 sermons, and led countless thousands to Christ. But who led *him* to Christ? It was one of the fellowship of James the Less.

Think also of Alexander Cruden, born in Aberdeen on May 31, 1701. He was known as Crazy Cruden since on several occasions he displayed evidence of mental instability. He became first secretary to the earl of Derby and later he worked as a tutor. Cruden saved his money and in 1732 he rented a shop in London just a stone's throw from the royal exchange and went into the bookselling business. Shortly after he moved into the shop, he began work on the project that made him famous: the compilation of a concordance of the Bible. There is no way we can estimate how helpful that concordance has been to the cause of Christ. Anyone knowing just one word in any Bible verse can find that verse with a *Cruden's Concordance,* a work still being published more than two hundred years after its completion.

Today there are other more sophisticated concordances.

Lexicons, word studies, and computer programs undreamed of in Cruden's day are available to us. Yet in his day and for generations afterward, armies of Bible students rose up to call Crazy Cruden blessed. But who led Alexander Cruden to Christ? Nobody knows. It was a member of the fellowship of James the Less.

Another member of that fellowship had an impact on the man who became known as General Booth. Called "the prophet to the poor," William Booth was born among the poor in Nottingham on April 10, 1829. He was born again at the age of fifteen. He launched his new mission in 1865 and called it The Salvation Army in 1878.

In Booth's day London's East End was a squalid slum of half a million people. There were gin shops on every corner and some of the shops even had steps up to the counter so that the smallest child could be served. Booth took the East End by storm. Uniformed Salvationists formed brass bands and marched through the streets, and thousands of people were saved. These militant Christians stirred up fierce opposition throughout Britain. The mayor of one English city advised the people to take the Salvation Army flag, tie it around the necks of the Salvationists, and hang them with it. In the early 1880s tavern keepers, enraged because so many of their customers were getting saved and giving up drink, urged people to attack Salvation Army soldiers in the streets. When William and Catherine Booth visited Sheffield in 1882, they were attacked by a gang of toughs. General Booth, surveying his troops covered with mud and blood and egg yolks, said, "Now is the time to have your photograph taken." In one year nearly seven hundred Salvationists were assaulted on the streets of Britain simply for preaching the gospel. Some were even punched and kicked to death.

Booth's army went after the poor and the wretched. It was designed, the founder said, for "wife-beaters, cheats and bullies, prostitutes and thieves." C. H. Spurgeon said, "If the Salvation Army were wiped out of London 5,000 extra policemen could not fill its place in the repression of crime and disorder."

General Booth died (or as his fellow soldiers would say, "He was promoted to Glory") on August 12, 1912. During his lying-in-state 150,000 people filed past his coffin and 40,000 people, including Queen Mary, wife of King George V, attended his funeral. In Booth's lifetime The Salvation Army had grown to include 15,945 officers serving in 58 countries.

But who led William Booth to Christ? Some biographers say that his conversion took place in Nottingham when the revivalist Isaac Marsden was conducting a campaign. Others say Booth was converted in a small prayer meeting. Nobody knows for sure. The person who led William Booth to Christ is another member of the fellowship of James the Less.

Consider next the case of John Knox. When George Wishart was burned at the stake as a heretic, his colleague John Knox escaped arrest but he watched his mentor die. Knox saw him being led to the stake by the executioner and heard about the words of forgiveness Wishart spoke to the man. Knox watched the flames leap up around Wishart as he ascended the ladder of martyrdom to his heavenly home. That martyr made a deep and a lasting impression on Knox.

In 1547 John Knox himself was arrested and sent to France where he was condemned to be a galley slave for nineteen months. While toiling at the oars of a French galley, he showed the stuff of which he was made by boldly defying the ship's Roman Catholic chaplain who tried to intimidate him.

When John Knox returned to Scotland from his enforced exile, he began to preach. He bluntly declared the mass to be idolatry and boldly stated that Catholic churches and monasteries should be closed. He lived to see Protestantism established as the national religion of Scotland. When Mary Stuart came to the throne in 1560, she promptly had John Knox arrested and tried for treason, but the court acquitted him. The triumph of the Scottish Reformation was complete. Thomas

Carlyle, the famous Scottish essayist and historian, said that in the history of Scotland he could only find one epoch: the Reformation wrought by John Knox. Carlyle described it as "a resurrection from the dead" for Scotland.

John Knox went to his rest in 1572, but his soul goes marching on. And who led him to Christ? We know that he was profoundly moved by Wishart, but who took the Bible and pointed John Knox to Calvary? It was another member of the fellowship of James the Less.

We might also ask about the conversion of John Bunyan. He's not so well-known today, but for three hundred years he was the best-known, best-loved, most-read author in the Christian world. His *Pilgrim's Progress* stood side by side with the Bible in almost every Christian home. He was born in Bedford, England, in 1628. Just a humble tinker by trade, he was arrested in 1660 for preaching without the permission of the established church. He remained in the Bedford jail for nearly thirteen years during which his wife, his little blind daughter, and his other children suffered much. He was in jail when the terrible bubonic plague ravaged England and he was there when the great fire of London reduced much of the city to smoking ashes and rubble.

The devil could lock Bunyan up, but he couldn't shut him up! During his incarceration he wrote his famous allegory of the Christian life. "As I walked through the wilderness of this world," he began, "I lighted on a certain place where was a Den, and I laid me down in that place to sleep; and, as I slept, I dreamed a dream…" The den was Bedford jail. The dream became *Pilgrim's Progress* with its host of colorful characters who have delighted Christians from that day to this. How can we ever forget Mr. Obstinate and Mr. Pliable, or Christian in the Slough of Despond, or Mr. Worldly Wiseman and Madam Bubble, or the man with the muck rake in his hand, or Mr. Hypocrisy, or Mr. Formalist, or Mr. Mistrust, or Giant Despair? And who can forget the Delectable Mountains, the Interpreter's house, Doubting Castle, Bypass Meadow, and Vanity Fair? To spend an hour or two with John Bunyan is to be thoroughly entertained and greatly helped on the straight and narrow way that leads to life. Who can measure the power, influence, and impact of a book?

For a long time before his conversion John Bunyan was tormented by his sin. He felt as though the sun in the sky begrudged the light it gave him. He felt as though the cobblestones of the street and the tiles on the houses banded together against him. Who led him out of this darkness into light? Bunyan mentioned being associated with a Master Gifford. He also mentioned overhearing a cluster of poor women discussing the kingdom of God as they sat in the sun outside their doors, and he mentioned being influenced by the members of the little church at Bedford. But who led him to Christ and thus gave the world *Pilgrim's Progress, The Holy War,* and *Grace Abounding to the Chief of Sinners?* We'll have to wait for the answer, for it was a member of the fellowship of James the Less.

James the Less stands in the forefront of a multitude that no man can number—anonymous men and women and boys and girls who are washed in the blood of the Lamb and whose names are written down in glory. They may stand as silent sentinels on earth, but they will be numbered among the aristocracy of Heaven. No bright lights shine on their names down here, but they will shine as the stars in the firmament forever over there.

III. HIS DESTINATION

One of these days the trumpet will sound. "The dead in Christ shall rise first: Then we which are alive and remain shall be caught up together with them in the clouds, to meet the Lord in the air" (1 Thessalonians 4:16-17). We will all be there, small and great—those who made a mighty mark for God and are mentioned in church history books, and little old ladies and shy retiring men who loved the Lord and like Mary of Bethany did what they could. Those who had the gifts of apostle and prophet, evangelists and pastors and teachers who filled great pulpits, those who blazed gospel trails into dark continents, and those who founded missions and movements will rise together with countless ordinary folk toward the sky.

We will all arrive at the celestial city. Before us will be the vast bulk of that city foursquare. We will see its jasper walls stretching far away on either side and soaring upward mile after mile until they are lost in the sky above. Our eyes will be drawn to the great foundations of that wondrous city, the city that haunted Abraham's dreams. He looked for "a city which hath foundations" (Hebrews 11:10) and here he will find a city with twelve foundations ablaze with precious stones. Twelve names are engraved on those foundations for all the universe to see. And just as prominent as the names of Peter, James, and John is the name of James the Less.

We will all go on in and stand at the judgment seat of Christ. The books will be opened. The name of James the Less will be called, and we will hear what he did and where he went and what he said and whom he won to Christ. James the Less will be James the Less no more! All those of his unsung fellowship will stand with him, honored and applauded "in the crowning day that's coming by and by."[2]

---

1. The family ties among the twelve disciples can become very confusing—mostly because opinions of commentators vary. W. Graham Scroggie stated his interpretation as follows: "Most of [the disciples] were closely related to Jesus or to one another. There were two pairs of brothers, Peter and Andrew, James and John. Tradition says that Thomas, Matthew and James of Alphaeus were brothers. Jude was either brother or son of James of Alphaeus, so that, perhaps, a father and a son were in that chosen circle. And James and John of Zebedee, Thomas, Matthew, and James of Alphaeus were first cousins of our Lord, and Jude was a first cousin once removed; so that the Twelve and their Master were a family group." (*The Gospel of Mark,* Grand Rapids: Zondervan, 1979, page 65.).
2. Quotation is taken from D. W. Whittle's hymn, "The Crowning Day."

4
James,
the Son of Zebedee

Matthew 4:21; 17:1; 20:20; Mark 1:19; 5:37; 13:3; 14:33; Acts 12:2

I. HIS FAMILY
II. HIS FAITH
III. HIS FIDELITY
IV. HIS FAME

I remember once being at sea on a troopship. Standing on the deck I could see in the distance the gray horizon where the tossing waves met the lowering sky. There was another ship out there. From time to time, riding an especially high wave, she would lift her masts above the skyline. Then she would sink back out of sight again. Such a ship, in such a sea, was the apostle James, who was the brother of John and the son of Zebedee and Salome. Once in a while we catch a fleeting glimpse of James in Scripture, but most of the time he is out of sight. We know he is there (usually when John or Peter is there); we catch the occasional glimpse of James, but most often we don't see him at all.

I. HIS FAMILY

James' father was Zebedee. Even more elusive than his son, Zebedee is seen on only one occasion in the Gospels

(Matthew 4:21-22; Mark 1:19-20). He lived at or near Bethsaida on the western shore of the sea of Galilee, where Peter and Andrew were raised. The place, often frequented by Jesus, was probably not far from Capernaum, where the Lord eventually had His headquarters during His Galilean ministry. Later on the Lord denounced Bethsaida for not receiving His teachings.

Zebedee was a successful fisherman who owned his own boats and paid other men to work for him. He was the kind of employer who keeps a watchful eye on his business. His two sons were in business with him, and there seems to have been some kind of partnership between them and Simon Peter and Andrew.

Zebedee probably had a house in Jerusalem too and was acquainted with the high priest Caiaphas and his household (John 18:15-16). We can gather that Zebedee moved in the upper social circles.

We do not know anything about his personal relationship with the Lord Jesus. Zebedee does not seem to have done anything to hinder his two sons from giving up the fishing business to become disciples of the young prophet from Nazareth. Doubtless he had hoped that his boys would continue in his fishing business and carry it on after he retired. Still he allowed them to go with Jesus and put no obstacles in their way. Some have criticized him for not going with them, but perhaps he thought it better to stay home and run the business so that he could contribute to their support.

It speaks well of a father when his boys want to follow in his footsteps. It also speaks well of a father when he unselfishly gives his sons to the Lord's work. Zebedee was a fine, hardworking man and a good father.

Salome, the mother of James, seems to have been a somewhat pushy, ambitious woman who wanted the best for her boys. We do not know how she reacted when her boys abandoned their future in the family business to trek up and down the countryside with the preacher from Nazareth. The early popularity of Jesus and His extraordinary miracles probably reconciled her to the decision her sons had made. Then when it dawned on Salome that Jesus was claiming to be Israel's rightful King, she was enthusiastically in favor of their choice.

In fact she attempted to push her sons forward in the anticipated kingdom (Matthew 20:20-28). Unknown to her, the Lord was actually on His way to Calvary when she made her move. She asked Him to give them the two highest and most important positions in His realm. We are not told what the two brothers thought of her behavior. Perhaps they were embarrassed. We do know what the other disciples thought. They were angry. In any case, the Lord denied her request.

It is possible that Salome was the sister of Mary, the Lord's mother. So perhaps Salome was trying to take unfair advantage of her family relationship. If on the purely human level Zebedee and Salome were indeed the Lord's uncle and aunt, they would have known Him from His infancy.

The circumstances of His birth were remarkable enough to have occasioned a considerable amount of gossip in the area. The character of the youthful Lord Jesus would also have been the likely subject of many conversations. He was never known to have said an unkind word or done an unkind deed. Luke said that He grew "in favour with God and man" (Luke 2:52).

Jesus was known in the area for His genius. He was a first-class scholar and a devoted student of the Scriptures. He carefully kept the letter and spirit of the Mosaic law, which He knew by heart. Stories must have been circulated about His encounter with the Jewish rabbis in Jerusalem when He was a lad of twelve.

For years the Lord labored at the carpenter's bench in Nazareth. Nobody ever had reason to complain about His workmanship. Nobody ever regretted doing business with Him. He was a craftsman whose creations were faultless. He was good and clever and kind. Nobody had a bad word to say about Him.

Doubtless He was a frequent visitor in Zebedee's home

during the thirty silent years, of which we know so little and
of which we should like to know so much. So perhaps Zebedee
and Salome were not at all surprised when Jesus quit the
carpenter's shop and announced Himself to be the Messiah.
They, of all people, would have known the truth about His
birth and lineage.

Salome became an early and enthusiastic supporter of
Jesus. She believed in His kingship (Matthew 20:20). She was
one of the women who ministered to Him of her own substance
(Luke 8:3; Mark 15:40-41). She followed Him on His last journey
to Jerusalem. She was at the cross and witnessed His final
suffering. She was one of the women who came first to the tomb
to complete the embalming of His body. Remembering her
devotion to Jesus, we can forgive her for being a bit pushy.

Salome and Zebedee's sons, James and John—the Lord's
cousins—would have amazing stories and countless unrecorded details to tell on their occasional visits home. Zebedee
would sit in his easy chair and listen to it all. Salome would
burst out with one exclamation after another.

Of the two brothers, James seems to have been the older.
Apparently it never occurred to James to be envious because
his younger brother was closer to Jesus than he was. Maybe
James recognized the unusual talents of his young brother who
went on to write five books of the New Testament. James and
John had something in common: they both loved the Lord
Jesus with an ever-growing love that would unite them in
everlasting bonds far more enduring than any earthly ties.

II. HIS FAITH

Reference is made to James in connection with the
healing of Peter's mother-in-law, for it was right after that
incident he responded to the call of Christ to become one of
His personal disciples. In time James, his brother John, and his
fishing partner Simon Peter formed a special inner circle
among the disciples. As part of that inner circle, James was

chosen by Jesus to be present on at least three significant occasions when his faith was greatly strengthened.

For instance James was in the house of Jairus, the ruler of the Capernaum synagogue, when Jesus had His first ministerial face-to-face confrontation with death. That day James saw something no one had seen for hundreds of years. Not since the days of the prophets Elijah and Elisha had anyone seen a person raised from the dead.

The daughter of Jairus had died and James saw the grief of the heartbroken parents. He witnessed the struggle in the soul of Jairus as he hoped against hope and battled so bravely with his understandable unbelief. Then James watched Jesus put out the professional mourners and turn His back on their mockery. James, John, and Peter, along with the stricken mom and dad, went into the child's bedroom. They looked at the once-fresh face of the twelve-year-old girl now cold and fixed in death. They saw Jesus take the little girl's dead hand in His and heard Him say, "Damsel, I say unto thee, arise" (Mark 5:41). They watched the blush return to her cheeks as she came back to life. James would never forget what he saw that day. He saw _the Lord's greatness_. It robbed death of all its terrors.

Later on James saw Jesus raise the widow's son and Lazarus, whose body was already rotting in the grave! No wonder James was such martyr material. He knew Jesus had conquered death and all its powers.

James was also with Jesus on the mount of transfiguration. Once more in the company of Peter and John, he walked with Jesus into the Anti-Lebanon mountains and climbed to the snow line of mount Hermon. There he saw the Lord's appearance change. James caught a glimpse of man as God intended man to be—inhabited by God and robed in a glory not of this world. Dazzled by the blazing whiteness of the Lord's home-spun robe, James saw His face shine like the sun. James saw Moses and Elijah and heard their conversation with Jesus. James heard them talk of the Lord's "decease which he should accomplish at Jerusalem" (Luke 9:31). James heard Peter's blundering words as well as the voice from Heaven. The Lord enjoined silence about the transfiguration, but James would never forget what he saw. He saw *the Lord's glory*.

Then James was with the Lord in dark Gethsemane. He heard the Lord say that His soul was "exceeding sorrowful, even unto death" (Matthew 26:38). Doubtless the mind of James was in a whirl. He had just come from the upper room where the Lord had talked more bluntly than ever before about His impending departure. James had partaken of the emblems of a new feast of remembrance, the significance of which was wholly beyond his comprehension at the time. He was bewildered by the talk of the Lord's body being broken and His blood being shed.

In the garden James promised the Lord that he would stay awake and watch and pray, but he promptly fell asleep. He was ashamed of himself, but he kept on falling asleep just the same. Jesus excused him and John and Peter so graciously: "The spirit indeed is willing, but the flesh is weak" (Matthew 26:41). But James saw the Lord's face drawn with anguish and stained with tears. He saw *the Lord's grief*.

James was with Jesus when Judas arrived with the rabble, the rulers, and the Romans. Like the other disciples, James ran away. Salome went to Calvary, but we have no intimation that James was there. John was there and the Lord consigned the future care of His mother to him, but there's no hint that James was there. If fear kept him away, he must have severely reproached himself for his desertion—until Pentecost changed everything forever.

James was in the upper room when the Lord appeared to the disciples after His resurrection. We can be sure he made up his mind then never to play the coward again. It was small comfort that the others had run away too. It was small comfort that he had not betrayed the Lord as Judas did or denied the Lord with fisherman's oaths as Peter did. It was great comfort that the Lord had forgiven him. James had learned his lesson and learned it well. He was determined that next time he found himself in a place of danger because of his confession of Christ, he would play the man. To that end he schooled his heart and mind and soul and will.

III. HIS FIDELITY

We see the fidelity of James in an incident that took place shortly after the transfiguration. Jesus had deliberately set His face toward Jerusalem and each step was bringing Him closer to the cross. His way led through Samaria. Hard feelings had existed between the Jews and Samaritans for centuries, and the city of Jerusalem stirred the religious envy of the Samaritans. When the Lord entered the province of Samaria He pointedly bypassed their holy mountain Gerizim, thus making it evident that He was on His way to Jerusalem. So when the Lord and His disciples passed through a small Samaritan village, they encountered a hostile crowd. Perhaps the Samaritans felt that Jesus had snubbed their holy site. Perhaps they resented a band of Jews taking a shortcut through their village. For one reason or another the Samaritans gave the Lord and His disciples an uncongenial reception.

James and John reacted at once. They had just seen Elijah on the mount of transfiguration—if Elijah could call down fire, they could do it too. "Lord," said James and John, "wilt thou that we command fire to come down from heaven, and consume them?" (Luke 9:54)

The call for fire was indeed appropriate: not penal fire, but Pentecostal fire! Not the fire of God's wrath, but the fire of God's grace! James and John did not yet know of what Spirit they were. They would understand better by and by.

In the meantime the Lord gave them a nickname. He called the pair *Boanerges,* "sons of thunder" (Mark 3:17). Some think that the designation was given to James and John earlier because of their hot tempers, but in any case the term comes to mind in connection with this incident.

They *were* hotheads, but they were loyal hotheads. If their zeal was mistaken, they meant well. They could not bear to see their beloved Master slighted—and by Samaritans of all people! However blameworthy James may have been at the time, the incident certainly gives us a glimpse of his fidelity.

We see another glimpse of James shortly before Calvary. The disciples were exclaiming over the wonders of the temple and the great stones in its foundation when Jesus at once foretold the impending destruction of the temple and the city. Mark 13:3-4 tells us that James was one of those who asked the Lord for more details regarding the prediction. James wanted his faith and fidelity to be intelligent and informed. In answer to James' question, the Lord picked up the threads of Old Testament prophecy and the threads of New Testament prophecy and wove them into the wondrous tapestry of His great Olivet discourse. We might say even at this belated date, "Thank you, James, for being so thoughtful as to ask that question."

Then in the last chapter of the Gospel of John we see James on the seashore after the Lord's resurrection. The Lord had promised to meet the disciples in Galilee, so off to Galilee they went, back to the towns and villages and scenes and memories of their earlier years. Before long Peter got tired of waiting for Jesus and announced that he was going back to fishing. James was one of the other six disciples who fell in step with Peter. Down to the shore they went, just like old times. It was as though nothing had ever happened and that the three years they had spent with Jesus were all a lovely but impossible dream. The familiar boat, the ropes, the sails, and the nets were still there. The disciples launched out into the water, let down the nets, and toiled all night. The result was—nothing! They had come back to nothing! Then Jesus came and told them what to do and called them afresh to His work.

Like the others, James sat there shamefaced enough and, in uneasy silence, ate the breakfast the Lord provided. He listened as the Lord dealt with Peter. James heard Him silence

Peter when he wanted to know what John's future would be. James heard the Lord's veiled but unmistakable prophesy of the terrible death Peter would die. And James made up his mind: he too would die, if need be, for the One who had died for him.

IV. HIS FAME

Around A.D. 44 James was murdered by Herod Agrippa I. The church was just ten years old. The Herods were a cruel and dangerous family. Three or four of them come into the gospel story and a quick glance at them will be useful.

Herod the Great, as the world calls him, was the man who murdered the babes of Bethlehem in an attempt to get rid of the infant Christ. He was an Edomite sitting on the throne of David and lording it over the people of God. He was such a brutal tyrant that even his own family was not safe. He had nine or ten wives and not only murdered his favorite, but also murdered her two brothers and some of his sons as well. Just five days before he himself died, he ordered the death of his son Antipater. No wonder the emperor Augustus said it would be better to be one of Herod's hogs than one of his sons! When Herod knew his life would soon be over, he rounded up all the leading Jews and gave orders for them to be massacred the day he died. "The Jews will not mourn me," he raved, "but they will mourn." Toward the end of his life he suffered terribly. A horribly painful and foul disease seized him and his agony was indescribable. His sores stank so badly that people dreaded having to be in his presence.

Then there was Herod Antipas, the son of Herod the Great. Antipas had a reputation for craftiness and cunning, and one historian called him "a wily sneak." He stole his half brother Herod Philip's wife Herodias, and she in turn goaded Antipas on to murder John the Baptist. That crime so haunted his conscience that he grew superstitious about Jesus, especially as the reports of His miracles circulated throughout the country.

Herod Antipas secretly hoped someday to witness a miracle. He thought his time had come when Pilate, finding that the trial of Jesus was likely to be a very dangerous business indeed, sent Jesus to Herod Antipas for judgment. Antipas was delighted, thinking now he would see a miracle. However, Jesus simply ignored him until at last Antipas, enraged by the Lord's silence, mocked Him and poured scorn on His claim to be King. So this Herod began by murdering John the Baptist and ended by mocking Jesus.

Herod Antipas was succeeded by Herod Agrippa I, a grandson of Herod the Great. The Herods had the confusing and unhealthy habit of marrying each other. Herod Agrippa I, for instance, was the child of two first cousins. He married another cousin who was the daughter of his aunt who was married to an uncle! Agrippa was a close friend of Caligula, one of the maddest of the caesars. Agrippa was the Herod who murdered James in an attempt to curry favor with the Jews. Later he accepted divine honors for himself and died under the stroke of God.

James was the first of the apostles to suffer martyrdom. One tradition is that before his martyrdom James went to Spain to preach to Jewish captives in exile there. Herod Agrippa I had sent the Jews to Spain as slaves, so if James did indeed go there to minister to them, Agrippa would have thought he had sufficient grounds for executing him. The execution of James pleased the Jews so much that Agrippa, wanting to humor his difficult subjects, went on to arrest Peter.

It is one of the mysteries of God's providence that Peter escaped and James was martyred. But it was only a decade or two before Peter was martyred also. Doubtless Peter was welcomed to his new home in Heaven by both Jesus and his old fishing partner James. James, through his mother, had once made a bid for a crown. Now he wears a martyr's crown in a land of fadeless day where he sits enthroned as one of the mighty apostles of the Lamb.

5
Matthew,
the Tax Collector

Matthew 9:9-13; Mark 2:14-17; Luke 5:27-32

I. HIS MONEY

II. HIS MASTER

III. HIS MANUSCRIPT

    A. The King Is Revealed

        1. His Person

           a. His Ancestry

           b. His Advent

           c. His Ambassador

           d. His Adversary

        2. His Purpose

           a. His Men

           b. His Mandate

        3. His Power

    B. The King Is Resisted

    C. The King Is Rejected

    D. The King Is Raised

Matthew is called "the son of Alphaeus" (Mark 2:14). So is James the Less, but it is possible that Matthew's father was not the same Alphaeus who was the father of James the Less. Matthew's name is usually linked with that of Thomas and it is not at all unlikely that they were brothers. Thomas is called *Didymus,* which means "the twin," so perhaps he and Matthew were twin brothers. Some scholars think that Thomas, Matthew, and James the Less were brothers.

There were several sets of brothers in the apostolic fellowship. Andrew and Simon Peter were brothers. James and John were brothers (since their mother Salome is thought to have been the sister of Mary, the Lord's mother, James and John may also have been the Lord's cousins). James the Less and Jude (Judas) may have been brothers. Half the company of the disciples was made up of pairs of brothers.[1]

Matthew always referred to himself as Matthew. Mark and Luke always referred to him as Levi. We usually think of Matthew first as a tax collector.

I. HIS MONEY

At one time Matthew had plenty of money. The trouble was that his money had been treasured up at the price of infamy, for he was a publican, a tax collector for the Roman government. Most Jews branded him an outcast, for they considered the publicans to be traitors in the pay of the detested occupying foreign power.

Moreover tax collectors were not at all scrupulous about how they amassed their private fortunes. They used the system to their own advantage. Roman officials farmed out the actual job of collecting taxes and gave each collector a quota. What he collected over and above the quota was his to keep. As a result extortion was common and the tax collectors preyed on rich and poor alike.

Matthew had an office in Capernaum, a busy town on the northwest shore of the sea of Galilee. There he collected taxes from the fishermen and from the caravans that came that way. We do not know how he came to be so employed. His choice of a profession must have broken his parents' hearts, for he was born a Levite.

To be born a Levite was considered a privilege, for that family was set apart by God for the handling of holy things. Children of the Levites were well-grounded in the Scriptures. Matthew's familiarity with the Old Testament is evident throughout his Gospel. The Levites were the experts in Mosaic law and rabbinic traditions.

Their tribal history was unique. Every other tribe was given a province of its own, but the tribe of Levi had no such territorial holding. Instead it was given a number of cities (including six "cities of refuge") scattered throughout the territories of the other tribes. Thus the Levitical tribe was supposed to have a godly, leavening influence on the more secular tribes. The Levites were denied property in this world so that they might lay up treasure in Heaven. The Levitical tribe derived its income from the tithes and offerings of the other tribes.

Young Matthew seems to have taken a dim view of this arrangement. We can imagine that when his mother asked him what he wanted to be when he grew up, he did not say he wanted to be a Levite. When she said, "What are you going to be?" he replied, "Rich!" The Levitical system of living on handouts from other Israelites was not for him. Matthew was sick of that kind of life. He intended, when he grew up, to get rich as fast as he could. When in his bed at night or in his wanderings here and there he thought about how to get rich quick, one sure-fire way became obvious. He would become a tax collector.

Why not? he reasoned. *I might as well accept the situation as it is. The country is occupied by Rome and that is a fact of life not likely to change in my lifetime. So what if tax collectors are despised and classified with harlots and sinners? I don't need to be an extortioner. I will just make a fair commission. My parents are wedded to the old ways, trying to earn a living teaching the Mosaic law. But surely the only law that really matters is Roman law. I cannot spend the rest of my life tied to my parents' apron strings. I'm sorry they will be upset by my decision, but it's my life after all. I'm going to become a tax collector.*

To that end Matthew gave attention to his education so that he would be literate and at home in both the Jewish and Roman worlds and able to handle basic math and bookkeeping. And eventually he became a publican and joined a small tightknit community of rich social and spiritual outcasts. He shrugged off the vision of his parents' anguished faces and their shame and went about the business of making money.

Matthew probably knew Zebedee and his sons quite well. They were prosperous fishermen and doubtless paid their taxes to him. So did Jonas and his boys Andrew and Peter.

Very likely Matthew saw Jesus when He visited the area. Probably he knew His reputation for integrity, workmanship, generosity, and plain old-fashioned goodness even before Jesus gave up the carpentry business in Nazareth, went down to Jordan to be baptized of John, and then reappeared as a preacher and miracle worker. Perhaps Jesus showed His scorn of gossip and cutting public opinion by occasionally stopping to pass the time of day with Matthew.

II. HIS MASTER

It is unlikely that Matthew was really a happy man. He may have laughed and joked when he was with his own company—that tight little circle of tax collectors who shrugged off the scorn of their fellows by throwing lavish parties for each other and hiring entertainers of questionable morals and few scruples. But the snubs and sneers of the Jews, his excommunication from temple and synagogue, and the pained stricken looks on the faces of his parents must have cut deeply into Matthew's soul. Perhaps he had already discovered that money—lots and lots of money—couldn't make a man happy.

Then one day, like a bolt out of the blue, a voice of authority and command offered the opportunity of a lifetime. There was Jesus of Nazareth hailing him, and there was a handful of His new disciples. The disciples were looking him over with very mixed feelings indeed, but the Master was looking into his very soul. The disciples saw the publican; Jesus saw the person. Jesus saw the man beneath the empty mask of indifference and bravado. "Follow me," He said. That was all. It was enough. Matthew did not hesitate for a moment. He handed his account book over to his assistant, appointed a successor, and then walked out of the tax-collecting business forever. Matthew was a changed man.

Perhaps the Master's call came to him as an unexpected challenge. Perhaps he had been thinking about a change for a long time. Perhaps he had heard some of Jesus' sermons, seen some of His miracles, and talked to Him privately at night like Nicodemus. Perhaps Matthew had been longing and yearning for just such a call. In any case, it did not take him long to make up his mind. He didn't say, "I'll think it over." He rose up and followed Jesus.

We can believe that Matthew's decision caused quite a stir in and around Capernaum. The gossip spread from village to village: "Guess what! Jesus of Nazareth has a new disciple—a publican. He must be hard up for disciples."

But Jesus wanted Matthew. He wanted him for Himself—He saw beneath the surface to the sound quality of the man. But He also wanted the skills that Matthew had. They would be invaluable later on in establishing His kingdom in the hearts and lives of men. He wanted the businessman in Matthew.

Most of the Lord's disciples were only average people. Judas was the only Judean; the rest were Galileans and the Galileans were despised in Jerusalem as provincial. Most Galileans had a very limited education. But Matthew could read, write, keep records, draw conclusions, weigh the pros and cons of a situation, and make firm decisions. He was used to assessing the value of all the different kinds of merchandise carried by the caravans on the great Damascus-Tyre highway that ran through Capernaum. His work as a tax collector had called for considerable knowledge and he would be an invaluable man to have in the apostolic circle.

Like all other Jews, the disciples had well-trained and retentive memories and would be able to recall much of what they heard and saw in their three and a half years with Jesus— especially when their capacious memories were quickened by the Holy Spirit. Yet it was in the interest of everyone to have someone along who could write things down. Making notes seems to have been Matthew's particular job, for he never opens his mouth in the Gospels. We see his name in the various lists of the apostles, but we read little else about him.

No sooner had Matthew responded to the royal invitation to become a personal follower of the Christ of God than he did a very sensible thing. He threw a party. He invited all his former friends, the whole fellowship of publicans and sinners, to be his guests. He also invited Jesus and all his new friends in Christ. It was Matthew's way of introducing his former associates to Jesus. It was his way of saying to his old crowd, "I'm through with the old way of life. Come and meet the Master. Come and meet the man who changed my life completely. Perhaps you would like to enthrone Him as Savior and Lord of your lives too."

We have no idea how many responded. Perhaps it was news of Matthew's changed life that touched the heart of Zaccheus. In any case, Matthew's dinner party marked a complete break with his old way of life. He had a new Master, a new fellowship, and new friends. His old friends could come and join him, but he would not be joining them anymore. What a wonderful way to begin a new life in Christ!

Committed now beyond recall, Matthew spent the next three years of his life in the personal company of Jesus and His disciples. He trudged the length and breadth of the promised land with Him. He saw His many miracles (only a scant three dozen of them are recorded in the Gospels). He heard His wonderful sayings. He saw how Jesus handled Himself in various situations. He listened to the sermon on the mount and made copious notes—Matthew was the only Gospel writer to give us the full text. He listened avidly to the Olivet discourse—and again Matthew gave us the fullest account of that remarkable sermon on things to come. He watched the growing opposition. He was in the upper room for the Lord's farewell messages. He had firsthand knowledge of the trial, the terrible miscarriage of justice, the crucifixion, the burial, and the resurrection. And all this time his pen was busy writing and recording. Of the 1,068 verses that make up Matthew's Gospel, 644 contain actual words of Christ, so about three-fifths of his Gospel is made up of the recorded words of the Lord Jesus.

III. HIS MANUSCRIPT

If Matthew never did anything else, he performed a service of the highest order for the world and for the church when he wrote the Gospel that bears his name. His Gospel was initially intended for the Jewish people. He wanted to demonstrate that the man Jesus, whom the Jews had so terribly rejected, was indeed their Messiah. There is ample evidence of this intent in the nature and content of the Gospel itself. Consider the following examples:

1. The Gospel of Matthew traces the Lord's ancestry back to David, the founder of the Hebrew royal family.
2. This Gospel traces that ancestry through Joseph, the lineal descendant of Solomon and the foster father of Jesus.
3. This Gospel makes constant reference to "the holy city" and refers also to "the holy place."
4. This Gospel calls Jesus the Son of David in various places.
5. This Gospel shows the fulfillment of Old Testament prophecy regarding the coming of Christ.
6. This Gospel alone makes reference to the kingdom of Heaven. The kingdom of Heaven is not the same as the kingdom of God. The kingdom of God is eternal, spiritual, and free from sin. It can only be entered by means of the

new birth and its empire is established in the hearts of the regenerate. The phrase "the kingdom of Heaven" refers to God's purpose and plan to establish a kingdom on earth. Its fortunes have fluctuated with the course of history and its establishment is postponed now until the second coming of Christ. Matthew's understanding of the Jewish role in the kingdom of Heaven led him to tell us most of what we know about it.

7. The Gospel of Matthew alludes frequently to Jewish customs, the Mosaic law, and the Hebrew prophets. Matthew generally assumed his readers were familiar with his quotations and allusions.

In all likelihood Matthew's Gospel was written just before the destruction of Jerusalem and the temple by the Romans in A.D. 70. By that time Jewish rejection of the claims of Christ, both in the homeland and among the diaspora, was deeply entrenched.

Matthew's plan was to group his material not necessarily in chronological order, but in a logical order to produce a cumulative effect. For instance, Matthew kept the remarkable sermon on the mount intact, whereas in Luke the substance of the discourse is found scattered here and there throughout the Gospel. Matthew recorded twenty specific miracles of Jesus and, in keeping with his pattern of grouping his material, half of these miracles are recorded in just two chapters (8–9).

Matthew recorded about forty of the Lord's parables. He alone told us about the wheat and the tares, the hidden treasure, the pearl of great price, the fish net, the householder and his treasure, the unmerciful servant, the laborers in the vineyard, the ten virgins, and the talents. Nearly all the parables recorded by Matthew alone are in keeping with his purpose of emphasizing the fact that Jesus was Israel's Messiah.

At least seven of the forty parables recorded by Matthew are parables of judgment. Doubtless the terrors inflicted on his native land as the Romans pursued their relentless war colored

Matthew's writing. Jesus had warned that judgment would come to the apostate nation of Israel. But the judgment at the hand of the Romans was only preliminary. Matthew focused on end-time judgments too. In keeping with the judgmental aspect of his Gospel, Matthew recorded the Lord's denunciations of the Jewish leaders. In this Gospel the Lord's public ministry thus begins with eight beatitudes (Matthew 5:3-10) and climaxes with eight curses (Matthew 23).

Matthew's Gospel can be divided into four parts: (A) in chapters 1–9 the King is revealed; (B) in chapters 10–16 the King is resisted; (C) in chapters 16–27 the King is rejected; (D) in chapter 28 the King is raised.

A. The King Is Revealed

1. His Person

First the Gospel of Matthew reveals *His ancestry*. Jesus was the Son of David and the rightful heir to David's throne. When Matthew wrote, the temple was still standing and anyone could verify the Lord's genealogy by consulting the registers in the temple.

Next the Gospel reveals *His advent*. Matthew recorded how it came to pass that Jesus was born, as prophesied, in the town of Bethlehem. Matthew told of the visit of the wise men from the East—the Gentile magi who bore tribute to Jesus as the King of the Jews. Matthew told also of the fulfillment of another prophecy: "Out of Egypt have I called my son" (Matthew 2:15).

The Gospel then reveals *His ambassador*. Matthew told of the coming of John the Baptist, in the spirit and power of Elijah, to herald the imminent unveiling of the King.

Moreover the Gospel reveals *His adversary*. Matthew gave us the fullest account of how the Lord was tempted in the wilderness and how He routed the ancient enemy of mankind.

2. His Purpose

The King's purpose is revealed in the choice of *His men*. Matthew told us how the Lord chose His disciples, the men with whom He intended to share the administration of His kingdom. Those who judged only by outward appearance thought the disciples were an unpretentious and insignificant collection of nobodies. It was obvious that here was a King who loved ordinary folk. He bypassed the religious establishment as represented by synagogue and Sanhedrin and went straight to the common people for His followers.

Matthew also revealed *His mandate*. The Gospel records the famous sermon on the mount, in which the King issued a series of astonishing precepts for the government of His kingdom. The Lord took the light of the Mosaic law (in itself impossible to obey completely), passed it through the prism of His divine intellect, broke that white light up into its glowing colors, and then lifted it like a rainbow as high as the heavens themselves. Then in answer to those who wrote the word *impossible* over His precepts, He lived by them—moment by moment, day after day, in all the various circumstances of life.

3. His Power

Then too Matthew revealed the King's power. The Gospel tells how Jesus cleansed the leper, stilled the storm, and raised the dead. He fed the multitudes, healed the sick, and gave sight to the blind. He made the dumb to speak, the deaf to hear, and the lame to walk. Such power had never been demonstrated on earth before.

B. The King Is Resisted

In chapters 10–16 of his Gospel, Matthew wrote of mounting resistance to the King. We would have expected His contemporaries to cheer Him all the way to Jerusalem, Rome, and the empire of the world. Instead the Jewish religious establishment instigated a rising tide of opposition. That resistance was *foretold* in Matthew 10, *felt* in Matthew 11, and *focused* in Matthew 12–13. When the Jewish leaders finally accused Him of doing His marvelous miracles in the power of Satan, He gave a series of parables ("the mystery parables") in which He officially postponed the establishment of the kingdom of Heaven until an unspecified future date. He interposed the age of grace (the church age in which we live), a period of time during which God would work out quite a different purpose of grace—He would build a spiritual *church* rather than establish a material *kingdom*.

C. The King Is Rejected

Matthew 16–27 tells of the King's rejection. After Peter's confession and the subsequent transfiguration, the Lord began to talk increasingly about His forthcoming death on the cross. He pronounced a series of woes upon the leaders of the Jewish religious establishment, and then in His great Olivet discourse He foretold the impending destruction of both Jerusalem and the temple and set the stage for His coming again.

Events happened swiftly after these warnings. Judas defected to the Sanhedrin and betrayed the Lord while He was praying in Gethsemane. A series of mock trials followed and Jesus was handed over by the Romans to the executioners. And so the Jews rejected their Messiah, and the Romans collaborated with them in His murder. An age had come to an end.

D. The King Is Raised

In the final chapter of his Gospel, Matthew told us of the King's resurrection. Matthew 28:1 says it was "the end of the sabbath" when Jesus rose from the dead. It was the end of the sabbath indeed! It was a new dawn, a new day, a new dispensation. Everything now centers not on the dead Jewish sabbath, but on the first day of the week, the resurrection morn, the day the King came back. The Sanhedrin did their best to squelch the tidings, but they might as well have tried to put out the sun. Today the tidings of a risen Christ are heralded around the globe.

Well, Matthew, you took good notes and the Holy Spirit inspired you as to how to use them. We are grateful to you. Little did you know that day when you walked out of the Capernaum customs office that you would eventually write a bestseller—a book that would become part of the divine library, a book that would be read and studied and loved and taught throughout the whole wide world, a book that would be translated into hundreds of languages, a book that would make your name famous for the rest of time. That was a good bargain you made when you forsook all to follow the Christ of God.

---

1. See note 1 on page 38.

6
Jude
the Obscure

Matthew 10:3; Mark 3:18; Luke 6:16; Acts 1:13; John 14:22

> I. HIS NAME
> II. HIS FAME
>> A. A Very Important Test
>> B. A Very Important Truth
>> C. A Very Important Trio
> III. HIS AIM

We can be quite sure that the Lord made no mistakes when He chose the twelve. Indeed He waited some time before He selected His disciples out of an ever-growing crowd of followers and ordained those twelve to be apostles. He made His selections after a night of prayer. Besides, He was incarnate omniscient wisdom. But why did He choose such a pale-faced nonentity as Judas (Jude), the brother (or perhaps son) of James?

Two other men by the name of Judas are prominent in the New Testament: Judas the betrayer, the man who sold the Savior for a handful of coins; and Judas the author of the book of Jude, the little memo on apostasy near the end of the New

Testament. The latter is commonly thought to be one of the Lord's half brothers.

But who was Judas, the son of James? He is barely mentioned outside the lists of the apostles and he is often overlooked by the average reader because in some of the lists he is not called Judas.

I. HIS NAME

He bore a name of infamy. After the nefarious and notorious behavior of Judas Iscariot, the name Judas was a heavy enough cross for anyone to carry. "Oh! So you're Judas?" people might say, having only heard of the other Judas and not knowing that he was dead.

"No! No!" Jude the Obscure would say. "I'm not *that* Judas."

"Who are you then?"

"I'm Judas the son of James."

The title "Judas the son (or perhaps brother) of James" opens up a complex field of investigation. Three people by the name of James appear in the New Testament. Two of them were disciples of the Lord and one was James the brother of Jesus. This third James was an ascetic. He became prominent in the Jerusalem church and wrote the Epistle that bears his name. He was not one of the Lord's disciples during the days of His earthly ministry and was an unbeliever until the Lord met him and saved him after the resurrection. This James is not thought to have been the father of Judas.

The disciple James the Less was the son of Alphaeus and is sometimes called James the Younger. We know next to nothing about him. Some scholars think that he and Judas were brothers—these relationships are not always so clear as we could wish![1]

Other scholars think that the disciple James who was the brother of John and the son of Zebedee, was the father of Judas. This James, the first martyr among the apostles, was one of the

Lord's inner circle along with Peter and John. If Judas was the son of this James, he was the grandson of Zebedee and the nephew of the apostle John.

If he is undistinguished in all else, this son (or brother) of James is outstanding among the apostles in that he has three names. In Matthew 10:3 he is called "Lebbaeus, whose surname was Thaddaeus." In Mark 3:18 he is called Thaddaeus. Luke 6:16 and Acts 1:13 refer to him as "Judas the brother [or son] of James." John 14:22 speaks of "Judas ... not Iscariot." We gather that Judas (Jude), Lebbaeus, and Thaddaeus are all names for the same individual, for the names always appear in the same position in the various listings of the twelve.

Perhaps out of kindness and consideration Matthew and Mark dropped the name Judas. Luke used it to help us identify the man. John wrote at the end of the first century when it no longer mattered that there were two men by the name of Judas, one of whom was infamous and the other more or less anonymous. By that time Jude the Obscure may have been dead. Just the same, out of respect for the memory of the faithful Judas, John distinguished him from the traitor by adding the words "not Iscariot."

Both *Thaddaeus* and *Lebbaeus* suggest the idea of being dear or beloved or close to the heart. Probably these were nicknames given to Judas either when he was young or after he became an apostle. In any case he apparently was looked upon with affection.

Jesus deliberately chose this Judas. If he was the grandson of Zebedee and Salome, Jesus knew him well. Salome was His mother's sister. So Jude's grandmother was the Lord's aunt, his grandfather was the Lord's uncle, and Jude's father James was the Lord's cousin! During the silent years of Jesus' life, He and His family must have made many trips from Nazareth to the seaside to visit His mother's family. Jesus would often have observed little Judas growing up. Perhaps He saw in him the character traits that earned the nickname Thaddaeus. Judas may well have been a lovable little fellow. Jesus and young

Judas were attracted to each other, and by the time Jesus was ready to call James to be a disciple, He had made up His mind to call young Judas as well.

Jesus knew Judas would never be a boisterous leader like Peter. He would never be a great visionary like his uncle John. He would never stand tall or stand out, but Jesus saw something in him. When we get to the judgment seat of Christ and the books are opened, we will understand why Jesus added this youngster to the apostolic band. Perhaps Jesus valued his youthfulness, which made him quiet and retiring around the older men. Perhaps Jesus desired diversity in age as well as in temperament and background among the twelve. In any case Judas found his place among the disciples. He was a follower rather than a leader, a listener rather than a talker. Indeed he only spoke once in Scripture, but what he said was very much to the point, as we will see.

Judas Iscariot tarnished a great name: that of Judah. Young Jude the Obscure went a long way to redeem it. *Judas, Judah,* and *Jude* are synonymous. Judah was the name of the royal tribe, the tribe of which Jesus was born.

II. HIS FAME

Judas is famous for only one thing: a question. Only once in the Gospels did he speak, and then it was to ask Jesus a question. The place was the upper room. The time was the last Passover and the institution of the Lord's supper.

By the following night Jesus would be dead and buried. Within an hour He would be weeping His heart out in Gethsemane. Soon Peter, usually so forward, would have denied the Lord three times, once with oaths and curses. Only Jude's uncle John would show any semblance of courage and he would become the tender guardian of Mary, the Lord's mother. Judas Iscariot would be both dead and damned—his name blotted out of God's book and indelibly written into the history of this world as the archetype of all traitors. In time and one by one the scattered disciples would find their way back to this upper room. Jude the Obscure and the other disciples—wishing they were as obscure as he was—would huddle there behind barred and bolted doors dreading to hear the footfall of the temple police or of Pilate's officers.

But let us refocus on Jesus sharing the last Passover meal with His disciples. Once Judas Iscariot had left their midst, a sense of foreboding prevailed in the upper room. Jesus addressed a hushed and unhappy group. "I'm going away," He said in effect. "I'm going home. But don't let that bother you too much. You know both where My Home is and how to get there." He went on to speak of other things. He told them about the Holy Spirit. He told them they could expect the hatred of the world. He talked to them about the true vine. He prayed for them. Jude the Obscure sat there at the table with all the others listening, hardly believing his ears, wondering what kind of world it would be without Jesus.

The Lord was interrupted three times. First Thomas *contradicted* Him. He told the Lord He did not know where He was going and certainly didn't know the way. Then Philip *confronted* Him. He said in effect: "You keep on talking about the Father. Who is this Father You talk about? Show Him to us and we'll be satisfied." Then Jude *consulted* Him. He asked Him a question.

There are various kinds of questions. The *scientist* asks why. Why does a magnetized needle point north? Why does light travel at the speed of 186,000 miles per second? Why does the gravity of the earth attract a falling object?

The *pragmatist* asks how. "So what if the square on the hypotenuse is equal to the sum of the squares of the two sides containing the right angle!" he says. "How does that fact affect practical everyday life?" The answer to his question leads him to the three-four-five-triangle, which enables him to lay out perfectly angled ninety-degree buildings.

The scientist asks why mass and energy and the speed of light are interrelated, and he comes up with an equation that explains the relationship of space, matter, and time. The pragmatist says how that equation relates to the real workaday world, and he invents the atomic bomb and the nuclear power plant.

Jude the Obscure heard what Jesus was saying. He followed the conversation and the interruptions. He heard Jesus say, "He that hath my commandments, and keepeth them, he it is that loveth me: and he that loveth me shall be loved of my Father, and I will love him, and will manifest myself to him" (John 14:21). The word "manifest" arrested young Judas. The original Greek word *emphanizō* means "to cause to be manifest or shown plainly and clearly; to see something that otherwise would not be recognized by the unaided mind or eye." Jude quickly extrapolated something of profound significance: Those who loved the Lord and were loved by Him would be enabled to see things hidden from the general run of men and women. This revelation of the Lord Jesus, in other words, would be a secret revelation.

At once Judas asked his question: not why, but how. "Lord, how is it that thou wilt manifest thyself unto us, and not unto the world?" (John 14:22) The question was penetrating and went to the heart of the matter.

All the disciples had expected the Lord to manifest Himself to the world. They had anticipated an earthly kingdom. They had looked forward to the day when He would come suddenly into the temple, announce Himself as the promised Messiah, take over the reigns of government from the ruling and unbelieving establishment, mobilize His forces, rid the country of the Romans, sit on the throne of His father David, and extend His empire to the ends of the earth. Doubtless Judas had gulped at the revelation that Jesus intended to do no such thing now. He could take in his youthful stride the total upset of all the conventional ideas about the Messiah. But the practical problem remained: How could Jesus possibly manifest Himself to some people and not to other people? And how could He show Himself if He was going home to Heaven?

The Lord did not deal with Jude's question directly. The answer on the pragmatic earthly level would be known soon enough. Within the next few days and weeks, the resurrection, the ascension, and the coming of the Holy Spirit would answer Jude's question more fully than anything the Lord could say that night. Moreover Jude and the others would be better equipped to understand the answer later on.

The last time the world saw Christ was when the authorities sealed Him into Joseph's tomb and set a guard to patrol the grounds. Nobody witnessed Christ's resurrection. Early in the morning just as the dawn was tinting the eastern sky, Jesus rose through the graveclothes and stepped silently and invisibly through the walls of the tomb. Nobody saw Him rise. For some time afterward the sentries continued to patrol up and down before an empty tomb. They did not know it was empty until the angel came and rolled back the stone to show to one and all that the tomb was tenanted no more. One sight of that angel was enough for even those Roman veterans. With a howl of terror they fled toward the city.

Then Jesus began to manifest Himself to His followers. He manifested Himself in His *resurrection* body. He appeared here and there to this one and to that one. He appeared to Peter and to James. He appeared to the two on the Emmaus road. He appeared in the upper room. He appeared again to convince Thomas. He appeared by the shore of the sea of Galilee. On one occasion He manifested Himself to about five hundred believers at one time, but never to the world.

He also manifested Himself in His *rapture*. He gathered the entire band of believers together and led them to the mount of Olives. He talked and answered questions as He went. Then right before their eyes He stepped from the earth into the sky and thence back into Heaven.

The Lord manifested Himself in *revelation* as well. In the upper room on the day of Pentecost the Holy Spirit came. The eyes of the disciples' understanding were then fully opened. They understood at last and in the full blaze of that understanding went out to evangelize the world and write the various books of the New Testament.

Jude the Obscure, of course, was to be in on all these events. The Lord had no need to give an explanation ahead of time. Everything would be made plain in the course of the next six or seven weeks. Instead the Lord went to the heart of Jude's question and taught him some very important lessons that are recorded in John 14:23.

A. A Very Important Test

"If a man love me," He said, "he will keep my words." This statement presents the ultimate test of genuine love for the Lord: Those who love the Lord do what He says. Those who love the Lord treasure His Word. His slightest wish is their command. Love can never do enough for the Beloved. If we say we love Him but spend little time reading His Word and even less time doing what He says, there is something radically wrong with what we call love.

B. A Very Important Truth

"If a man love me, he will keep my words," Jesus said, "and my Father will love him." Imagine being the special object of the love of the Father. The Lord Jesus was always talking about His Father. God is rarely called Father in the Old Testament—probably fewer than six times—but the name Father was constantly on the lips of the Lord Jesus. In His first recorded utterance He said to Joseph and Mary, "Wist ye not that I must be about my Father's business?" (Luke 2:49) As a boy of twelve He already knew who His Father was and He had already made it His goal to "do always those things that please him" (John 8:29).

Speaking His last words on the cross He said, "Father, into thy hands I commend my spirit" (Luke 23:46). Jesus spoke the name again in His first conversation after the resurrection. He said to Mary Magdalene, "I am not yet ascended to my Father" (John 20:17). Almost the last word He uttered on earth was

Father. On the way to Olivet He told the disciples to go back to Jerusalem and wait for the promise of the Father. Jesus knew that all times and seasons are in the Father's sphere of authority.

The Lord Jesus loved His Father and His Father loved Him. Now if we love the Lord Jesus with the kind of love that does what He says, and if we treasure His Word, the Father will love us too. He will love us with the *agape* kind of love—the kind of love that is stronger than death, the kind of love that many waters cannot quench, the kind of love that suffers long and is kind. What a truth! Imagine being the object of God's personal affection and tender loving care.

C. A Very Important Trio

"My Father will love him, and we will come unto him, and make our abode with him." What a trio! The Father, the Lord Jesus, and the person who loves the Lord Jesus and does what He says will dwell together. The Father and the Son will come and take up their abode with such a believer.

Think for a moment of what that promise means. God the Father and God the Son will move in with us. They will live in our houses. They will ride in our cars. They will join us where we work. They will be with us when we gather with others of like precious faith. Imagine it! Sometimes we read this awesome statement and hardly let its significance penetrate our minds. The two most wonderful, most powerful, most loving, most infallible persons in the universe will take up their abode with us.[2] They control all the factors of space, matter, and time. They are the objects of the ceaseless adoration of the angels and the theme of the seraphs' song, and they choose to come and live with us!

The word translated "abode" in John 14:23 is the same word that is translated "mansions" in John 14:2. The Father and the Son will turn even the humblest cottage into a mansion, into a place more important by far than the White House or Buckingham Palace.

Jude the Obscure listened to Jesus' words and took them

all in. He said to himself, "I love Him. I intend to do what He says. I love His words. So I'm going to count on having some very exclusive and magnificent company from now on."

III. HIS AIM

Aided after Pentecost by the baptizing, indwelling, filling, and anointing of the Holy Spirit, Judas set out to live the life of one who keeps the words of Christ.

For some time he tarried in Jerusalem with the other apostles. He witnessed the great influx of souls after Pentecost and helped organize and supervise the church. He probably came in contact with Paul and heard his impassioned defense of liberty in Christ for an ever-growing Gentile church. Perhaps Judas and Barnabas had some long talks about the work in Syria, especially in Antioch.

Then the time came to move out of Jerusalem. Reasonably reliable Christian tradition leads us to believe that Jude the Obscure headed north to Syria. He is thought to have helped plant the gospel in Armenia and to have gone to Mesopotamia and Persia. So as Paul headed west with the gospel, this little-known foot soldier of the cross went East. In the end, it is believed, Judas suffered martyrdom in Persia. Wherever he went, this unsung saint of God carried another presence with him. God the Father and God the Son accompanied him on his travels and stood by him in his efforts to spread the glad tidings of salvation.

For the most part Judas remains obscure, but one day the books will be opened. When they are, we will join hands with him around the throne in Heaven and he'll invite us to come along and see his heavenly mansion eternally graced by the abiding presence of the Father and the Son.

---

1. See note 1 on page 38.
2. The coequal Holy Spirit's ministry is not in view in this passage.

7
Simon
the Zealot

Luke 6:15

```
I. THE MAN HE WAS
II. THE MAN HE MET
III. THE MAN HE BECAME
```

imon is called the Zealot and that's all we know about
him beyond the fact that he was a disciple of the Lord
Jesus and one of the twelve apostles of the Lamb. The
silence about him in Scripture is all the more arresting
because the other Simon in the apostolic company is made
highly visible. The name *Simon* means "one who hears." His
name may be some kind of clue to the mystery of the Zealot,
for "faith cometh by hearing, and hearing by the word of
God" (Romans 10:17). Perhaps we can deduce that he was
a good listener, but Scripture does not give us any additional
insights. In an attempt to synthesize a character sketch of
Simon, we will consider the man he was, the man he met,
and the man he became.

As we think of the man Simon was, we will be drawn into
a study of a man's convictions. We will also see how Jesus
CHOOSES a man.

As we think of the man Simon met, we will be undertaking

a study of a man's confrontation. We will also see how Jesus CHALLENGES a man.

As we think of the man Simon became, we will be engaged in *a study of a man's conversion*. We will also see how Jesus CHANGES a man.

I. THE MAN HE WAS

When Pompey conquered Judea and Jerusalem, the country became a Roman province and thereafter its people were subject to Roman taxation. The Romans paid no attention to the fact that the Hebrew people were already heavily taxed— they had to pay a double tithe to support the Levites, priests, and temple. Most pious Jews paid these religious taxes willingly enough, but the new tax was harsh and rapacious and the Romans farmed out the job of collecting it to self-seeking opportunists. One estimate is that the Jews were paying at least 30 to 40 percent of their income in taxes. So heavy was the burden that it threatened to bring the country to the verge of economic collapse. Neither the religious leaders nor the Roman masters would give way. This is the situation which gave rise to the Zealots.

The Roman administrators of the country were often insensitive and heavy-handed. Most of them were hack appointees—rough-and-ready soldiers who had risen up through the ranks. They had little or no administrative skill and cared nothing about social niceties. They made crude mistakes and backed them up with cruelty. Their idea of statesmanship was simple: when all else fails, use force.

The Roman procurators were often incompetent. The last of them, Florus, turned out to be the worst. He had learned nothing from the history of the previous governors of Judea. During a Passover celebration he seized the high priest's vestments. Then Florus added insult to injury by violating with obscenities the most sacred beliefs of the Jews. He had a consuming passion for wealth so it is not surprising that he raided the temple treasury. A riotous demonstration ensued and Florus chose to treat this demonstration as an act of rebellion. He called in the troops, arrested a number of the leading citizens, crucified them, and then handed Jerusalem over to his soldiers to plunder. This was the last straw and a revolt against Rome broke out.

The Jews stormed the Roman garrison outside Jerusalem and routed the troops stationed there. Rebellion spread like fire throughout the country and the Zealots saw the magic moment they had been waiting for. They captured the impregnable fortress of Masada. The tiny Jewish nation had thrown down the gauntlet to Rome, the giant oppressor of the world, and the Zealots became national heroes.

This group of rebels was the party Simon had joined. The Zealots were an intolerant crowd. Josephus described them as *sicarii,* a term that refers to people armed with daggers. Until open insurrection against Rome was possible, the more extreme Zealots relied on simple terrorism to achieve their ends. These extremists would conceal daggers in their robes, mingle with the crowds, and stab those they regarded as traitors.

The Zealots were in the thick of the fight against Rome. At the time the Roman army drew its compass around Jerusalem, the city was in the hands of three rival groups: the city itself was in the hands of Simon Bar Giora; the outer temple court was held by John of Gischala; and the inner courts were held by the Zealot leader Eliezerben Simon. The unfortunate people of Jerusalem suffered as much from the brigandry, oppressions, and squabbles of these bandit leaders as they did from the Roman siege. When the three rival gangs were not fighting Rome, they were fighting each other and pillaging and ravaging the inhabitants of the city. Anyone suspected of wanting to defect to Rome was killed—often simply flung over the wall of the city to be dashed to pieces by the rocks below. The scenes of horror and terror inside the city were almost indescribable. Josephus heaped much of the blame for the suffering on the Zealots.

The last stand of the Zealots was at Masada in A.D. 71. After a long and bitter fight the fortress was taken by the Roman general Silva. Masada, a remote "fortress in the sky" in one of the most desolate places on earth, frowned down on the Dead Sea. Herod the Great had made the fortress virtually impregnable and the Romans were compelled at last to build an enormous and expensive ramp up to the walls. When they finally stormed the fortress, they found only a few people still alive. All the rest had committed suicide rather than fall into the hands of the Romans. To this day the Zealots' defense of Masada is legendary.

Simon was a Zealot, but not all Zealots were nationalist fanatics. Some were pure idealists. However all of them longed to see their country forever rid of the Romans.

When Jesus decided to pour Himself into just a dozen men, one of the men He chose was Simon the Zealot. Simon, after all, was a man of conviction. He may have been inclined to carry his convictions to the extreme, but the beliefs he held, he held with passion. Jesus needed a man like him.

On the purely human level Simon might have been a potential liability to Jesus. We can be sure that the procurator's palace had a list of men to be kept under surveillance and high on this list were members of the Zealot party. They were known troublemakers, forever fomenting riot and rebellion. To be marked down as a Zealot in those days would be like being marked down as a Jew by the Nazis or as a communist in the days of the cold war. Jesus took the risk in His stride. He was as willing to associate Himself with a Zealot as with a publican.

There was considerable variety within the ranks of the apostolate. Simon was a Zealot; Matthew was a publican. They stood at opposite ends of the political spectrum. One was an ardent patriot, the other an outcast collaborator. Peter was a doer; John was a dreamer. Nathanael was a thinker. Thomas was a doubter. Philip was a realist, Andrew was an optimist, and Judas Iscariot was an opportunist. They were as diverse a collection of men as you would find today in the average local church.

Yet they all were attracted to Jesus, and Jesus was attracted to them. He chose them after a night of prayer. He knew what He was doing when He called Simon the Zealot. He knew the man's secret heart. He knew that he ached and longed for the Messianic kingdom. He knew that the spark and fire that made him a Zealot would also make him a grand apostle—once all his fiery passions had been extinguished and rekindled by Calvary love.

Simon the Zealot was made out of the same stuff as the Old Testament prophet Jonah, a man who was fearless, single-minded, and mightily used of God. Jesus had a future field of service for a man like him.

So we can surmise what kind of man Simon was: a man of conviction. We never read anything about him except that Jesus chose him and called him—and he came. We do not know how long Jesus knew him or when he was called. We do not know what kind of home he came from. We do not know if he moved in the same circles as Barabbas and his band of insurrectionists. We do not know anything except that he was willing to lay all his passionate convictions at Jesus' feet. In the Gospels he never raised his voice in debate. He never pushed himself forward. He asked no questions. Simon ("one who hears") was just there—listening, learning, longing, looking.

II. THE MAN HE MET

Before Jesus began His public ministry, a notable prophet appeared among the Jews—his voice raised in the wilderness, his message strangely stirring to the soul, and his appeal widespread among the masses. "Repent," John the Baptist cried, "for the kingdom of heaven is at hand" (Matthew 3:2). Thousands of people were moved to the depths of their beings. They flocked in droves to the Jordan to hear him. Large numbers responded to his call for baptism as a token of repentance.

The fact that the religious establishment wrote John off as a public nuisance probably helped confirm to Simon the Zealot that the man was indeed a true prophet of God in the Old Testament sense of the word. The Sanhedrin and the synagogue had sunk to a sorry level of compromise, materialism, hypocrisy, formalism, and impotence, so Simon would be inclined to listen to John. Perhaps Simon thought that John was the prophet Elijah who was to herald the coming of the Messiah. Probably Simon determined to keep his eyes and ears open.

Then Jesus came. He took up John's cry: "The kingdom of heaven is at hand." John did no miracles and he kept himself in the backwoods and in the wilderness. But the new teacher, Jesus of Nazareth, took the Jewish world by storm. Stories of miracles came pouring in from all over. Not even in the days of Moses and Elijah had such wonders been seen. It seemed that neither demons nor disease nor even death could exist in His presence. Moreover He was preaching about a kingdom now being offered to Israel. The common people heard Him gladly. The establishment suspended judgment, but as usual were inclined to be negative.

Perhaps the action of Jesus in the temple in Jerusalem finally persuaded Simon the Zealot of His authenticity (John 2:14-17). Jesus looked around the courts with growing wrath. He used a scourge of cords to drive out the money-changers and overturned their tables. He drove out the merchants who marketed sacrificial animals. "Make not my Father's house an house of merchandise," He said. When Simon the Zealot heard about the cleansing of the temple, he said to himself, "Good for Him!" Perhaps Simon remembered the Old Testament text about the promised Messiah: "The zeal of thine house hath eaten me up" (Psalm 69:9). Here was a Zealot indeed.

Perhaps the Lord's social program first appealed to Simon. Here was a man who was actually doing something about the sick and the hungry. What had the Zealots ever done? True, they were against injustice, tyranny, and the Roman occupation of their native land. The program of the Zealots, however, seemed to begin and end with clandestine meetings. It was a program of deception, violence, guerilla warfare, and for those who were caught, a cross.

One day the confrontation came. Jesus challenged Simon to become one of His disciples. We know nothing whatever about the meeting. We can be quite sure, however, that Jesus made the issues crystal clear. He was the last, the rightful, and the only surviving legitimate claimant to David's throne—a fact that could be checked by consulting the records in the temple—and He was going to establish a kingdom. He was indeed the Messiah, the King of Israel. He was the Son of God.

Simon was being invited to become part of a revolution! However, unlike any other revolution, this was to be a revolution of love. The problem was much more serious than the Roman occupation. The problem was sin. Jesus had come to destroy sin's empire in the human heart.

Doubtless Jesus said much the same to Simon the Zealot as He said to Nicodemus: "Except a man be born again, he cannot see the kingdom of God" (John 3:3). Jesus was indeed going to found an empire—but the ruling principle in that empire was to be love. There would be a revolution, but it would be based on regeneration. Human nature has to be changed before nations can be changed.

Simon certainly had a lot to think about. He also had to consider that indefinable "something" about Jesus. It was not just His clear thinking, His great vision, His captivating personality, and His demonstrated power. It was not just His radiant humanity. There was His evident deity. He was so essentially good. Indeed *holy* would be a better word to describe Him. His wisdom, love, and power were absolute, beyond any ever displayed by sinners of Adam's ruined race.

So Simon the Zealot made his decision for Christ. Then Jesus must have introduced him to the others. "This is Simon

Peter and his brother Andrew, fishermen from Capernaum. This is James and his brother John. Their mother Salome and My mother are sisters. They too used to be fishermen. This is Thomas. These two are Philip and Nathanael. Here's someone you'll be interested to meet: Matthew or Levi, to give him his Hebrew name. He used to be a tax collector, a publican, but now he is My disciple and My friend. Here's Judas. We have two Judases. This one is Judas Iscariot. He's our treasurer ... "

Under any other circumstances and in any other setting, the Zealot would have had little or nothing in common with most of these men. What made him one of them, and one with them, was their common love for the Lord Jesus. The apostles were like the spokes of a wheel, radiating out from their common center to the circumference of the circle. As those spokes draw closer and closer to the hub, they draw closer and closer to each other. They depict the secret of the apostolic community. Each of the twelve, except Judas Iscariot, loved the Lord Jesus. He was the hub that held them all together. As they drew nearer to Him, they drew nearer to each other. Apart from Him there would have been no apostolate. Apart from Him there can be no church.

Simon the Zealot accepted Christ's challenge. He exchanged his membership in a band of hotheaded revolutionaries for membership in a fellowship based on love for the Lord Jesus Christ. He would never regret his decision. The man he met became all-in-all to him. The man he met eclipsed all others, dominated all horizons, controlled all situations, filled his heart and mind, and thenceforth ruled his life—for the man he met was Jesus!

III. THE MAN HE BECAME

Conversion is both a crisis and a process. The crisis comes when Jesus is enthroned in the heart as Savior and Lord. The process goes on for the rest of the believer's life. The crisis is often sudden; the process is usually slow. We grow in grace and increase in the knowledge of God. Both growing and acquiring knowledge are gradual processes.

Surely it did not take Simon long to realize that his zeal would need to be redirected. The sermon on the mount must have convinced him of his need. It would take the death, burial, resurrection, and ascension of Christ, followed by the baptism, indwelling, filling, and anointing of the Holy Spirit to bring him and the other apostles into some measure of the fullness of the stature of Christ.

Tradition tells us that after the concentration of the apostles in Jerusalem was finally broken up and the apostles began to take seriously the Lord's call to "the uttermost part of the earth" (Acts 1:8), Simon the Zealot headed for North Africa. He journeyed westward through what was called Mauretania and probably took the gospel to the great city of Carthage. Then Simon and Joseph of Arimathaea, it seems, went to Britain.

Britain had been conquered by Julius Caesar half a century before the birth of Christ. London was founded in A.D. 43 and within a couple of decades became an important city. When Nero became emperor the British people, led by the indomitable Queen Boadicea, revolted against Roman rule and a savage war broke out. About this time Simon would have arrived in Britain with the gospel.

One tradition is that the Zealot's activities were brought to the attention of Caius Decius, who nursed in his pagan soul a deep hatred of Christianity. Simon was arrested, given a mock trial, and sentenced to death by crucifixion. He is said to have been martyred at Caistor, Lincolnshire, where he was buried on or about May 10, A.D. 61.

A different tradition is that he did preach to the Latin community in Britain, perhaps even in London, but the Boadicea uprising prompted him to leave the country since the climate was no longer favorable to the gospel. Simon is thought to have returned to Palestine and made his way to Persia, where he was martyred by being sawn asunder.

Simon remained zealous to the end. His vision for the liberation of Palestine from the rule of Rome was expanded by Christ to a vision for the salvation of the whole lost Gentile world. Once he advocated the use of the sword, but after his conversion he proclaimed God's offer of peace to all mankind.

The church needs men like Simon the Zealot. So many Christians are lazy, apathetic, half-hearted, and careless; they cannot find it in their hearts to give even minimal support to the evangelistic and Bible-teaching efforts of the church. We need the zeal of a John Knox, who said, "Give me Scotland or give me death!" We need men like D. L. Moody; when he heard someone say that the world had yet to see what God could do through a man wholly sold out to Him, he declared, "By the grace of God I'll be that man." We need men like David Livingstone, who was willing to go anywhere as long as it was forward. We need men like George Verwer, who motivated thousands to get up and get going for God; he was driven by the life-text, "Nothing shall be impossible unto you" (Matthew 17:20). The church needs men who are willing to be fuel for the flame of God.

8

Thomas
the Twin

John 11:16; 14:1-6; 20:24-29

> I. HIS CAUTION
>
> II. HIS COMMITMENT
>
> III. HIS CONCERN
>
> IV. HIS COLLAPSE
>
> V. HIS CONFESSION

He is usually called Thomas, but sometimes Didymus. Both names mean "the twin." Because he is usually paired with Matthew in the various listings of the twelve apostles in the New Testament, it has been surmised that he was perhaps the twin brother of Matthew.

One commentator, Matthew Poole, speculated that Matthew was the original prodigal son, for before his conversion Matthew was a renegade Jew who had sunk so low as to sell his soul to Rome. The far country is not always defined in terms of miles; it can often be defined in terms of morals. If Matthew was indeed the prototype for the prodigal in the Lord's parable, Thomas (if he was Matthew's twin) must have been the original elder brother. In the case of twins, being the elder brother can hinge on a matter of minutes. Esau and Jacob were twins, but

Esau was always considered the elder and Jacob the younger even though their births were only minutes apart. These are interesting speculations, but probably nothing more.

Archbishop Trench saw a connection in Thomas between being a twin and being twin-minded. The twins of belief and unbelief battled each other in Thomas's heart just as Esau and Jacob struggled in Rebekah's womb. Regardless of whether there is any truth in these suggestions, the fact remains that Thomas was a twin and that somewhere he had a twin brother or twin sister. It would be interesting to know whether he or she also became a follower of the Lord Jesus.

We are indebted to the apostle John for all we know about Thomas as a person. The synoptic writers only mentioned him in their various listings of the twelve apostles. John, writing toward the end of the first century and looking back to those wonderful years of his youth, evidently thought of Thomas as one who was a personality in his own right. Perhaps they had been boyhood friends, since both were Galileans.

I. HIS CAUTION

We call him Doubting Thomas, but it might be fairer to say he was cautious. He always wanted to be sure of his ground. He was not the kind of man to sign a document without first reading it all the way through. In a debate his favorite defense would be "Prove it!" He was the kind of man who had to see things for himself. Once he was convinced, he would hold tenaciously to what he believed.

It is not a bad idea to be cautious, especially about what we accept as the articles of our faith. The Bible urges us to be cautious. In his first Epistle John warned against deceiving spirits that lurk in the unseen world. He warned us not to accept ideas just because they were imparted by ecstatic utterance or by a so-called prophet. The Holy Spirit commended the people of Berea because they put even the preaching of an apostle to the test. They searched the Scriptures daily to see if the teachings of Paul were true.

There was a high brick wall around the playground of the high school I attended in Britain. The wall was topped with a thick layer of cement in which was embedded pieces of jagged broken glass. The idea, of course, was to discourage boys from scaling the wall. I once saw a cat walking along the top. He took each step with great caution. He would put out a paw, gingerly feel the surface, and when he was quite sure that cement and not glass was beneath his feet, he would take the next step. That cat's name might well have been Thomas! Thomas wanted to be sure of his ground before he made a move. There's not much fault to find in that philosophy of life.

But sometimes even the most careful of men will throw all caution to the winds. Thomas did so and thus earned honorable though gloomy commendation in John's memoirs of Jesus.

II. HIS COMMITMENT

It will be helpful to review the circumstances surrounding the time when Thomas made his daring commitment. The Lord Jesus was in Peraea, a rural area beyond the Jordan river. Originally Peraea was the tribal territory of Gad and Reuben. The northern section was densely wooded; the southern section was rich pastureland fading off to widening tracts of desert as the area reached toward the Dead Sea.

Jesus had been up to Jerusalem to keep the feast of tabernacles, a joyful occasion when even Jews from the far-flung lands of the diaspora made their pilgrimage to the holy city to pay their tithes and taxes. The Lord had been watched with great suspicion by the Sanhedrin as He taught in the temple. Their spies were everywhere.

Between the feast of tabernacles and the last Passover feast was a period of about six months, which the Lord spent in Peraea. There His ministry was mostly a teaching ministry devoted to parables and discourses. The time in Peraea was interrupted by a brief visit to Jerusalem in December for the feast of dedication. This feast was personally significant to the Lord Jesus, for it was at the time of His birthday.

There was speculation among the Jews as to whether or not He would come to Jerusalem at all, since official opposition to Him was mounting in the capital. But come He did. He appeared suddenly in the temple and taught the people. He claimed that He was the true Shepherd and they were not His sheep. When He said that He was coequal with the Father, "the Jews took up stones again to stone him" (John 10:31).

He escaped and went back across the Jordan to Peraea. Except for a brief interlude when He went to Bethany to raise Lazarus from the dead, He stayed in Peraea. With the river rolling between Him and His enemies, He gathered the people around Him. There, near the scene of the early labors of John the Baptist and not far from the place where He had been baptized, He taught the people.

What wonderful stories He told on those Peraean hills! We are indebted to Luke for the preservation of most of them. They poured out of Him: stories of the good Samaritan; the importunate neighbor; the rich fool and his barns; the barren fig tree; the great supper and the silly excuses made for not coming; the lost sheep; the lost silver; the lost son; the unjust steward; the rich man and Lazarus; the unjust judge; the self-righteous Pharisee; and the unmerciful servant. Meanwhile the shadows of His rejection were gathering deeper and darker in Jerusalem. The Lord prepared Himself, the people, and His disciples for what lay ahead.

Then came the urgent message: "Lazarus is sick. He's going to die. Please come! Come quickly." But Lazarus was already dead and Jesus knew it. However He sent the messenger back with a word of hope and cheer, and He stayed where He was. The disciples must have breathed a sigh of relief. The last place they wanted to go was the vicinity of

Jerusalem. Two days later Jesus suddenly announced that He intended to go to Bethany to deal with the unfinished business of His friend Lazarus. Immediately a storm of protest arose from the ranks of the disciples. They remembered the angry mob. They could still picture the stones in the hands of the crowd. They could have been stoned with Him.

To his lasting honor, Thomas spoke up. "Let us also go, that we may die with him," he boldly said (John 11:16). Thomas had no doubt whatsoever that if they once ventured back into the vicinity of the capital, the Sanhedrin would orchestrate their death. But if Jesus was determined to go to His death, he was determined to go to his too. Thomas's commitment made him willing to die for Christ if the call of duty demanded such a sacrifice.

So the disciples rallied around this unexpected leader and trooped back toward Jerusalem. Instead of facing the anticipated stoning, they witnessed the greatest of all the Lord's miracles: the resurrection of a man already dead, buried, and decomposing.

III. HIS CONCERN

When Thomas spoke up in Peraea, he spoke with the voice of his heart. When he expressed himself in the upper room, he spoke with the voice of his mind.

So much happened between the two occasions. Jesus entered Jerusalem triumphantly, and the disciples, their hearts pounding with excitement, thought that at last He was going to seize the reins of power and re-establish the throne of David on earth. But the excitement passed and even the densest of them could see that the storm clouds were gathering thick and heavy across their sky. The Sanhedrin was openly plotting to get rid of this unwanted Messiah.

In the upper room Jesus and the disciples observed the Passover and the Lord instituted a new feast of remembrance. The Lord, performing a servant's task to teach a lesson in humility, washed the disciples' feet. Judas departed on his unexplained mission.

Then Jesus began to talk again about the subject they dreaded. Over the past few months He had kept coming back to it. He was going to die, by crucifixion of all things. He was going to be buried, but they were not to worry. He would be back three days later. Then He would go home to His Father. "In my Father's house are many mansions," He told them (John 14:2). Although Heaven is infinitely better than earth, in some ways that other world is very much like this one, He assured them.

Adding to the consternation and confusion of the disciples, Jesus said, "Whither I go ye know, and the way ye know" (John 14:4). That was too much for Thomas. He blurted out what was probably on all their minds. They did not have the faintest idea where He was going or how to get there! "We know not whither thou goest," Thomas said. "How can we know the way?" (14:5) In all this incomprehensible talk, one ominous and terrifying fact was clear: He was going away. Thomas spoke up for them all. They did not want Him to go away.

Thomas's outburst gave the Lord Jesus an opportunity to make one of His greatest statements: "I am the way, the truth, and the life: no man cometh unto the Father, but by me" (John 14:6). In His reply to Thomas He answered the three most important questions of the human heart. Man asks, "How can I be saved?" He replies, "I am the way." Man asks, "How can I be sure?" He replies, "I am the truth." Man asks, "How can I be satisfied?" He replies, "I am the life." So long as the disciples knew Him, they knew the way because He was the way.

For a nominal fee one can go into the Hampton Court maze and find out what it is like to be lost. Hampton Court is the famous palace built by Cardinal Wolsey in the days of England's notorious Henry VIII. Having seen the covetous gleam in the king's eye when that imperious monarch saw the palace, Wolsey deeded it over to the king. The maze on the grounds of the palace consists of narrow lanes bordered by high and impenetrable hedges. All paths seem somehow to lead to the middle. When I was quite young an uncle of mine took me into that maze and, sure enough, we ended up in the center where the authorities had thoughtfully provided a seat where one could sit down and think things over. We wandered in the maze for a considerable time and just when I was getting weary, an attendant came along and offered to show us how to get out. Very soon we were on the outside! The secret to all those perplexing pathways was a man—a man who knew the way.

Likewise Jesus knew the way home. In essence Jesus was saying to Thomas and the others, "Don't worry about the way. I am the way. Just follow Me. If you know Me, you know the way because I am the way!"

IV. HIS COLLAPSE

Thomas was almost as overwhelmed by the arrest, betrayal, trial, crucifixion, and burial of Jesus as Peter was. Thomas played the coward and sought to save his own skin, as all the disciples did. Some of them recovered sooner than others and slowly the sad little group began to reassemble in the upper room. They would at least stay around Jerusalem for a few more days to see what might happen. If they kept a low profile, doubtless the authorities would leave them alone.

The Lord's tomb was sealed and guarded. There was no point in going anywhere near it. A couple of days passed. Then early Sunday morning some of the women decided to take the risk. Perhaps they could find someone to open the tomb for them so they could finish embalming the body. Soon they returned with news: the tomb was empty! The guards were gone. The women had seen some angels who told them that Jesus was alive. Peter and John went to see for themselves, but they only saw an empty tomb and some discarded wrappings.

By evening all the disciples were back in the upper

room—all except Thomas. The Lord appeared to them all—all except Thomas. Around that absence of Thomas, scores of suggestions gather themselves and countless sermons have been preached.

Why did Thomas stay away? Why did he make himself the patron saint of believers who stay away from the meetings of the Lord's people? We can suppose that he made the usual excuses people make today.

Thomas might have said, "I'm too tired, too overwrought. This has been a terrible few weeks. I need a rest." Or "I'm too busy. I have to get my life reorganized and pick up the threads of my old fishing business." Or "It's too dangerous to go out right now. The political and religious climate in Jerusalem is particularly unhealthy for believers in Jesus of Nazareth. The city is swarming with Sanhedrin spies. Why, the moment I step outside this house I'm likely to be arrested. I didn't mind dying for Christ when there was still time for another miracle to happen. But all hope for a miracle is gone." Or "I'll stay home and read my Bible. I can get just as much out of Moses and the Psalms as I would get out of a meeting with the others. All they'll do is pool their ignorance anyway. Besides, Peter will probably be there and he'll do all the talking. The last thing I need is to hear that man talk after the way he cursed and swore the other day. But he'll be up at the front as bold as brass telling everybody what to do." Or "It's going to rain." Or "I can't imagine a meeting without Jesus in the midst. Any meeting without Him will be dead and dull and meaningless."

So Thomas stayed home and missed Jesus. That evening He came in—through the walls! He talked to those who were there, let them handle Him, ate a meal, and vanished. And Thomas missed everything.

We can be sure that when he did bump into one of the other disciples and heard the astounding news, he was quite taken aback. Then his native caution would have come to his aid. He would have said, "I don't believe it. You are all mistaken. You've been seeing things." The united testimony of the other ten made no impression on him at all. "Except I shall see in his hands the print of the nails, and put my finger into the print of the nails, and thrust my hand into his side," he said, "I will not believe" (John 20:25).

The first time Thomas spoke, he spoke with the voice of his heart (John 11:16). The second time he spoke with the voice of his mind (14:5). Now we hear the voice of his will. In the last analysis, the outcome of the battle between doubt and faith always hinges on the will. We doubt, not because we *cannot* believe, but because we *will not* believe.

V. HIS CONFESSION

Thomas did not miss the next meeting. The following Sunday he was in his place in the upper room, as skeptical as ever, but there just the same. He was still muttering to himself, "I won't believe. I have to see. I have to feel...."

Then all of a sudden Jesus was there in the midst of the disciples! The doors were barred and bolted. There was no knock at the door, no hailing voice asking to be let in. He was just there! Having proved His omnipotence by coming through a barred and bolted door, He proved His omniscience by singling Thomas out and responding to his skeptical words: "Reach hither thy finger, and behold my hands; and reach hither thy hand, and thrust it into my side: and be not faithless, but believing" (John 20:27). Sad to say, the Lord used the same word (translated "faithless") He had used to describe the chronic unbelief of the world in Matthew 17:17.

Thomas was won over. "My Lord and my God," he exclaimed (John 20:28), placing Jesus on the throne of his heart ("my Lord") and on the throne of the universe ("my God"). "Thomas," the Lord rejoined, "because thou hast seen me, thou hast believed: blessed are they that have not seen, and yet have believed" (20:29).

We of course are among the blessed. We are in that succession of multitudes of men, women, boys, and girls who have believed without seeing—who have simply taken God's word that the gospel is true. With all such believers the Lord is well-pleased.

After John 20:28 the Bible records no more words spoken by Thomas. It does, however, include his name in John 21:2 and in the roll call of the apostles present in the upper room on the day of Pentecost (Acts 1:13). He was, therefore, one of those upon whom the Holy Ghost came with mighty power.

Eventually, tradition says, Thomas went eastward with the gospel—first to Babylon, then across the Euphrates to Parthia, and then on to India. Everywhere he went he told about the One who was risen from the dead, who could walk through walls, who still wears the nail scars in His hands, and who is now in Heaven preparing a place of many mansions. All Thomas's doubts were replaced by certainties once Jesus became not only his Lord but also his God.

9
John
the Beloved

John 1:35-39

By the time John took up his pen to write his Gospel, his Epistles, and the Apocalypse, the first century of the Christian era was about to close. As an old man he looked out on a world much different from the one he had known as a boy. Jerusalem was no more. The Jewish people had been uprooted and scattered to the ends of the earth. The church was spreading over the entire world and had already endured the terrible persecutions of Nero and Domitian. The roots of apostasy were everywhere. Gnosticism threatened to change Christianity into something unrecognizable. Peter was gone, James was gone, and the apostle Paul was gone.

John wrote for the third generation of Christians. By its third generation a movement stands in desperate need of revival or else it will either disappear altogether or linger on as a ghost of its former self. In the first generation truth is a *conviction*. Those who hold a conviction, hold it dearly. They do not know the meaning of compromise. They are willing to die for what they believe to be true. In the second generation the conviction becomes a *belief*. Sons hold to the truths they have been taught by their fathers and defend their beliefs in discussion and debate. However the keen edge of conviction has been blunted and adherence to a body of beliefs inherited from the fathers is not so much a passion as a persuasion. In the third generation the belief becomes an *opinion*. By then some members of the movement are willing to trade their opinions in. They feel it is time for a change, they start talking about renewal, and they look to the world for ideas.

John wrote for this third generation. He wrote with a sense of urgency. He did not write, as did the synoptists, from the viewpoint of an infant church; he wrote from the standpoint of an infirm church, one that was in dire peril from persecution without and subversion within.

We will look at John as a person, as a pupil, as a pastor, as a prophet, and as a prisoner.

I. JOHN AS A PERSON

His father was Zebedee, a successful fisherman of Bethsaida on the sea of Galilee. His mother was Salome. She had ambitious plans for her son. A devoted follower of the Lord Jesus, she sometimes traveled with the apostles. She was present at the crucifixion and at the tomb on resurrection morning. From Matthew 27:56, Mark 15:40, and John 19:25 it may be inferred that she was a sister of Mary, the mother of Jesus. John's brother was James, the first of the apostles to pay the price of martyrdom. The two brothers appear to have been cousins of the Lord Jesus, so they doubtless had known Him most of their lives. The Zebedee family was prosperous. They had hired servants and ministered unto the Lord of their substance (Luke 8:3). Moreover they were influential in official circles in Jerusalem.

A follower of John the Baptist before becoming a follower of Jesus, John the Beloved was one of the first two disciples to be called by Christ (John 1:35-39; Matthew 4:18-22). Along with his brother James and Simon Peter, John was one of the inner circle of three in the apostolic fellowship and as such was given a special vision of the Lord's *greatness* at the raising of Jairus's daughter, of the Lord's *glory* on the mount of transfiguration, and of the Lord's *grief* in the garden of Gethsemane.

John was one of the four who prompted the Olivet discourse by asking the Lord questions about eschatology (Mark 13:3). John was one of the two sent by the Lord to prepare for the Passover (Luke 22:8). John was called "the disciple whom Jesus loved" (John 21:20) and he was the disciple to whom the Lord Jesus entrusted the care of His mother (John 19:25-27). Although John was of a contemplative disposition, he was capable of being greatly aroused—so much so that Jesus called him "a son of thunder" (see Mark 3:17).

John was with Peter when Peter healed the lame man at the temple gate (Acts 3:1). John appeared before the Sanhedrin with Peter (Acts 4) and the two refused to obey the command to cease from speaking in the name of Jesus. John went with Peter to Samaria to give the apostolic blessing to the Samaritan revival spearheaded by Philip the evangelist (Acts 8:14).

John was banished to the island of Patmos by the emperor Domitian and died a natural death at Ephesus during the reign of the emperor Trajan (A.D. 98-117).

II. JOHN AS A PUPIL

If we were to ask John what he learned during the three and a half amazing years he spent with Jesus, he would point us to that wonderful book we know as the Gospel of John. In that Gospel we have John's memoirs of Jesus. John wrote his Gospel when he was an old man, but he had forgotten nothing. Indeed he had mused over the miracles of Jesus and meditated deeply on His teachings for many years. A remarkable memory, quickened by the Holy Spirit, enabled John to write a Gospel that was *contemplative, complementary* to the works of Matthew and Mark and Luke, and *conclusive* regarding the gnostic heresy.

John's Gospel is the basis of our chronology of the life of Christ. We gather from this Gospel that the Lord ministered for three and a half years. John recorded the Lord's visits to Jerusalem in connection with the national feasts, and from him we learn that Jesus had six periods of ministry in Judea, five in Galilee, one in Samaria, and one in Peraea.

John's favorite words were *know* (used 142 times), *believe* (used 100 times), *Father* (used 118 times), *world* (used 78 times), *see* (used 105 times), *verily* (used 50 times in 25 pairs), and *love* (used 36 times).

John struck the dominant notes in his Gospel again and again. Pre-eminently he wanted to demonstrate the fact that Jesus was indeed whom He claimed to be: the Son of the living God. The miracles and messages of Jesus in John's Gospel were carefully chosen to this end.

The thoughts, imagery, and language in John's Gospel were drawn from the Old Testament. Graham Scroggie said that there are probably 124 references rooted in the Old Testament. Seven times John referred to Scripture being fulfilled.

Scroggie also pointed out that John evidently had Luke's Gospel in front of him when he wrote his Gospel. What Luke put in, John left out; what Luke left out, John put in.[1]

It is from John that we learn how our Lord Jesus (as man) made Himself available to the Father, so that God could in turn make Himself available to the Son. Now we can enjoy the same type of relationship. As men we can make ourselves available to Jesus so that He (as God) can make Himself available to us.

John taught us nearly all we know about the Father and

much of what we know about the Holy Spirit. John was the one who emphasized the absolute deity of the Lord Jesus.

The Gospel of John revolves around three focal points: the signs, the secrets, and the sorrows of the Son of God. John first set before us various *signs* and proofs that Jesus of Nazareth was the One who was in the beginning with God, who was God, and who became flesh and dwelt among us as God incarnate. Then John set before us the *secrets* revealed in those heart-to-heart upper-room talks of Jesus with His disciples prior to His crucifixion. Finally John set before us the *sorrows* of the Son of God as he bypassed Gethsemane and took us straight to the trials and the tree.

John was a very good pupil! By the time he started to write his Gospel, he had been taught not only by the Son of God but also by the Spirit of God. Because he was a good student he was able to give us facts that the synoptic writers omitted from their narratives and to show us the Lord's thought-life. John's Gospel is of incomparable worth.

John lingered long at the cross. One half of his Gospel is devoted to just one week in the Lord's life: Passion week. To him the great wonder of the universe was that the Son of God should die for sinful man.

III. JOHN AS A PASTOR

In the New Testament a pastor is a shepherd, one who has a heart for the flock. The Lord Jesus is the Chief Shepherd, the great Shepherd of the sheep. A pastor is an undershepherd who cares for the people of God as Jesus cares for them.

When the Lord Jesus from the cross committed the care and keeping of His own mother to His dear friend John, John's work of shepherding began. He took Mary home with him and became a son to her. In later years when John went to Ephesus to help with the pastoral care of the great Pauline church in that city, he may have taken Mary with him. What a blessing that godly woman would have been to that particular flock!

We can formulate an idea of what John was like as a pastor by studying his three Epistles, all of which are short and two of which are little more than memos. His first Epistle deals with fellowship, the second with faith, and the third with family.

A. A Word about the Fellowship

In his first Epistle, as in his Gospel, John took us back to basics. Peter and Paul had both been dead thirty or thirty-five years and John was all alone, the only surviving apostle. Old men dwell much in the past and John referred to the past about fifty times. He referred to "the beginning" ten times (nine of the ten times in connection with Christ and His ministry).

In his Gospel John set forth the life of God *in Christ;* in his first Epistle he set forth the life of God *in us.* The life of God is inherent in Christ; the life of God is imparted to us.

The First Epistle of John gives evidence of its writer's pastoral care. It was written to *banish distance,* for we are called into intimate fellowship with one another and with the Father Himself. It was written to *banish distress* so that the believer's joy might be full. It was written to *banish deception.* One of John's key words is "light" as opposed to darkness. In this Epistle there are no shades of gray. All is black or white, true or false, right or wrong. First John was also written to *banish defilement.* John condemned sin in the life of the believer, called for confession, and reminded us that the blood of Jesus Christ cleanses us from all sin. Finally the Epistle was written to *banish doubt.* John listed about two dozen things we can know. We can know that we have passed from death unto life. We can know that we have been born again.

B. A Word about the Faith

The Second Epistle of John is a brief memo addressed to a lady. Here again we see the pastor at work, for John was concerned about the lady. She was in *danger* since the faith was under attack. It was very likely that she would receive a visit from the emissaries of a cult. Someone would come offering new lamps for old as in the story about Aladdin, so she must be on her guard.

Should such a person come, she should not let him get his foot in the *door*. Christian courtesy did not require her to open the door to a cultist or invite him in to spread forth his wares. The door must be firmly closed on him—in his face if necessary.

When sending this person about his business, she must not even wish him godspeed. She must not shake his hand or bid him good day. The *duty* of the woman of the house was to send the man packing without even the most common courtesies. John knew how persistent cultists could be. They were not to be given the slightest encouragement to come back.

C. A Word about the Family

The Third Epistle of John is a brief memo addressed to a man. Here again we see in action a great undershepherd of the sheep. We also learn about four men.

The first man is *Gaius the believer*. We are to recognize men like him. Gaius was gentle and hospitable, the kind of man whose ministry is a benediction to a local church.

The second man is *Diotrephes the bully*. We are to resist men like him. He wanted to be a local pope and made it his business to decide who could or could not be received into the fellowship. Diotrephes even prated against the highly esteemed, benevolent, and patriarchal apostle John.

The third man is *Demetrius the brother*. We are to receive men like Demetrius. He seems to have been a traveling preacher whose ministry Diotrephes rejected. John gave Demetrius his own personal word of commendation.

The fourth man is *John the Beloved*. We are to respect men like John. If anyone ever had a right to be a pope it was John, but he held an office better than that of a pope. He was an apostle—and he was not too old to wield the power of an apostle if necessary.

John closed this brief memo with a gentle word. "I hope to see you again before too long," he said in effect. "I plan on coming your way." His glove may have been velvet, but there was a resolute hand in that glove. Many years had passed since John and his brother had been called "the sons of thunder," but let Diotrephes and his kind beware. There are times when even the mildest and most patient of pastors has to assert his authority and power.

John must have been a very good pastor. He had the very best of teachers. He could remember how patiently the Lord had shepherded His own little flock in those far-off Palestinian days. Jesus had even laid down His life for His sheep. John was ready to do the same.

IV. JOHN AS A PROPHET

John was given the task of writing the book that completed the sacred Canon of Scripture. Appropriately enough, Revelation is a book that looks ahead; it is in many ways the greatest book of prophecy in the Bible.

John, as mentioned before, was one of the disciples who asked the question that prompted the Lord to give them His great Olivet discourse. In that sermon on eschatology the Lord Jesus drew together all the threads of New Testament prophecy. Although John never discussed this prophetic discourse in his own Gospel, he doubtless remembered it. Doubtless too he had copies of Matthew's account, and Mark's and Luke's as well.

John's Apocalypse, "the unveiling," is saturated with Old Testament quotations and allusions. The Gospel of Matthew has 92 and the Epistle to the Hebrews has 102, but the Apocalypse has 285 references to the Old Testament. John knew his Bible and must have spent many years poring over its prophecies.

The Apocalypse is closely related to the book of Genesis.

Three chapters from the beginning of Genesis we meet the serpent for the first time. Three chapters from the end of Revelation we meet the serpent for the last time. There are at least two dozen other comparisons and contrasts involving Genesis and Revelation. In Genesis it all begins; in Revelation it all ends.

In the book of Revelation all the forces of Heaven and Hell are seen ranged in conflict and the chief arena of battle is the planet Earth. Arrayed against God's Lamb are the scarlet beast, the scarlet woman, the miracle-working false prophet (with the appearance of a lamb and the voice of a dragon), and the red dragon himself with his seven heads and ten horns! But God's Lamb is no ordinary lamb. This Lamb has seven eyes and seven horns—all the attributes of deity.

Throughout Revelation the scenes alternate between Heaven and earth. God's word is decreed and declared in Heaven and then in spite of all the power of the enemy, His will is done on earth. Revelation unveils the full and final answer to the Lord's prayer: "Thy kingdom come. Thy will be done in earth, as it is in heaven" (Matthew 6:10). But supremely John's prophetic book is an Apocalypse, a Revelation, an unveiling, of Jesus Christ.

The book proceeds in an orderly fashion. First there is a series of seven _seals,_ broken so that "the beginnings of sorrows" (Mark 13:8) might overtake the earth. This section of Revelation is all about man. Man reduces the world to a state of utter chaos and the terrified people left on the planet desperately look for any man who can bring order out of chaos.

Then there is a series of seven _trumpets,_ blown so that Satan's false messiah, the antichrist, might come and take over the planet. This section of Revelation is all about Satan. He brings his man to total mastery over the globe, inaugurates the great tribulation, and unleashes untold woes on a Christ-rejecting world.

Finally there is a series of seven _vials,_ outpoured to bring events to a climax at the final return of Christ. This section of

Revelation is all about God. He steps down at last into the arena of human affairs. He begins to break the antichrist's stranglehold on the planet, mobilizes the Asiatic hordes against him, and draws the armies of the world to Megiddo. When He has His foes where He wants them, He suddenly reappears and puts an end to man's mismanagement of the planet.

The account of John's soaring visions ends with a description of the eternal state and the eternal city—as seen from Heaven's point of view. Thanks to the keen vision of John the prophet, the Bible ends on a triumphant note. The Lord, Revelation tells us, is now sitting on His Father's throne in glory, waiting until the earth is made His footstool.

V. JOHN AS A PRISONER

In the Aegean sea between Asia Minor and Greece, lies a small rocky island called Patmos. About ten miles long and six miles wide, Patmos consists of two segments joined by a narrow isthmus. On this island of rugged volcanic hills and valleys, wrapped by blue waters of the sea, the Romans had a penal colony. Criminals banished to Patmos were compelled to work in its mines and marble quarries. Among the prisoners was the apostle John, who was banished to Patmos by the emperor Domitian in A.D. 95.

We can picture this venerable old man, bowed down beneath his chains, working at hard manual labor all day long. Perhaps out of consideration for his age he was allowed to toil at some lesser task, but we can still picture him as a lonely exile—cut off from his home in Ephesus where he had been respected as a beloved apostle and pastor. Yet this old man was by no means defeated, and we can also picture him out among the angels and the heights of heaven by night.

All the might of Rome could back the emperor's decree banishing the aged apostle to Patmos. But all the power of Hell could not keep John from his dreams and visions. Little did that wicked old tyrant Domitian know that he was setting the stage for a prophet to catch a glimpse of glory!

Tradition says the Romans had tried boiling the apostle in oil, but he had come through unscathed. Over him the tormentor had no power! What could the devil do with a man like John? Turned loose, he would bless the church and win souls to Christ. Martyred, he would be promoted to glory. Locked up in a penal colony, he was "in the isle that is called Patmos" one moment (Revelation 1:9) and "in the Spirit on the Lord's day" the next (1:10). The time will come when we will hear the Lord say, "Well done, John."

---

1. W. Graham Scroggie, *A Guide to the Gospels* (London: Pickering and Inglis, 1948) 426,437-444.

10
Joseph,
the Husband of Mary

Matthew 1:18–2:23

> I. HIS EMPLOYMENT
> II. HIS ENGAGEMENT
> III. HIS EMBARRASSMENT
> IV. HIS ENCOURAGEMENT
> V. HIS ENLIGHTENMENT
> VI. HIS ENJOYMENT
> VII. HIS ENNOBLEMENT

Joseph was not rich, but he must have been a remarkable man. God would not have chosen a mean man, a miserly man, a moody man, a mediocre man, or a merciless man to be the foster father of His Son. Although we only catch a brief glance of Joseph in the Bible, we see enough to know he was careful, conscientious, concerned, and compassionate—a fitting foster father for Jesus.

I. HIS EMPLOYMENT

Joseph was a village carpenter. He knew what it was like to toil at a workbench and barely make ends meet. We can be sure he was honest in his business dealings and we can be sure he worked hard, but he does not seem to have made much money. We gather that he was poor because when the time came for the presentation of the infant Christ in the temple in Jerusalem, the best offering he and Mary could afford was the smallest and least expensive sacrifice the Mosaic law allowed.

Yet this poor humble laboring man was a prince in his own right. We cannot imagine him boasting about his ancestry, but he could have. He could have said to his friends: "I'm a direct descendant of good King Josiah. I am related to King Hezekiah. My family tree goes back to Solomon. I am of the lineage of David. I am a member of the Hebrew royal family. The blood of princes flows in my veins. If I had my rights, I would be sitting on the throne of David in Jerusalem right now in place of that scoundrel Edomite Herod." (If Joseph had made such boasts, Herod would have had his head.)

Joseph probably was not a braggart, but he was a direct descendant of David. However, the fortunes of the imperial house of David had sunk so low that instead of sitting on a throne in Jerusalem, the rightful heir to that throne was living in a despised Galilean village and laboring for his daily bread at a carpenter's bench. The tools of his trade were a hammer, an adze, and a saw. He made yokes for oxen, doors for houses, handles for plows, and tables and chairs.

Joseph brought his adopted son up to this trade. Significantly the One who had created a hundred million galaxies labored from His youth at creating things for people. Being thus employed, Jesus forever ennobled manual labor and the crafting of useful and beautiful objects for the benefit of one's fellow men.

II. HIS ENGAGEMENT

A young girl in Nazareth caught young Joseph's eye. She was not immaculately conceived, as some say. The Bible does not support any such idea. But she was as perfect as any daughter of Adam's fallen race could be. She was humble and holy, loving and lowly, patient and pure, thoughtful and kind. God had waited for some four thousand years for this particular woman to be born, so we can be sure that she was as near perfection in character, personality, and disposition as a human woman could be.

Young Joseph knew one thing: he wanted to marry Mary. His sun rose and set on her. She was all anyone could ever want in a wife. He was thrilled when his proposal was accepted and the betrothal arrangements were made.

There were two forms of betrothal among the Jews. We do not know which form was used in the case of Mary and Joseph. In one form the agreement was spoken in the presence of witnesses. The vows were confirmed by the pledging of a piece of money (we can be sure any dowry was small in Mary and Joseph's agreement). In the other form the transaction was confirmed in writing.

Either form of betrothal was probably followed by a supper, a benediction, and a statutory cup of wine for the engaged couple. From that moment on, the prospective bride and groom were pledged to be married. Their relationship was as solemn and sacred as the marriage relationship and any breach of it would be regarded as adultery. The engagement could not be dissolved except by a formal divorce. Yet months—sometimes even a year—elapsed between the engagement and the marriage.

Joseph was the happiest man in Nazareth. Mary filled his whole horizon. He was engaged to be married to a princess of the house of David. She was also related to the priesthood— her mother seems to have been a blood relative of Elizabeth, the wife of Zacharias the priest. This engagement was a remarkable event—not that Joseph cared that much about the lineage of Mary. She was going to marry *him!* That was all that mattered. That good, pure-minded, Bible-believing, spiritual, and capable girl was going to marry him!

For Joseph, heaven above was deeper blue; earth around

was deeper green. We can imagine that he whistled while he worked. He sang as he delivered his wares to his customers. Each week he looked forward to seeing her in the synagogue on Saturday. He counted the days and hours to the wedding. He gazed in rapture at the moon. He was going to marry Mary and all was well with the world. He slept with a lock of her hair under his pillow. He dreamed of the day when the two would at last become one.

III. HIS EMBARRASSMENT

Then one day Mary approached him. "I need to see you, Joseph," she said. "Something has happened. I have something to tell you." We can imagine the shock he received when she broke the news: "I'm going to have a baby."

The news was devastating. Joseph was absolutely stunned. He knew he had never touched her in a dishonorable way. If she was going to have a baby, he was not the father.

Joseph could not believe what he was hearing. He could not imagine his pure and spiritually-minded fiancée doing anything wrong. She was not that kind of girl. She said she had not been raped. She had not committed adultery. She had not betrayed him. She was not interested in anyone else; she never had been and never would be. But she *was* going to have a baby. Joseph could not believe Mary was lying to him. He had always believed her honesty and integrity to be above suspicion.

"Well," he must have said at last, "what *is* your explanation?"

"About six months ago," she might have answered, "my cousin Elizabeth's husband Zacharias was visited by the angel Gabriel. He told Zacharias that Elizabeth was going to give birth to a son. Well, since Elizabeth was too old to have a baby, Zacharias did not believe what Gabriel said, so Gabriel smote Zacharias with dumbness. Then, sure enough, Elizabeth became pregnant. That was six months ago and Zacharias is still dumb. The whole incident caused quite a stir in the priestly confraternity."

"What does that have to do with you?"

"I'm coming to that, Joseph. The angel told Zacharias that his son would be a special child, the forerunner of the Messiah."

"I still don't see what that has to do with you."

"It has everything to do with me. A little while ago that same angel visited me."

"Come on, Mary! You never told me that."

"I'm telling you now. The angel Gabriel visited me. He told me I was to become the mother of the Son of God--that God was going to send His Son into the world as a baby and that I was the chosen vehicle for that birth. Gabriel told me that I would be overshadowed by the Holy Ghost, that I would miraculously conceive, and that the Son of God would be born of me. Now, just as the angel said, I'm going to have a baby. I waited until I knew for sure before I told you. What do you think of that?"

Joseph simply did not believe the story. He could not believe that Mary was with child. He could not believe she had been unfaithful to her betrothal vows, but he could not believe her explanation. He didn't know anyone else who would believe the story either. He wondered whether he was dealing with a moral issue or a miraculous issue. Since Mary's explanation was incredible, the issue had to be a moral one.

"You do believe me, don't you, Joseph?" we can hear Mary say.

"I don't know what to believe. I'm going to have to think it over."

"Well, while you think it over, I'm going to visit my cousin Elizabeth. At least she'll believe me."

And so Mary left and Joseph began to think it over. As far as he was concerned, it was going to take a great deal of thinking over. *Pregnant by divine conception indeed!* he thought. *Who in his right mind will ever believe a story like that?*

IV. HIS ENCOURAGEMENT

Anyone who has suffered a broken engagement will be able to enter into the mind and heart of Joseph. For him there was deep, deep sorrow and a gnawing anguish of soul. There was a sense of shock and disbelief. Perhaps there were sudden surges of outright anger and resentment. But most of all, there was the nagging ache of a broken heart.

The more Joseph thought over Mary's story, the more it became evident to him that for his own protection under the stern Mosaic law, he would have to break the engagement. The provisions of that law added a new dimension of horror to his agony. For a single girl to become pregnant, especially when betrothed, was a capital offense. The law demanded the death penalty for the guilty parties. Joseph would have to accuse Mary publicly and go on the witness stand to denounce her. Worst of all, when the death sentence was passed he would have to cast the first stone.

He could never do that, but he couldn't marry her now— that would be tantamount to admitting his own guilt. Besides, Mary had betrayed him. How else could her condition be explained? He couldn't believe her story about angelic visitations and a virgin birth. She must be living in a dream world, a world of fantasy and wishful thinking and make-believe.

On the other hand, Mary had spoken with candor and she had always exhibited a stainless character before. Moreover she had rushed right off to Elizabeth of all people. Elizabeth's husband was a priest and would be the first to sit in judgment on an adulteress. Surely Mary's visit to Elizabeth was profoundly significant. If Mary were guilty of immoral conduct, the last place she would go would be Judea, where the laws were more rigidly enforced. The last place she would go would be the house of a priest who would be duty-bound to report her.

So a disconsolate Joseph thought the situation over as he wandered the streets of Nazareth. Every corner, every tree, every hill, and every dale reminded him of her. The place was haunted now by a ghost. Mary was gone and Nazareth was a place without a soul. His hometown had suddenly become a city of sepulchers, the grave of all his hopes.

The wind in the trees reminded him of the sound of Mary's voice blithely singing the Psalms of their great ancestor David. The village fountain where the girls gathered and chatted brought back memories. The synagogue was a place of torture. On the sabbath Mary's place was empty now. He could only sit and stare at it sadly, choking back his tears. Joseph felt like abandoning the synagogue and its services altogether.

The mental torture continued until one day, we can imagine, he flung down his hammer and strode out of the carpenter's shop. He went out of the town and up the hill to the place, perchance, where years later the villagers would seek to throw Jesus to His death. There Joseph halted and, frightened, drew back from the drop. He sank down to the ground and wept bitter tears. He had to come to a decision one way or another. In his agony he decided to break the engagement privately and let matters take their course. Exhausted, but glad that some decision, however wretched, had been made, he fell asleep.

Suddenly his sleep was ablaze with light. Scripture tells us the angel of the Lord appeared—not just Gabriel, but the Jehovah angel. The words of the angel rang in his soul: "Joseph, thou son of David, fear not to take unto thee Mary thy wife: for that which is conceived in her is of the Holy Ghost. And she shall bring forth a son, and thou shalt call his name JESUS: for he shall save his people from their sins (Matthew 1:20-21).

The storm clouds rolled away and the sun broke through again. The words of the prophet Isaiah came to Joseph's mind: "Behold, a virgin shall be with child, and shall bring forth a son, and they shall call his name Emmanuel, which being interpreted is, God with us" (Matthew 1:23). Within an hour, we can imagine, Joseph was running as fast as his legs could carry him to Judea. From then on his steps would be ordered of the Lord.

V. HIS ENLIGHTENMENT

After Mary and Joseph were married, a decree came from Caesar Augustus. They were to go back to the city of their birth to be enrolled for taxation purposes. Mary was approaching the time of her confinement, but the word of the caesar had to be obeyed. In the providence of God, the decree meant that in keeping with an ancient prophecy the holy child would be born in Bethlehem. Perhaps the couple were glad to leave Nazareth. Indeed it took a special divine revelation to bring them back to Nazareth (Matthew 2:19-23).

The journey from Nazareth to Bethlehem must have taken at least three days. Probably Mary and Joseph followed the route along the eastern bank of the Jordan to avoid going through hostile Samaria. As they approached the heights of Bethlehem, they could see one of Herod's frowning castles perched on the highest hill southeast of Bethlehem. On they went until the mountain ridges of Tekoa came into view. East of the travelers lay the sullen waters of the Dead Sea. To the west the road wound away to Hebron. To the north was undulating countryside behind which Jerusalem was hidden. And in front of them at last was Bethlehem.

Mary must have been exhausted and Joseph not a little anxious to get her settled for the night, for her time had come. But alas there was no room in the inn and thus the Son of God came from the mansions of glory, from the ivory palaces of Heaven, to a wayside cattle shed. We can be sure, however, that Joseph did what he could to clean up the worst of the filth. He found a manger and filled it with straw and hay so that the newborn babe might have a clean and comfortable bed.

The shepherds came and the angels sang. Joseph moved his family into a more convenient place and the wise men came with their timely gifts. Then the angel of the Lord appeared again and said to Joseph, "Arise, and take the young child and his mother, and flee into Egypt, and be thou there until I bring thee word: for Herod will seek the young child to destroy him"

(Matthew 2:13). That child was Lord and Creator of the universe—He could have called ten thousand angels to stop Herod and his men of war dead in their tracks. Instead He fled to Egypt! God had His own timetable for bringing judgment on Herod.

Joseph and his family stayed in Egypt until the death of Herod. And a terrible death it was. The cup of Herod's crimes was full and his torments and terrors came. He was haunted by visions of a rival to the throne and he sacrificed thousands of innocent people to that fear, including his favorite wife and various sons. He died demented of a dreadful disease that devoured his body. According to Edersheim the visit of the Magi took place in February. In March Herod rounded up all the rabbis he could lay his hands on, locked them up, and left orders for them to be executed on the day of his death. At the end of March or beginning of April he murdered his son Antipater and Herod himself was dead five days later.

He was succeeded by his son Archelaus, who spent the night of his father's death carousing and rioting with his friends. One of his first acts as king was to massacre three thousand Jews within the sacred precincts of the temple. Vile as his father had been, Archelaus was worse. He surpassed him in cruelty, oppression, opulence, pride, and sensuality.

Soon after the death of Herod, Joseph returned to Palestine. It seems he wanted to settle in Bethlehem, a proper setting for great David's greater Son, but Joseph was directed to go back to Galilee and thus Jesus grew up in Nazareth.

VI. HIS ENJOYMENT

What greater joy could any man on earth have had than the joy of being foster father to Jesus, the Son of the living God? Christ's presence in Joseph's humble home was a benediction.

Jesus grew up giving Joseph the courtesy title of "father." When Mary reprimanded Him for tarrying in the temple on the occasion of His first Jerusalem Passover, she said, "*Thy father* and I have sought thee sorrowing" (Luke 2:48, italics added). So Joseph parented Jesus. Joseph surrounded Him with love and kindness and counsel and all the necessities of life. And Jesus responded by being the only absolutely perfect child and teenager who ever blessed a human home.

We can imagine how Joseph delighted in the willing, cheerful obedience of Jesus to every command; in His loving, joyful, peaceable disposition; in His uniformly excellent grades at school; in His enjoyment of the Word of God; and in His wisdom and universal popularity. There never was such a boy in all this world, and it was Joseph's privilege to provide the setting for that jewel to be displayed. A humble setting it was: a small, primitive, but comfortable house and a nearby carpenter's shop.

Joseph must have felt an inner glow when the neighbors were impressed. One of them would ask, "How's that boy Jesus doing at school?" And Joseph could reply, "Jesus? He's a straight-A student. He has already memorized the Pentateuch and mops up languages like a sponge." Another neighbor would add to the pleasure: "I say, Joseph, your son Jesus was at our place the other day. He brought my wife some flowers from the field to cheer her sickroom. She says it was a tonic just to have Him visit."

So Joseph played the part of protector, provider, and parent to the Son of the living God, and he enjoyed every minute of it.

VII. HIS ENNOBLEMENT

We will not find this Joseph in *Who's Who in the World,* but we can be quite sure that his name is written down in the book of God's kingdom. When the roll of that kingdom's great ones is called, we will hear the name of Joseph. Yes indeed, and we will also hear the part of the story that is not recorded in the Bible.

11
Pilate,
the Judge of Jesus

John 19:19

I. A PEOPLE HE DESPISED
II. A PLACE HE DERIDED
III. A PERSON HE DISOWNED
IV. A PRINCE HE DENIED

When Pontius Pilate left Rome for Palestine, the emperor Tiberius gave him a special gold ring. It identified Pilate as an *amicus Caesaris,* "friend of the caesar." To keep that ring, as much as for any other reason, Pilate allowed Christ, a man he knew was innocent, to be crucified.

Pilate's ancestors were Roman nobles of the equestrian order. He had served a tour of duty in Syria as an administrative military tribune with the Twelfth Legion and had earned the reputation of being a tough commander. His wife, Claudia Procula, is said to have been the granddaughter of Caesar Augustus, so Pilate had the highest connections in Rome.

As procurator of Judea, Pilate carried a heavy responsibility. Judea was the capital of the seven million Jews who lived in the Roman empire—7 percent of its entire population.

Moreover Judea commanded the trade routes and lines of communication between Syria and Egypt. Judea was also important because it was the only outpost preventing Parthia from moving in and blocking Roman access to Egypt. Rome depended on Egypt for her grain supply, so Egypt itself could not be allowed to fall into hostile hands either. And the ships that carried their precious cargoes of wheat to Rome must never be endangered. So the governorship of Judea was a trust of some magnitude.

Pilate was not going to allow some local messiah to imperil his position as friend of the caesar and guardian of Rome's Egyptian gate, so he caved in to political expediency. If he let Jesus go, he would incur the wrath of the Sanhedrin. If he let Jesus go, he would in effect be endorsing Christ's claim to be a king—the King of the Jews.

Having rejected the claims of Christ against the advice of his wife and the instinct of his own soul, having signed the death warrant that consigned Jesus to a particularly cruel and horrible death, and having uselessly washed his hands of the whole business, Pilate gave Jesus a title. As was customary in the case of a public execution, the governor wrote a placard naming both the criminal and the crime. Much to the annoyance of the Jews, Pilate wrote: "JESUS OF NAZARETH THE KING OF THE JEWS" (John 19:19). "This title," John recalled, "then read many of the Jews: for the place where Jesus was crucified was nigh to the city: and it was written in Hebrew, and Greek, and Latin" (19:20). The placard was written in Latin, the language of government; in Greek, the language of culture; and in Hebrew, the language of religion. The title was written in all three languages so that all the world could read and consider both the Christ and His claims.

Doubtless Pilate wrote the title tongue-in-cheek. He was annoyed at the Jews for pushing this case off on him. He knew perfectly well that at the bottom of their maneuvering was a deep-seated envy of Jesus of Nazareth. Pilate knew from his spies scattered throughout the country that Jesus was a good man and that He posed no threat to Roman rule. Had He not said, "Render to Caesar the things that are Caesar's, and to God the things that are God's" (Mark 12:17)? At His trial He had conducted Himself with extraordinary self-control and poise. Pilate had been impressed. Pilate knew He was innocent of the charges brought against Him. Jesus confessed to be a King but at once declared that His kingdom was not of this world. He claimed to have come from another world altogether, and Pilate more than half believed Him and was more than a little afraid of Him.

So to get even with the Jews for the annoyance, inconvenience, embarrassment, and anxiety they had caused him, Pilate wrote: "Jesus of Nazareth the King of the Jews." And he would not change the wording. "What I have written I have written," he said (John 19:22).

The placard that Pilate wrote and had nailed to Christ's cross was more significant than he realized. The title revealed a people Pilate despised, a place he derided, a person he disowned, and a prince he denied.

I. A PEOPLE HE DESPISED
"Jesus of Nazareth the King of the JEWS"

The Jews were much older than the Romans. Before Pompey marched into Jerusalem, the Jews were a great people. When the Romans were still bearded barbarians, the Jews were already a great people. Before the story of Romulus and Remus and the she-wolf was circulated, the Jews were a great people.

Before Alexander the Great was crowned king of Macedonia in 336 B.C., the Jews were a great people. Before the Athenians began building the Parthenon in 447 B.C., the Jews were a great people. Before Xerxes invaded Greece, before Cyrus the Persian conquered Babylon, before Nebuchadnezzar rose to power, before the Phoenicians founded Carthage, before the Assyrians forged their cruel empire, before Ramses the Great began construction of the temple of Abu Simbel—the

Jews were already a great people. Their roots and their history
go far back—back before Hammurabi of Babylon hammered
out his legal code, back before the Hyksos kings subdued
Egypt. When the Bronze Age was coming to flower in Egypt,
the Jews were a people to be reckoned with in this world.

Perhaps Pilate did not know his history book, but the
Jews, a people he despised, were a people not to be despised.
They had a legal code greater than Rome's. They had a religion
greater—far greater—than Rome's. Even in Pilate's day the
Jews were the world's bankers. But Pilate despised the Jews
because Rome measured a man by his might and the Jews were
not famous as fighters.

In sizing up the Jews, however, Pilate was ignoring the
wars of the Maccabees. And before the century was over, the
Jews would teach Rome a lesson it would not soon forget. To
quell the Jewish revolt, the Romans were forced to assemble
an army of eighty thousand men. Alexander the Great had
carved out his vast empire with thirty-two thousand men. Julius
Caesar needed only twenty-five thousand soldiers to conquer
Gaul and invade Britain. To fight the Jews, however, Titus was
forced to mobilize ten thousand cavalrymen and seventy
thousand infantrymen, and even against those odds the Jews
kept the Romans at bay for four long years. In the end the
Romans won, not because of greater skill but because of
greater numbers. After the Romans conquered Jerusalem, they
still had to subdue Masada. And the Jews led by Bar Kokhba
tried to resist Rome again in A.D. 135.

The Jews would outlast Pilate, the caesar he served, and
the empire he represented. When the Huns and Goths and
Vandals at last descended on Rome, the Jews were still a mighty
people. They are a mighty people today. Every nation or
empire that has ever turned its hand against the Jews has in the
end found itself fighting against God.

But Pilate despised this people. He wrote his contempt
into the title he made for the cross: "Jesus of Nazareth the King
of the *Jews*." To him the title was ludicrous. Everybody knew

the Jews had no king. The king who reigned over them was Herod. And the king who ruled over Herod was a Roman. Pilate thought of the Jews as moneylenders. He thought of them as religious fanatics. He thought of greedy men like Annas and guileful men like Caiaphas. The idea that the Jews should have a king struck him as ridiculous.

II. A PLACE HE DERIDED
"Jesus of NAZARETH the King of the Jews"

Nazareth! Even the Jews regarded this Galilean town with a measure of contempt. They despised Galileans because they were of mixed blood; because so many Gentiles lived in Galilee; and because its chief city was Tiberius, doubly unclean since it was named after a despised emperor and it was built on the site of an old graveyard. The Jews despised Galileans because they were "unlearned and ignorant men" (Acts 4:13) and because they spoke the native Aramaic with a thick, north-country accent.

The Jews despised Nazareth even more. "Can there any good thing come out of Nazareth?" asked Nathanael when Philip told him he had found the Messiah, a man named Jesus of Nazareth (John 1:45-46). Pilate had been governor of Judea long enough to know how much Nazareth was despised by the Jews. "Jesus of *Nazareth*," he wrote, hoping to annoy the Jews still further. If the accused had been Jesus of Rome, Jesus of Athens, Jesus of Carthage, or even Jesus of Jerusalem, Pilate may have paid more heed to the case. For a Jesus of Nazareth to claim kingship struck Pilate as absurd.

Nazareth wasn't much of a place by worldly standards. We can imagine there were cypress trees reaching toward the sky, terraces of fig and olive trees, poor homes, a fountain supplying the town's only water, a market, and a carpenter's shop. With a clientele of struggling farmers and agricultural workers, the carpenter was paid once a year at harvest time in produce and grain.

Jesus, His mother, Joseph, and His half brothers and sisters would have lived in a room above a cave where a donkey was kept. The room would have been virtually bare of furniture. Bedding mats would have been rolled up and tucked away in a corner. Such cramped quarters were typical of Nazareth.

Although Nazareth was not in his province, Pilate doubtless knew all there was to know about the place. In a way the town was significant as a dividing line. To its south were Jerusalem and Judea and Old Testament religious norms. To the north was upper Galilee. To go from Judea to Galilee was almost to turn one's back on the Old Testament world. Galilee was crossed by the great north-south military roads and by the east-west caravan routes. Galilee was an international corridor and Nazareth was its gateway.

The sophisticated Judeans spoke the name of Nazareth with a sneer and Pilate would have preferred Caesarea any time. Sophisticated Caesarea was a transplant of Rome. Caesarea had a fine harbor where Roman warships could drop anchor. It had magnificent theaters, a hippodrome, a marble temple, and the great palace of Herod. Pilate chuckled as he wrote *Nazareth* on the sign. It was a place to be derided.

III. A PERSON HE DISOWNED
"JESUS of Nazareth the King of the Jews"

Jesus was a common name among the Jews of Pilate's day. The name had its roots in the Hebrew for Joshua, pronounced *Yeshua*. Whether Pilate knew or appreciated the meaning of the name is questionable. *Jesus* means "Jehovah the Savior." To the Christian, Jesus is the sweetest name on earth. To Pilate it was the name of just another Jew. Ultimately Pilate had to choose between two names: Jesus and Tiberius—the King of the Jews or the emperor of Rome.

Caesar Tiberius was the adopted stepson of Caesar Augustus. In the early days of his reign, Tiberius had the reputation of being an able soldier and administrator. But he had a vicious streak in him and before long he was thoroughly detested in Rome, not only for his cruelties but also for his abominable vices. He retired to the island of Capri and abandoned himself to all forms of lust. When he finally died, there was such rejoicing in Rome that people ran about shouting, "To the Tiber with Tiberius!" Others offered prayers to the infernal gods to give him no room below except among the damned. To this disgusting and debauched individual Pilate owed his promotion. There was little doubt in Pilate's mind about whether he would choose the caesar or the Christ. Pilate would choose the caesar.

Everything Pilate had ever heard about Jesus was extraordinary and we can be sure nothing happened in the provinces that wasn't known in Pilate's palace. "He goes about doing good," his spies would tell him. "He performs astounding miracles. Herod Antipas is dying to see one of them. Jesus heals sick people. He casts out evil spirits. He feeds the hungry. He has even cleansed lepers and raised the dead. Many of the common people take His name to be prophetic and consider Him to be their Savior."

When face to face with Jesus, Pilate felt the awesome goodness and power of the man. Pilate had never ever met a man like Him before. Indeed the procurator seems to have been superstitious about Jesus, but he banished his superstitious fears and decided that Jesus was just another Jew—a remarkable one, but just a Jew. Thus when Pilate sat down to write the title for the cross, he wrote the name of Jesus without any real understanding of the significance of that name.

It is *the saving name*. When Joseph was trying to make up his mind what to do about Mary, he had a visit from an angel who set his mind at rest. The angel told him that the child about to be born was indeed the very Son of God, then added, "Thou shalt call his name JESUS: for he shall save his people from their sins" (Matthew 1:21). The name was not an everyday name; it embodied an eternal truth. Jesus is the Savior of His people.

"Neither is there salvation in any other," Peter bluntly told the Sanhedrin, who were responsible for the murder of the Messiah. They were equally responsible for efforts to hush up stories about the resurrection and attempts to stop the spread of the gospel. Peter added, "There is none other name under heaven given among men, whereby we must be saved" (Acts 4:12).

Years later when the apostle Paul was a prisoner in Rome, he sent some sound advice to the church at Colosse: "Whatsoever ye do in word or deed," he wrote, "do all in the name of the Lord Jesus" (Colossians 3:17). We cannot go far wrong when His name governs our character, conduct, and conversation. The name of Jesus is *the sanctifying name.* When it is the dominant color on the canvas of one's life, His name sets a very high standard indeed. We should take Paul's advice and echo the words of hymnist James Rowe:

> Be like Jesus—this my song—
> In the home and in the throng;
> Be like Jesus all day long!
> I would be like Jesus.

Pilate asked, "What is truth?" when Truth was staring him in the face (John 18:38). Jesus had said just the day before, "I am the...truth" (14:6). Face to face with Truth incarnate, Pilate sold Him for a lie. The procurator persuaded himself that it was in his own best interest to stay in the good graces of Caiaphas and his crowd and to do nothing that the suspicious old tyrant back in Rome might interpret as treason. So Pilate signed a death warrant and wrote a title. In effect it said, "This is Jesus ...just another Jew."

IV. A PRINCE HE DENIED
"Jesus of Nazareth the KING of the Jews"

When Pilate sent Jesus to Herod Antipas, Herod arrayed Him in mocking purple. Herod had the right idea. Pilate went further. He let his soldiers crown this King of the Jews with a crown of thorns. Would Pilate himself *crown* Him or *crucify* Him? Would he dismiss all charges against this innocent man or would he sign the most infamous death warrant in history? Pilate crucified Him and the same day made friends with Herod Antipas. The man who mocked Christ and the man who murdered Christ shook hands that day.

Contrary to all appearances, the man on the center cross was indeed the King of the Jews. But He was more than that—much more. In the book of Revelation He is called King of kings and Lord of lords!

Pilate soon had an inkling that He was a Prince indeed. A crucified man often lingered on for days in his death agony, but the Sanhedrin urged Pilate to hasten the end of the current victims because of the approaching Passover. Pilate cooperated, ordering that the victims' legs be broken. Then the centurion came in to report that Jesus was dead—not from crucifixion, not from further action ordered by Pilate, but by a sovereign act of His will. He had simply dismissed His spirit and died. Other phenomena had occurred. A supernatural darkness had descended on the country from the sixth to the ninth hour. The temple veil had been torn asunder in some mysterious way. An earthquake had shaken the ground. Reports began to come in from all over the country that graves and sepulchers had burst open.

Three days later Pilate was faced with the news that the tomb was empty and the man he had murdered was alive, back from the dead. At the same time the open graves had discharged their dead. As Matthew 27:52-53 records, "Many bodies of the saints which slept arose, And came out of the graves after his resurrection, and went into the holy city, and appeared unto many."

Jesus was more than the King of the Jews. The centurion ventured his own opinion: "This," he said at the cross, "was the Son of God" (Matthew 27:54). Perhaps he was bold enough to repeat those words to Pilate. But Pilate had denied Him. To the end of his days he would carry with him the memory of eyes that had looked into his and read his very soul. Pilate's assessment of Jesus had been wrong. If only he could rewrite that title! If only he had never written it at all! He should have crowned Him. Perhaps when, as one tradition tells us, he was a lonely outcast banished from power, he belatedly did crown Him as King of his own life.

12
Antichrist,
the Beast of the Apocalypse

Revelation 13,17

```
I. HIS PARENTAGE
II. HIS PROPHET
III. HIS POLICY
IV. HIS PERSECUTION
V. HIS PARALYSIS
VI. HIS PUNISHMENT
```

He is known by many names. He is called the Assyrian, the lawless one, the man of sin, the son of perdition, the little horn, and the prince. We often call him the antichrist. In the Apocalypse he is usually called the beast.

The antichrist has been foreshadowed in history time and time again. *Cain* was the first in a long series of men who by their wicked works and willful ways prefigured him. Cain went out from the presence of the Lord a marked man. Having refused to become a pilgrim and a stranger on the earth, he became instead a fugitive and a vagabond. He laid the foundations of a thriving and energetic civilization that became so utterly godless and vile that it had to be divinely overthrown by the waters of the flood.

Nimrod was another type of the antichrist. His name means "the rebel." He determined to build a society to suit himself. It was to be a humanistic and rebellious kingdom. Three times the words "Let us" occur in the story of the tower Nimrod's civilization built. All the emphasis was on man. "Let us make us a name," they said (Genesis 11:4). Nimrod's society was to be a new-age civilization, a united-nations organization, a world federation of nations—with God left out. There was to be a one-world *sovereignty* symbolized by the city, a one-world *society* symbolized by the common language, and a one-world *sanctuary* symbolized by the tower. And Nimrod, the great rebel himself, would preside over it all. Babylon was to be center of his empire and idolatry was to be its religion.

One of the strongest types of the antichrist in history and Biblical revelation was *Antiochus Epiphanes*. This Syrian tyrant conquered Jerusalem in 168 B.C. and massacred the worshipers in the temple. He issued a decree that everyone had to join a universal religion and obey universal laws—or face the death penalty. He seized the Jewish temple and consecrated it to Jupiter (Zeus). Antiochus identified himself with this pagan god and ordered everyone to worship him. He also ordered an immediate cessation of all Jewish sacrifices and suspended all Jewish religious observances. He destroyed all the copies of the Scriptures he could find. He replaced the annual feast of tabernacles with a feast dedicated to Bacchus. Antiochus built an idol altar over the brazen altar in the temple court. In the temple itself he installed an image of Zeus, the thunderer of Olympus. Antiochus sacrificed a sow on the altar, made broth of its flesh, and sprinkled the broth all over the temple. He perverted the youth of the city and taught them vile practices. He massacred thousands of Jews, although there were numerous apostate Jews who admired and followed him. Antiochus was one of Satan's forerunners of the coming antichrist.

There have been other men in the long course of history who have staged dress rehearsals for the coming of the antichrist. The devilish *Nero,* for example, staged a fearful persecution of the Christian church. *Napoleon,* who aimed to resurrect the old Roman empire and conquer Palestine, used the Roman Catholic Church as a pawn in much the same way the antichrist will. *Hitler* sought to bring Europe under his control, and his holocaust against the Jews was a precursor of the coming great tribulation.

The Bible tells us many things about the actual antichrist. It reveals his parentage, his prophet, his policy, his persecution, his paralysis, and his punishment.

I. HIS PARENTAGE

In Revelation 12 the great red dragon appears in Heaven. He has seven heads and ten horns and is easily identified as the devil. We see his malice toward the nation of Israel and his thwarted effort to destroy the man-child, the Lord Jesus, at His birth.

In Revelation 13 we see "a beast rise up out of the sea" (13:1). It too has seven heads and ten horns. We read about this beast again in Revelation 17, which emphasizes the seven heads and ten horns and provides the additional information that he is "a scarlet coloured beast" (17:3).

The great red dragon is Satan and the scarlet-colored beast is the antichrist. The beast betrays his parentage, for he looks and acts like the great red dragon. In other words, the father of the beast is the devil himself.

Revelation 17 gives us more information about the beast. He is to be killed and brought back to life again, so he has two comings. When he comes the first time, he rises out of the sea. In other words, the beast is an ordinary human being who rises out of the sea of the nations and out of *the* sea, namely the Mediterranean world. He will probably be a Roman because he is identified with the little horn of Daniel 7.

Some people think that the beast will be only part human, that he will actually be fathered by Satan. Since Jesus said concerning Judas, "Have not I chosen you twelve, and one of you is a devil?" (John 6:70) some assume that both Judas and the antichrist are of Satanic origin. Since Jesus called Judas "the son of perdition" (John 17:12) and this title is only used elsewhere for the antichrist (2 Thessalonians 2:3), some surmise that Judas and the antichrist are the same individual. People who make this assumption point to Acts 1:25, which says that Judas, after he hanged himself, went "to his own place." They speculate that Judas is presently being groomed in the underworld to come back as the antichrist.

More likely the beast out of the sea will be a Gentile—a Roman who will revive the old empire. He will rule as the last of the caesars. He will also be the final heir to Nebuchadnezzar's lordship of the world. The antichrist, at his first coming, will be a very attractive, dynamic, clever individual who will charm and fascinate the nations. Probably he will sell himself to the devil, as Hitler did. The antichrist will be taught and led by principalities and powers and rulers of this world's darkness (see Ephesians 6:12).

Revelation 17 tells us he will be killed, but it does not tell us how. Perhaps the antichrist will be slain when God's two witnesses (Revelation 11) and Satan's two representatives (the beast and the false prophet) wage war against each other. That war will be a battle of miracles similar to that which took place in Egypt when Moses and Aaron confronted the pharaoh's two false prophets.

God will permit Satan to bring the antichrist back to life again. Thereafter he will be known not as "the beast out of the sea" (Revelation 13:1-4) but as "the beast out of the bottomless pit" (11:7; 17:8-11). From this point on he will be a supernatural being and will be universally worshiped. The antichrist will be Satan incarnate, the visible expression of the invisible devil and the vehicle through whom Satan will try to accomplish his purposes for this planet.

II. HIS PROPHET

Revelation 13 chronicles the coming of two beasts. The first rises out of the sea and is therefore a Gentile. The second comes up out of the earth and is therefore a Jew because the earth stands in contrast to the sea in Old Testament typology and symbolism. The second beast will be subordinate to the first one, but they will be soul twins. The second beast looks like a lamb, but speaks like a dragon. Thus he too betrays his Satanic origin. He is called "the false prophet" (Revelation 16:13) and he will exercise all the power of the first beast. The false prophet will be the first beast's high priest and spokesman. The false prophet will persuade the world that the first beast is the long-awaited messiah and that the world's interests lie in submitting to him.

The Lord Jesus warned that as the last days begin to dawn, numerous false prophets will arise and deceive many (Matthew 24:11). All the world's false religions have been founded by false prophets. The church has had its false prophets too. Today false cults in Christendom deceive millions. But these false prophets are simply part of Satan's general attack on the Christian faith. He is the father of lies, and deception is the idiom of his language. He uses false religions to keep lost people lost. Satan is not against religion; he is all for it; he invented most of it.

However a false prophet of quite a different kind is still to come. He will be known as *the* false prophet. He will come with deceit and lying wonders and will wield all the power and authority of his master, the antichrist. The false prophet will be a golden-tongued orator and will appear to be harmless. Satan will enable him to speak as one inspired and only those enlightened by the Holy Spirit will be able to withstand his persuasive eloquence. The false prophet will make wickedness seem right. His miracles will dazzle and deceive. Except for those whose names are written in the Lamb's book of life, the human race will fall for him and follow him. The false prophet will lead them to the antichrist, the antichrist will lead them to Satan, and Satan will lead them to Hell.

The only safeguard for the human race will be the Word of God. But since men will long since have abandoned that for the countless false religions and philosophies abroad in the world, the false prophet will persuade men that the antichrist is their long-sought savior.

III. HIS POLICY

When the antichrist first appears, he will be just a "little horn" (Daniel 7:7-8,16-26)—that is, he will not have a great deal of power. But he will be the consummate master of craft and cunning. He will arise somewhere in southern Europe, probably in Rome, and will be given a seat in the councils of the ten kings, the European leaders who control a shadow Roman empire. He will make short work of three of them and then control all ten of them.

The details in Scripture are sketchy, but we do know from Revelation 17 that the antichrist will make common cause with the Roman Catholic Church. The Vatican will think it can control him, but it will soon discover that it has allied itself to a tiger. The antichrist will use this religious system to gain the upper hand in Europe and in all countries where Catholicism is entrenched. The Vatican will think it can use this "little horn" to get back its lost power and authority in the world, but as soon as the antichrist has made the ten kings subservient to his will, he will turn on the ecclesiastical system and tear it to pieces. The ten kings themselves will gleefully fall upon the enormous wealth and riches of the Roman Catholic Church and divide the spoils among themselves.

As soon as the antichrist is securely enthroned as the ruler of Europe and the revived Roman empire, he will act swiftly to expand his power. We are not told specifically what part the United States and the western hemisphere will play in all this. The "old lion" (the European powers—Isaiah 60:9; Ezekiel

38:13) will be loose. The lands of the Americas are the young lions spawned centuries ago by the old lion. Perhaps the antichrist will simply pull the economic rug out from beneath the United States and thus bankrupt the United States, Canada, and Latin America. Then he may form a new Atlantic alliance in which the countries of the western hemisphere take orders from Rome. Once he has the western world at his command, the antichrist will prepare to satisfy larger ambitions, for his goal is to rule the world.

The rule of the world was granted in principle to Nebuchadnezzar, with whom the "times of the Gentiles" began (Luke 21:24). He only ruled a tithe of the whole. His successors in the prophetic world were the leaders of Medo-Persia, Greece, and Rome, but none of these men ruled the whole world. With the revival of the Roman empire and the formation of the new Atlantic alliance, the way will be clear for the antichrist to pursue his plans for a truly global empire. All the economic, industrial, and military might of the West will be at his disposal and he will be ready to further his schemes.

The antichrist will sign a treaty with Israel—an agreement with Hell (Isaiah 28:15). This seven-year treaty will activate the seventieth and final "week" of seven years still hanging in abeyance (see Daniel 9 for the vision of the seventy weeks). Under the terms of this treaty the antichrist apparently will guarantee Israel's security and authorize them to rebuild their temple. He will allow that temple to be built for a reason.

We can imagine the howl of rage that will come from the Muslim world when the Jews start to rebuild their temple on its ancient site. But the Muslims will be powerless. They fear that at the slightest hint of opposition the antichrist will want to occupy all Arab territory down to the Euphrates. He will not want a huddle of quarrelsome Middle East Arab states to spoil his global plans. He will want to get rid of Islam if it looms as an obstacle to the accomplishment of his ultimate goals.

So the Islamic powers will appeal to Russia, which will be looking for a chance to reassert itself as a world superpower.

Russia will seize this invitation to move into the Middle East. Ezekiel 38 seems to indicate that a united Germany will join Russia and the Islamic states in a massive antisemitic alliance. Russia and its allies will move swiftly and the combined armies will cross the frontier into Israel. Then God will act. The terrible disasters spoken of in Ezekiel 38–39 will overtake the invading powers, and their armies will be virtually annihilated. Their homelands will also be visited by divine judgment. Suddenly Russia, Germany, and the Islamic powers will no longer exist.

The way will thus be open for the antichrist to achieve his goal of global sovereignty. Before the rest of the world can recover from the astounding news that Russia and her allies have been destroyed, the armies of the antichrist will occupy their territories. He will issue an ultimatum to the eastern nations: Join me—or else. They will say: "Who is like unto the beast? who is able to make war with him?" (Revelation 13:4)

The eastern nations will quickly submit to the all-conquering antichrist, who will now have three capitals: *Rome,* his political capital; *Jerusalem,* his religious capital; and rebuilt *Babylon,* his economic capital. He will have achieved the goal of hundreds of would-be world conquerors. He will rule the whole world.

IV. HIS PERSECUTION

Having no more use for the Jews, the antichrist will tear off the mask of friendship and show his real face. He will seize the rebuilt temple in Jerusalem and put an image of himself in the temple. The false prophet will give the image life and endow it with power to destroy those who refuse to worship it.

The antichrist will order a test of allegiance: People will be required to prove their loyalty to the new world order by receiving the antichrist's mark on their right hands or on their foreheads. Without that mark no one will be able to buy or sell. A total economic boycott of those not wearing this badge will be globally enforced. A little boy will not even be able to buy an ice cream cone without the mark.

"The mark of the beast" (Revelation 16:2; 19:20) will be related to the name of the beast. Revelation 13:17-18 tells us "the number of his name." In Hebrew and Greek every letter is also a number, so every word is not only a collection of letters but also a collection of numbers. Thus every word has a numerical value. The Greek letters that make up the name of Jesus add up to 888. The numerical value of the antichrist's name, when it is finally revealed, will be 666.

Those with a Judeo-Christian background, those who have been converted by the preaching of the 144,000, and those who fear God more than they fear man will be persecuted. Those who refuse to wear the mark of the beast will pay the price. Satan will launch his most determined effort to rid the world of all lingering traces of the true and living God. The resulting holocaust will make the horror camps of the Nazis look like a Sunday school picnic.

But God will not abdicate the throne. Not for one moment will He surrender His sovereignty. The antichrist's day of reckoning will come.

V. HIS PARALYSIS

Even as the antichrist rides the crest of his power, things will begin to go wrong. The vials of God's wrath will be outpoured. The first four vials will be aimed at the antichrist's power structure on the planet. Under the hammer blows of Heaven he will lose his grip and his might will begin to ebb away.

The eastern half of the antichrist's empire, the nations east of the Euphrates, will break away. (The Euphrates has always been the dividing line between East and West.) A new eastern coalition will be thrown together and the "kings of the east" will mobilize against him (Revelation 16:12). Japanese technology will be married to Chinese manpower. The great eastern hordes will rally to the rebel cause. The united armies of the East will march westward, cross the Euphrates, and deploy on the plains of Megiddo. The antichrist will mobilize the West, and the vast armies of East and West will face each other, determined to decide once and for all who is going to rule the world. The stage will be set for the battle of Armageddon.

VI. HIS PUNISHMENT

Before the battle can begin, there will be an invasion from outer space: Jesus will come again! This time He will be backed by the armies of Heaven. The church will be there in all its glory. All the Lord's might and majesty will be revealed. The sword will go forth from His mouth and the conflict will be over. The armies of earth will be swept away, and the antichrist and his false prophet will stand alone gazing at an enormous field strewn with dead bodies.

The judgment of the antichrist and the false prophet will be swift and sure. They will be seized and flung headlong into the lake of fire, and the smoke of their torment will rise up on high. The antichrist's rickety empire will be quickly dismembered. The survivors—Jew and Gentile alike—of the years of famine, pestilence, earthquake, persecution, and war will be summoned to the valley of Jehoshaphat. There, near the site of Gethsemane, the Lord Himself will separate the sheep from the goats. The world will be fully cleansed of all those who wear the mark of the beast, of all those who joined the great conspiracy. Those who pass judgment will be regenerated and sent to pioneer the millennial kingdom in the name of Christ. But that's another story!